ZAGATSURVEY®

1999

WASHINGTON, D.C.
BALTIMORE
RESTAURANTS

Edited by Olga Boikess

Contributing Editor for Baltimore
and the Annapolis area
by Katz

distributed by
LLC

Acknowledgments

Besides thanking the nearly 3,750 Washington/Baltimore restaurant-goers who shared their dining experience with us, we are especially grateful to Barbara Alexander, Alicia Ault, Susan Austin, Darcy Bacon, Jay Block, Nicolas Brown, Mary Ann Brownlow, Tom Bryant, Al and Ellen Butts, Karen Cathey, Edward Cogen, Susan Cullman, Fred Deutsch, Elaine Eff, Donna Ellis, Lorraine Fitzsimmons, the Justin Franks, Mark Freeland, Phyllis Frucht, Sue and Sandy Greenberg, Bill Greene, Colleen Holt, Henry Hopkins III, Jim Jacobi, Rochelle Jaffe, Barbara Johnson, Jane and Danny Katz, Bill Kopit, Judy Levenson, Paige Mason Littleton, Suwanee Nivasabutr, Liz Schade, Alan Schlaifer, Robert Singleton, George D. Stewart, Bob and Bonnie Temple, and Joe Trabert for their support. Our special thanks go to Jami Yuspa for her editorial assistance.

Second Printing
© 1998 Zagat Survey, LLC
ISBN 1-57006-141-6

Contents

Introduction	5	
Foreword	6	
Key to Ratings/Symbols	8	
	DC	**BA**
Map	10	152
Favorite Restaurants	11	153
Top Ratings		
• Top Food and by Cuisine	12	154
• Top Decor, Outdoor Dining, Rooms, Views, Service	15	156
Best Buys	17	158
ALPHABETICAL DIRECTORY, RATINGS AND REVIEWS	19	161
INDEXES		
• Types of Cuisine	114	220
• Neighborhood Locations	123	227
• Breakfast	130	232
• Brunch	130	232
• Buffet Served	130	232
• Business Dining	130	232
• BYO	–	232
• Caters	131	233
• Cigar Friendly	131	233
• Dancing/Entertainment	132	233
• Delivers/Takeout	132	234
• Dessert & Ice Cream	133	234
• Dining Alone	133	234
• Family Style	134	234
• Fireplaces	134	235
• Game in Season	–	235
• Health/Spa Menus	134	235
• Historic Interest	134	235
• Hotel Dining	134	235
• "In" Places	135	236
• Jacket Required	–	236
• Late Late – After 12:30	135	236
• Meet for a Drink	136	236
• Noteworthy Newcomers	136	236
• Offbeat	136	237
• Outdoor Dining	136	237
• Outstanding Views	138	237

INDEXES (Cont.)	**DC**	**BA**
• Parking	138	238
• Parties & Private Rooms	141	239
• People-Watching/Power Scenes	142	239
• Pre-/Post-Theater Dining	143	240
• Prix Fixe Menus	143	240
• Pubs/Bars/Microbreweries	143	240
• Quiet Conversation	143	240
• Raw Bars	144	240
• Reservations Essential	144	240
• Romantic Spots	144	241
• Saturday Lunch	144	241
• Sunday Dining	145	242
• Senior Appeal	–	242
• Singles Scenes	146	242
• Sleepers and Teflons	146	242
• Smoking Prohibited	147	243
• Teas	147	243
• Teenagers & Other Youthful Spirits	–	244
• Transporting Experiences	147	–
• Visitors on Expense Accounts	148	244
• Wheelchair Access	148	244
• Winning Wine Lists	148	244
• Worth a Trip	148	244
• Young Children	148	244
Rating Sheets	245	
Wine Chart	252	

Introduction

Here are the results of our *1999 Washington, D.C./Baltimore Restaurant Survey* covering some 1,052 restaurants in the area.

By regularly surveying large numbers of local restaurant-goers, we think we have achieved a uniquely current and reliable guide. We hope you agree. Nearly 3,750 people participated. Since the participants dined out an average of 3.2 times per week, this *Survey* is based on about 624,000 meals per year.

We want to thank each of our participants. They are a widely diverse group in all respects but one – they are food lovers all. This book is really "theirs."

Of the surveyors, 52% are women, 48% are men; the breakdown by age is 13% in their 20s, 25% in their 30s, 23% in their 40s, 27% in their 50s and 12% in their 60s or above.

To help guide our readers to the area's best meals and best buys, we have prepared a number of lists. On the assumption that most people want a quick fix on the places at which they are considering eating, we have tried to be concise and to provide handy indexes.

We are particularly grateful to Olga Boikess, a Washington lawyer and avid restaurant-goer, who has organized, edited and updated this *Survey* since it was first published in the fall of 1986. Our special thanks also go to contributing editor Marty Katz, photographer and writer, for his insights on the Baltimore and Annapolis-area food scene.

We invite you to be a reviewer in our next *Survey*. To do so, simply send a stamped, self-addressed, business-size envelope to ZAGAT SURVEY, 4 Columbus Circle, New York, NY 10019, so that we will be able to contact you. Each participant will receive a free copy of the next *Washington, D.C./Baltimore Restaurant Survey* when it is published.

Your comments, suggestions and even criticisms of this *Survey* are also solicited. There is always room for improvement with your help.

New York, New York
September 29, 1998

Nina and Tim Zagat

Foreword

As the Nation's Capitol races towards the millennium, stimulating developments in its dining scene foreshadow the decades that lie ahead. Eating out (or carrying in) is now a part of most people's everyday lives. Indeed, the participants in this *Survey* report that they rely on restaurants for almost half their weekly lunches and dinners. Responding to this demand, savvy enterprises, on every level, are offering diverse menus and multipurpose settings that are suitable for anything from a snack to a serious meal.

In the latter category, there's been an amazing acceleration of activity in the past year. Exciting new establishments, including Ardeo, DC Coast, El Catalan and Villa Franco, combine spectacular decor with sophisticated menus that draw inspiration from multicultural sources. At the same time, well-regarded local chefs are trading places and bringing new energy and ideas to high-profile spots, such as Elysium, New Heights, Nora, Pesce, Red Sage, the Tabard Inn and Thyme Square.

With the MCI Center revitalizing Chinatown and the Penn Quarter exploding with smart venues (Austin Grill, BET on Jazz, Fadó Irish Pub, M & S Grill and The Mark), the Downtown restaurant scene is more happening than ever. Yet, other DC neighborhoods and suburban sites are beginning to rival it as mealtime meccas. Successful dining venues have cloned themselves and followed their customers home to Tysons Corner (Sam & Harry's, Tara Thai and Taste of Saigon), Bethesda (the Donna Group's Cesco), Reston (McCormick & Schmick's) and Cleveland Park (Firehook Bakery, Nam Viet).

Our upscale demographics and knowledgeable customers are also attracting upper-tier chains from various regions of the United States and from abroad, including the Daily Grill, La Madeleine, Levante's, Maggiano's Little Italy, McCormick & Schmick's and P.F. Chang's China Bistro. With their eye-catching decor, commodious seating and please-all menus, they have become business and neighborhood hubs virtually overnight.

However, homegrown enterprises like the Capitol Restaurants (J. Paul's, Paolo's), Carlyle Grand Cafe (Great American Restaurants) and Clyde's are proving more than a match for these chains. Participating in the area's phenomenal growth, their spiffy outlets and wide-ranging menus are well-calibrated to the needs of each locale. Further down the dining scale, an impressive assortment of international ethnics, contemporary bistros, storefront eateries, coffeehouses and pubs proliferate with their endless budget-friendly possibilities.

While we lost a French classic with the closing of Jean-Pierre Goyenvalle's Le Lion D'Or, celebrated toques, like Roberto Donna (Galileo), Gerard Pangaud (Gerard's Place, Vintage), Bob Kinkead (Kinkead's) and, most recently, Michel Richard (Citronelle), have made this town their home. Their restaurants earn top marks in this *Survey* and provide edible evidence that DC has come of culinary age.

In Baltimore, local talents and out-of-area chains are invigorating the Inner Harbor and Downtown district with handsome, business-class establishments, such as Charleston, McCormick & Schmick's and Lenny's Chop House, as well as with the super sports haven, ESPN Zone. The same dynamic operates upcountry at the hunt-clubby Oregon Grill and the (happily) revived Milton Inn. While City Cafe (Mt. Vernon), Golden West Cafe (Hampden), Helen's Garden (Canton) and SoBo Cafe (Cross Street) join the roster of hip bean bars, bakeries and markets that are setting up tables and satisfying appetites for innovative, anytime food.

But, at heart, Baltimore is a 'shot-and-a-beer kind of town.' Although there is plenty of energy and elegance at the high-end of the dining spectrum here, the good value and genuine fellowship found in neighborhood bars like Kelly's, Jennings and McCabe's or in personable places, such as Samos and Vera's Bakery, have led them to become gathering places and part of the backbone of their communities.

Speaking of value, dining in Baltimore continues to be relatively reasonable. This year it ranks 14th among major US cities in the overall cost of a meal ($22.43), as compared to slightly pricier DC, which ranks 8th and averages $25.46 per meal.

It'll be midnight on December 31, 1999 before we know it. In the meantime, let's explore the area's exciting new entries to see what the future holds and revisit old favorites to affirm their enduring values. Now, and into the 21st-century, we hope that this *Survey* will guide you to many marvelous meals.

Washington, DC Olga Boikess
September 29, 1998

Key to Ratings/Symbols

This sample entry identifies the various types of information contained in your Zagat Survey.

(1) Restaurant Name, Address & Phone Number

(2) Hours & Credit Cards

(3) ZAGAT Ratings

F	D	S	C
23	5	9	$19

Tim & Nina's ◐ S ≠

4 Columbus Circle (8th Ave.), 212-977-6000

■ "What a dump!" – open 7 days a week, 24 hours a day, this successful "deep dive" started the "deli-tapas craze" (i.e., tidbits of pastrami, corned beef, etc. on cracker-size pieces of stale rye); though the place looks like a "none-too-clean garage" and T & N "never heard of credit cards or reservations", "dirt cheap" prices for "great eats" draw demented crowds.

(4) Surveyors' Commentary

The names of restaurants with the highest overall ratings, greatest popularity and importance are printed in **CAPITAL LETTERS**. Address and phone numbers are printed in *italics*.

(2) Hours & Credit Cards

After each restaurant name you will find the following courtesy information:

◐ .... *serving after 11 PM*

S .... *open on Sunday*

≠ .... *no credit cards accepted*

(3) ZAGAT Ratings

Food, **Decor** and **Service** are each rated on a scale of **0** to **30**:

F	D	S	C

F .... *Food*
D .... *Decor*
S .... *Service*
C .... *Cost*

23	5	9	$19

0 - 9	.... *poor to fair*
10 - 15	.... *fair to good*
16 - 19	.... *good to very good*
20 - 25	.... *very good to excellent*
26 - 30	.... *extraordinary to perfection*

▽ 23	5	9	$19

▽ .... *Low number of votes/less reliable*

The **Cost (C)** column reflects the estimated price of a dinner with one drink and tip. Lunch usually costs 25% less.

A restaurant listed without ratings is either an important **newcomer** or a popular **write-in**. The estimated cost, with one drink and tip, is indicated by the following symbols.

–	–	–	VE

I .... *$15 and below*
M .... *$16 to $30*
E .... *$31 to $50*
VE .... *$51 or more*

(4) Surveyors' Commentary

Surveyors' comments are summarized, with literal comments shown in quotation marks. The following symbols indicate whether responses were mixed or uniform.

◪ .... *mixed*
◼ .... *uniform*

Washington's Favorites

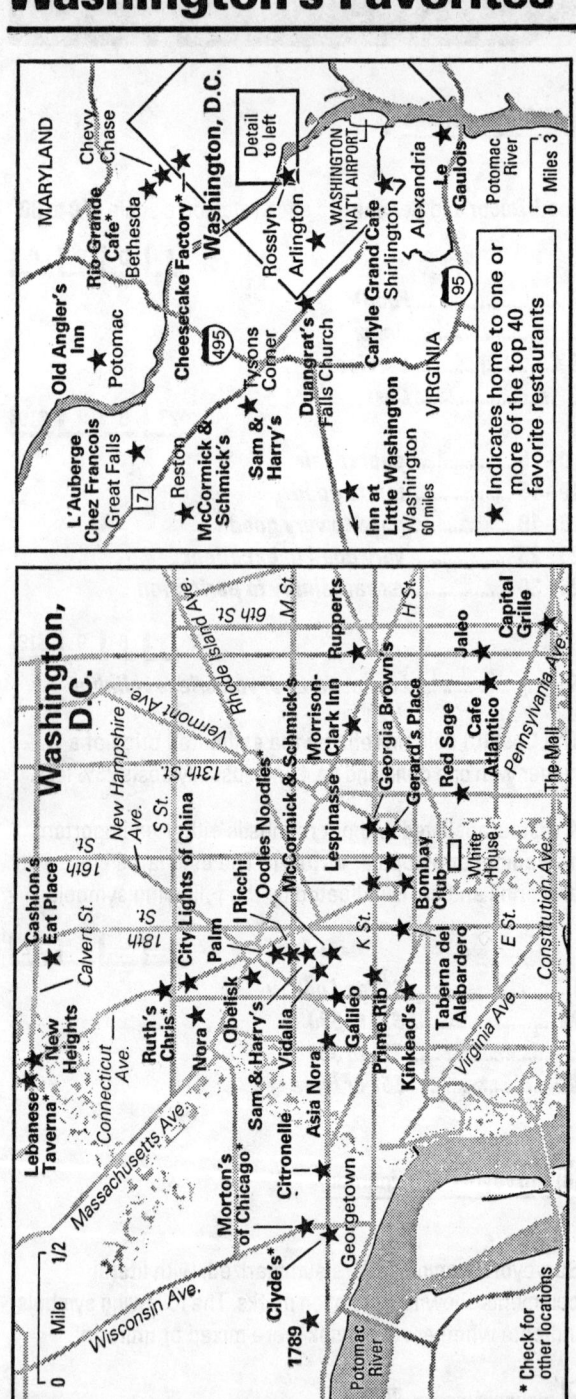

Washington's Favorite Restaurants

Each of our reviewers has been asked to name his or her five favorite restaurants. The 40 spots most frequently named, in order of their popularity, are:

1. L'Auberge Chez Francois
2. Kinkead's
3. Inn at Little Washington
4. Galileo
5. Vidalia
6. Carlyle Grand Cafe
7. Nora
8. Obelisk
9. Gerard's Place
10. 1789
11. Jaleo
12. Prime Rib
13. Ruth's Chris
14. Morrison-Clark Inn
15. Cheesecake Factory
16. Red Sage
17. Taberna del Alabardero
18. Bombay Club
19. I Ricchi
20. Rio Grande Cafe
21. Palm
22. Morton's of Chicago
23. Cashion's Eat Place
24. New Heights
25. Capital Grille
26. City Lights of China
27. Lebanese Taverna
28. Sam & Harry's
29. Georgia Brown's
30. Citronelle
31. Cafe Atlantico
32. Clyde's
33. Oodles Noodles
34. Le Gaulois
35. Rupperts
36. McCormick & Schmick's
37. Old Angler's Inn
38. Asia Nora
39. Duangrat's
40. Lespinasse

It's obvious that many of the restaurants on the above list are among the most expensive, but Washingtonians love a bargain. Were popularity calibrated to price, we suspect that a number of other restaurants would join the above ranks. Thus, we have listed over 135 Best Buys on pages 17 and 18.

Top Ratings*

Top 40 Food Ranking

- 29 Inn at Little Washington
- 28 Kinkead's
- 27 Makoto
  - L'Auberge Chez Francois
  - Obelisk
  - Gerard's Place
  - L'Auberge Provencale
  - Lespinasse
- 26 1789
  - Galileo
  - Seasons
  - Prime Rib
  - Morrison-Clark Inn
  - Vidalia
  - Four & Twenty Blackbirds
  - Melrose
  - Patisserie Cafe Didier
  - Nora
  - Sushi-Ko
  - Morton's of Chicago
- 25 Duangrat's
  - Ritz-Carlton, The Rest.
  - Taste of Saigon
  - New Heights
  - Rupperts
  - Tachibana
  - Pizzeria Paradiso
  - I Ricchi
  - Taberna del Alabardero
  - Pesce
  - Goldoni
  - Lafayette
  - Rabieng
  - La Bergerie
  - Bombay Club
  - Coeur De Lion
  - Connaught Place
  - Peking Gourmet Inn
  - Cashion's Eat Place
- 24 Bistrot Lepic

Top Spots by Cuisine

Top American (New)
- 28 Kinkead's
- 26 1789
  - Seasons
  - Morrison-Clark Inn
  - Vidalia

Top Bar-B-Q
- 22 Rockland's
- 19 Red Hot & Blue
  - Houston's
  - Old Glory BBQ
- 18 George Starke's

Top Breakfast**
- 26 Galileo
- 24 La Colline
- 21 Bread Line
- 19 Old Ebbitt Grill
  - Cafe Promenade

Top Brunch
- 28 Kinkead's
- 26 Seasons
  - Morrison-Clark Inn
  - Melrose
- 24 Ritz-Carlton, The Rest.

Top Business Lunch
- 28 Kinkead's
- 27 Gerard's Place
  - Lespinasse
- 26 Galileo
  - Seasons

Top Chinese
- 25 Peking Gourmet Inn
- 24 City Lights of China
- 23 Mr. K's
- 22 Fortune
  - Seven Seas

---

* Excluding restaurants with low voting.
** Other than hotels.

Top Continental
- 25 Ritz-Carlton, The Rest. Lafayette
- 24 Jockey Club
- 23 Village Bistro
- 22 Two Quail

Top Creole/Cajun/New Orleans
- 23 R.T.'s
- 22 Warehouse Bar & Grill Sea Catch
- 20 219 Cafe Marianna*

Top Family Dining
- 23 Lebanese Taverna Matuba
- 22 Rio Grande Cafe
- 21 Cheesecake Factory
- 19 Red Hot & Blue

Top French Bistro
- 24 Bistrot Lepic Le Gaulois La Provence
- 23 La Chaumiere Lavandou

Top French Classic
- 27 L'Auberge Chez Francois
- 25 La Bergerie
- 23 Le Refuge Jean-Michel Le Vieux Logis

Top French (New)
- 27 Gerard's Place Lespinasse
- 24 Willard Room Citronelle La Colline

Top Hamburgers
- 24 Addie's
- 23 Carlyle Grand Cafe
- 22 Occidental Grill
- 21 Mike's American Grill
- 19 Old Ebbitt Grill

Top of the Hill
- 24 La Colline
- 22 Two Quail
- 21 La Brasserie
- 20 B. Smith's
- – Barolo*

Top Hotel Dining
- 27 Lespinasse/Sheraton Carlton
- 26 Seasons/Four Seasons Morrison-Clark Inn Melrose/Park Hyatt
- 25 Ritz-Carlton, The Rest.

Top Indian
- 25 Bombay Club Connaught Place
- 24 Haandi Bombay Bistro
- 23 Bombay Palace

Top Italian
- 27 Obelisk
- 26 Galileo
- 25 I Ricchi Goldoni
- 23 Cesco

Top Japanese
- 27 Makoto
- 26 Sushi-Ko
- 25 Tachibana
- 23 Tako Grill Matuba

Top Mex/Tex-Mex
- 22 Rio Grande Cafe
- 21 Las Placitas
- 20 Lauriol Plaza Mi Rancho Los Chorros

Top Middle Eastern
- 23 Lebanese Taverna Pasha Cafe Moby Dick
- 22 Bacchus
- 20 Skewers/Cafe Luna

Top Newcomers/Rated
- 23 Cesco Tahoga
- 22 McCormick & Schmick's
- 21 Bread Line
- 19 Sostanza*

Top Newcomers/Unrated
- Ardeo
- BET on Jazz
- DC Coast
- Mark
- Villa Franco

* Low votes.

Top Pizza
- 25 Pizzeria Paradiso
- 23 I Matti
- 21 Primi Piatti
  Faccia Luna
- 20 Coppi's

Top Saturday Lunch
- 28 Kinkead's
- 26 Patisserie Cafe Didier
- 25 Duangrat's
  Ritz-Carlton, The Rest.
  Taste of Saigon

Top Seafood
- 28 Kinkead's
- 25 Pesce
- 22 Seven Seas
  Sea Catch
  McCormick & Schmick's

Top Southeast Asian
- 24 Asia Nora
- 21 Oodles Noodles
  Germaine's
- 20 Straits of Malaya
  Spices

Top Southern
- 26 Morrison-Clark Inn
  Vidalia
- 23 Georgia Brown's
- 20 B. Smith's
- 18 Southside 815

Top Southwestern
- 23 Gabriel
- 22 Rio Grande Cafe
  Red Sage
- 21 Sweetwater Tavern
- 20 Santa Fe East

Top Steakhouses
- 26 Prime Rib
  Morton's
- 24 Sam & Harry's
  Ruth's Chris
  Capital Grille

Top Thai
- 25 Duangrat's
  Rabieng
- 24 Tara Thai
- 23 Dusit
  Crystal Thai

Top Vegetarian-Friendly
- 26 Morrison-Clark Inn
  Nora
- 25 Greenwood's*
- 22 Udupi Palace
- 20 Thyme Square

Top Vietnamese
- 25 Taste of Saigon
- 23 Nam Viet
  Cafe Dalat
- 22 Pho 75
  Saigon Gourmet

Top Worth a Trip
- 29 Inn at Little Washington/
  Washington, VA
- 27 Prince Michel*/
  Leon, VA
  L'Auberge Provencale/
  White Post, VA
- 26 Four & Twenty Blackbirds/
  Flint Hill, VA
- 24 Bleu Rock Inn/
  Washington, VA

---

* Low votes.

Top 40 Decor Ranking

- **29** Inn at Little Washington
- **28** Willard Room
  L'Auberge Chez Francois
  Lespinasse
- **27** Ritz-Carlton, The Rest.
  Lafayette
  L'Auberge Provencale
  1789
- **26** Seasons
  Ritz-Carlton, The Grill
  Morrison-Clark Inn
  Taberna del Alabardero
- **25** Coeur De Lion
  Bombay Club
  Melrose
  Jockey Club
  Red Sage
  Bleu Rock Inn
  El Catalan
- **24** Old Angler's Inn

Capital Grille
Prime Rib
Two Quail
B. Smith's
Jefferson Rest.
Rainforest Cafe
Sequoia
Makoto
Asia Nora
Nora
Gadsby's Tavern
La Ferme
- **23** La Bergerie
  701
  New Heights
  Galileo
  T.H.A.I.
  Sam & Harry's
  I Ricchi
  Cafe Atlantico

Top Outdoor

Firehook Bakery
Gerard's Place
La Brasserie
L'Auberge Chez Francois
Old Angler's Inn

Perry's
Sequoia
701
Straits of Malaya
Tahoga

Top Rooms

BET on Jazz
Bombay Club
DC Coast
El Catalan
Fadó Irish Pub
Inn at Little Washington
Lespinasse
Morrison-Clark Inn
Old Ebbitt Grill

Red Sage
Ritz-Carlton, The Grill
Ritz-Carlton, The Rest.
Seasons
1789
Taberna del Alabardero
Two Quail
Villa Franco
Willard Room

Top Views

Bleu Rock Inn
Chart House
Le Rivage
Perry's

Potowmack Landing
Roof Terrace Ken. Ctr.
Ruth's Chris
Sequoia

Top 40 Service Ranking

- **29** Inn at Little Washington
- **27** L'Auberge Chez Francois
  - Makoto
- **26** Lespinasse
  - L'Auberge Provencale
  - Seasons
  - Ritz-Carlton, The Rest.
  - 1789
- **25** Obelisk
  - Coeur De Lion
  - Willard Room
  - Melrose
  - Prime Rib
  - Jefferson Rest.
  - Bombay Club
  - Morrison-Clark Inn
  - Jockey Club
  - Kinkead's
- **24** Gerard's Place
  - Lafayette
  - Kazan
  - Bleu Rock Inn
  - Ritz-Carlton, The Grill
  - Rupperts
  - Taberna del Alabardero
  - Four & Twenty Blackbirds
  - La Bergerie
  - Sam & Harry's
  - Vidalia
  - Nora
  - Connaught Place
- **23** Galileo
  - Morton's of Chicago
  - 701
  - Aquarelle
  - New Heights
  - Capital Grille
  - Ruth's Chris
  - I Ricchi
  - Mr. K's

16

Best Buys

Top 100 Bangs For The Buck

This list reflects the best dining values in our *Survey*. It is produced by dividing the cost of a meal into the combined ratings for food, decor and service.

1. Firehook Bakery
2. El Pollo Rico
3. California Tortilla
4. Burro
5. Bob & Edith's Diner
6. Bread Line
7. Burrito Brothers
8. Wrap Works
9. Chicken Out
10. Capital Wrapps
11. Food Factory
12. Teaism
13. Crisp & Juicy
14. C.F. Folks
15. Moby Dick
16. Hard Times Cafe
17. Florida Ave. Grill
18. Delhi Dhaba
19. Cafe Parisien Express
20. Le Bon Cafe
21. A&J Restaurant
22. Xando
23. Parkway Deli
24. Vienna Inn
25. Olney Ale House
26. Generous George's
27. Metro 29
28. Faccia Luna Pizzeria
29. Crystal Thai
30. Dean & DeLuca Cafe
31. Cafe Dalat
32. Dusit
33. Eat First
34. Patisserie Cafe Didier
35. Rockland's
36. La Madeleine
37. Haad Thai
38. Full Kee
39. Benjarong
40. Oodles Noodles
41. Las Placitas
42. King Street Blues
43. Pizzeria Paradiso
44. Los Chorros
45. Pilin Thai
46. Bangkok St. Grill
47. Taipei/Tokyo Cafe
48. Luna Grill & Diner
49. Silver Diner
50. Royal Restaurant
51. Bombay Bistro
52. La Lomita
53. Pho 75
54. Polly's Cafe
55. Bangkok Bistro
56. Good Fortune
57. Taste of Saigon
58. Bangkok Garden
59. Vegetable Garden
60. T.H.A.I.
61. Bertucci's
62. Little Viet Garden
63. Rabieng
64. Udupi Palace
65. Queen Bee
66. Cafe Saigon
67. Mi Rancho
68. Hunan Number One
69. Fortune
70. Foong Lin
71. Austin/S. Austin Grill
72. Aditi
73. Red Tomato Cafe
74. Pasha Cafe
75. Tara Thai
76. Panjshir
77. Louisiana Express
78. Meskerem
79. Silverado
80. Rio Grande Cafe
81. George Starke's
82. Hunan Lion
83. Saigon Inn
84. Haandi
85. California Pizza Kit.
86. El Tamarindo
87. White Tiger
88. Memphis Bar-B-Q
89. Skewers/Cafe Luna
90. Connaught Place
91. Thai Kingdom
92. Burma
93. Nam Viet
94. Rainforest Cafe
95. Zed's
96. Red Hot & Blue
97. City Lights of China
98. Nam's
99. Sabang
100. Amphora's Diner

17

Additional Good Values
(A bit more expensive, but worth every penny)

Appetizer Plus
Atami
A.V. Ristorante
Banana Cafe
Bistro Francais
Blue Plate
Bombay Club
Bombay Curry Co.
Cafe Marianna
Cajun Bangkok
Carlyle Grand Cafe
Charlie Chiang's
Clyde's
Coppi's
Evening Star Cafe
Greenfield Churrascaria
Houston's
Il Raddichio
Ivy's Place
Jaleo

Lebanese Taverna
Levante's
Little Fountain Cafe
Malibu Grill
Maggiano's Little Italy
Martin's Tavern
Mehak
Music City Roadhouse
Old Brogue Irish
Original Pancake Hse.
Outback Steakhouse
Pasta Plus
Ramparts
Rhodeside Grill
Samadi Sweets
Spices
Stardust
Thyme Square
Umberto's
Zuki Moon

Alphabetical Directory of Washington, D.C. Restaurants

Washington, D.C.

F	D	S	C

A&J Restaurant S ⊄   20 | 6 | 15 | $11
Woodmont Ctr., 1319-C Rockville Pike (bet. Talbott St. & Templeton Pl.), Rockville, MD, 301-251-7878
■ "Dim sum all the time", noodles and exotic meats, "sparse surroundings" and the "amazingly low prices" at this Rockville Taiwanese bespeak its authenticity; note, however, that some "strange, yet tasty" dishes are not for the squeamish and most people are speaking Chinese, so "order carefully" and "be patient."

Aangan S   18 | 16 | 19 | $19
4920 St. Elmo Ave. (bet. Norfolk Ave. & Old Georgetown Rd.), Bethesda, MD, 301-657-1262
■ An "intimate" courtyard setting and "attentive" staff make this "middling" Bethesda Indian a comfortable place for doing biz; while much of the food is "subtle", be "bold in your choices and you won't be disappointed."

Aaranthi S   ∇ 19 | 19 | 21 | $20
Dana Plaza, 409 Maple Ave. E. (Beula St.), Vienna, VA, 703-938-0100
◪ In Vienna, this "bright", "noisy" Indian does a workmanlike job with an "ordinary" menu of tandooris and curries; it's "not a fun place", but neither are most nearby options.

Addie's   24 | 14 | 18 | $28
11120 Rockville Pike (Edson Ln.), Rockville, MD, 301-881-0081
■ "Best food in the Maryland suburbs", "on a par with Downtown DC" rave reviewers about this "funky", "cheerful" cottage and its "excellent", "imaginative" Contemporary American food; given its intimate size and well-deserved popularity, it's "noisy" and there are often waits, but once you're seated, the "enthusiastic" staff is "eager" to please.

Aditi S   22 | 16 | 20 | $20
3299 M St., NW (33rd St.), 202-625-6825
◪ Overcoming a "lackluster" second-story setting, this "well-polished" Indian's spicy standards draw crowds; a loyal clientele touts "top-notch" food, yet a few cons counter that "everything tastes the same."

Adobe Grill S **(CLOSED)**   16 | 17 | 16 | $20
2218 Wisconsin Ave., NW (Calvert St.), 202-965-0665
◪ Somewhere between "SoHo" and the "Pottery Barn" appearance-wise, this young Southwesterner's food and service are "not quite there" yet, either; still, in Upper Georgetown, its "generally harmless" fodder might suffice.

Washington, D.C. | F | D | S | C |

Aegean Taverna | 17 | 14 | 18 | $20 |
2950 Clarendon Blvd. (N. Garfield St.), Arlington, VA, 703-841-9494
■ Finding a "slice of the [Greek] Islands" in Clarendon, an area best known for Asian dining, can be a pleasant surprise; while the "hearty" platters and "cheesy" decor at this "friendly" Hellene aren't overwhelming, neither is the bill.

Akasaka S | ▽ 18 | 15 | 16 | $33 |
Van Dorn Station Shopping Ctr., 514C S. Van Dorn St. (bet. Edsall & S. Pickett Rds.), Alexandria, VA, 703-751-3133
■ This "small", "quiet place for sushi, tucked into a strip mall" near Landmark Plaza, is something of a find; it's made with very "fresh fish", attractively presented, and "not too expensive for the DC area."

Alamo ●S | 13 | 17 | 15 | $19 |
100 King St. (Union St.), Alexandria, VA, 703-739-0555
☒ Dominating the best "people-watching" corner in Old Town, this Tex-Mex party place and "pickup scene" is filled with youngsters "having such a fun time imbibing" "killer margaritas", "they don't seem to notice" food and service shortfalls; to enjoy its "redeeming virtue", which is a "great location", sit "by the open windows on a summer night."

Al Tiramisu S | 23 | 18 | 22 | $35 |
2014 P St., NW (bet. 20th & 21st Sts.), 202-467-4466
■ Luigi Diotaiuti, the "exuberant" host, and his brother Giovanni, the "talented chef", bring "*Big Night* to life" at this "richly romantic" Dupont Circle Italian; backed by "handsome waiters" and a "cave-like" setting, they produce "fantastic" fish and pastas in a "warm atmosphere" that works best in the evening – lunch is a bit "too slow."

America S | 12 | 16 | 14 | $19 |
Union Station, 50 Massachusetts Ave., NE (N. Capitol St.), 202-682-9555 ●
Tysons Corner Ctr., 8008-L Tysons Corner Ctr. (Rte. 7), McLean, VA, 703-847-6607
☒ "Majestic" space and Capitol views provide "great visuals for out-of-towners" at this "very loud" Union Station megalith; but while both it and the Tysons Corner mall location are handy for business lunches and pre-movie snacks, their "phone book"–size menus, "mediocre" American food and "assembly-line" service lead some cynics to sneer: "huge, tasteless, incompetent."

American Grill ●S | 15 | 15 | 16 | $24 |
Loews L'Enfant Plaza Hotel, 480 L'Enfant Plaza, SW (bet. C & 7th Sts.), 202-484-1000
☒ Suitable for a "pleasant" New American business lunch in a part of town lacking alternatives, this L'Enfant Plaza hotel dining room is geared to expense accounts – "portions for l'enfant, prices for full-adult wallets"; while service is "competent", the kitchen sometimes "tries too hard."

Washington, D.C.　　　　　F | D | S | C

Amphora's Diner Deluxe ●S　　13 | 11 | 15 | $14
1151 Elden St. (Alabama Ave.), Herndon, VA, 703-925-0900
■ "Breakfast rocks" 'round-the-clock at this "overgrown diner" near Dulles, where towering desserts and a vast Greek-American menu comfort loyalists' late-night cravings; however, while critics concede it's "convenient", they say the "food is pre-fab" and "it's not a place to linger."

Andalucia S　　21 | 18 | 20 | $31
4931 Elm St. (Arlington Rd.), Bethesda, MD, 301-907-0052
12300 Wilkins Ave. (Park Dr.), Rockville, MD, 301-770-1880
■ Is Spanish cuisine "underappreciated"? – not at these Andalusian bastions of "wonderful fish", rioja and "lovely" flamenco guitar music that are separately run by Joaquim Serrano (the "more sophisticated" Bethesda branch) and his former wife Maria Serrano (the "homey" Rockville location); while they can be "very uneven" and "hectic when crowded", they're "great when they're on."

Appetizer Plus S　　– | – | – | M
1117 N. 19th St. (Lynn St.), Rosslyn, VA, 703-525-3171
Bargain "all-you-can-eat sushi pulls cubicle dwellers" out of Rosslyn towers to this bare-bones Japanese; while its buffet (and setting) may leave something "to be desired", you won't need a bank loan to eat your fill – a point well taken by local twentysomethings.

Aquarelle S　　23 | 23 | 23 | $54
Watergate Hotel, 2650 Virginia Ave., NW (New Hampshire Ave.), 202-298-4455
■ "Romantic" Potomac vistas from this legendary hotel dining room, a "wonderful pre-theater menu" and easy parking turn an evening at the nearby Kennedy Center into a "celebration" since the New American kitchen usually "rises to the occasion", even if the show's a bust; however, a minority maintains the "'60s Watergate chic decor" and "inconsistent" food are at odds with the "high rent."

Ardeo S　　– | – | – | M
3311 Connecticut Ave., NW (Macomb St.), 202-244-6750
The spring '98 debut of this smashing art deco Contemporary American in a duplex on Cleveland Park's restaurant row is yet another indication that this neighborhood has come of culinary age; its founder, Ashok Bajaj (Bombay Club, 701, Oval Room), knows what DC wants: interestingly seasoned, light tasting fare served in sophisticated settings; start-up problems can be expected, but it's likely to last.

Aroma S　　20 | 14 | 18 | $20
1919 I St., NW (bet. 19th & 20th Sts.), 202-833-4700
■ "Pink and perfect for business lunches", this K Street corridor Indian isn't fancy, but the food is "fine" and the staff "helpful"; if you take advantage of the "executive special", you can "taste a little of everything" for chump change.

Artie's [S] 21 18 20 $23

3260 Old Lee Hwy. (south of Fairfax Circle), Fairfax, VA, 703-273-7600

■ "Always crowded" and "noisy", nonetheless this American "oasis" in the Fairfax "dining desert" quickly "becomes your place", largely due to its late hours and "friendly" crew; the highlight of the daily specials is the "excellent blackened prime rib" on Saturday night.

Arucola [S] 16 15 15 $26

5534 Connecticut Ave., NW (Morrison St.), 202-244-1555

◪ "Better get there early" before the "family crowd" swarms into this Chevy Chase trattoria for pastas, antipasti and desserts dispensed from rolling carts; enthusiasts insist eating alfresco is "lovely", likewise dining in the "old-country room" upstairs; however, foes feel what is "fun in theory" can be "annoying in practice" – when it gets "too crowded", the food is "uneven" and service gets "slow."

Ashby Inn [S] – – – M

Ashby Inn, 692 Federal St. (Rte. 759), Paris, VA, 540-592-3900

It's a "beautiful drive" to a "wonderful setting" – a pre–Civil War Virginia residence with period dining rooms and a taproom with a stone fireplace – where John and Roma Sherman have realized their escapist dream; their "good" Contemporary American food and "remarkable wine prices" will help you realize yours.

Asia Garden [S] ▽ 18 13 15 $18

11401 Woodglen Dr. (Nicolson Ln.), Rockville, MD, 301-230-0088

■ "Lots of veggie options" are only a small part of this basic Rockville storefront's "great variety" of Pan-Asian offerings, which include Chinese, Japanese, Thai, Vietnamese and Malaysian dishes; if you don't know where to begin, give the bargain lunch a try.

Asia Nora 24 24 22 $38

2213 M St., NW (bet. 22nd & 23rd Sts.), 202-797-4860

■ A "challenging", exotic East-West menu, "exquisite presentations" and "romantic surroundings" make dining at this sophisticated West End Asian a "great adventure"; as a result, even skeptics find paying "big bucks for small food psychologically satisfying."

Atami [S] 18 12 17 $21

3155 Wilson Blvd. (Hudson St.), Arlington, VA, 703-522-4787

◪ Unless you're a sumo-sized "big eater", you probably won't get your money's worth at this all-you-can-eat sushi stalwart in Clarendon; while dissenters decry the "low-end" surroundings and "heavy on rice, low on fish" selections, its meal-in-a-bowl soups, buffet and lunch specials are good enough that, when more is more, it's a deal.

Washington, D.C. | F | D | S | C |

Au Pied du Cochon ●S | 13 | 13 | 13 | $18 |
1335 Wisconsin Ave., NW (Dumbarton St.), 202-333-5440
■ "Seedy" seems chic at 4 AM when you're sipping onion soup and "people-watching" at this "cheap", collegiate 24-hour Georgetown "dive"; although "great eggs Benedict" and frites have their takers, probably the kindest thing that can be said about the French bistro fare and the help is that the "hours are better" than both.

Austin Grill S | 18 | 17 | 18 | $18 |
2404 Wisconsin Ave., NW (bet. Calvert & Hall Sts.), 202-337-8080
750 E St., NW (bet. 7th & 8th Sts.), 202-393-3776
7278 Woodmont Ave. (Elm Ave.), Bethesda, MD, 301-656-1366
8430 Old Keene Mill Rd. (Rolling Rd.), W. Springfield, VA, 703-644-3111

South Austin Grill S
801 King St. (Columbus St.), Alexandria, VA, 703-684-8969
■ Sure, you can find "reasonably priced" Southwestern "comfort food", swirly margaritas and "pleasant eye candy" elsewhere, but something about these "fun", "laid-back", "kid-friendly" Tex-Mex cantinas allows them to find a niche in widely varied 'hoods; the stampede to the smashing Downtown AG (near MCI) is evidence of their appeal.

A.V. Ristorante Italiano | - | - | - | M |
607 New York Ave., NW (6th St.), 202-737-0550
Some say its "time has come and gone", yet this "old-fashioned" Italian "institution" with the prerequisite fireplace, "drippy candles, checkered tablecloths", "opera music" and "funky" charm is still here; and with the nearby MCI Center reviving the area (and offering its own on-site parking), it looks like its time has come again.

Bacchus | 22 | 18 | 20 | $26 |
1827 Jefferson Pl., NW (bet. 18th & 19th Sts.), 202-785-0734
7945 Norfolk Ave. (Del Rey Ave.), Bethesda, MD, 301-657-1722 S
■ For many, sharing *meze* (Middle Eastern appetizers) is the "way to go" at these "very accommodating" Lebanese, although the full menu tempts too: either way, for an "offbeat" business lunch "tucked away" near Dupont Circle, or dinner at the "showing some wear" Bethesda locale, they are "maybe not better than Beirut, but a lot safer."

Banana Cafe S | - | - | - | M |
500 Eighth St., SE (E St.), 202-543-5906
"Mango daiquiri" madness strikes young Hillclimbers at this nearby "fun" Caribbean and why not?; the colorful dining room, sidewalk cafe and "upstairs piano bar" have "atmosphere", the daily specials taste "good" and the Sunday brunch is a sleeper.

Washington, D.C. | F | D | S | C |

Bangkok Bistro S | 21 | 22 | 20 | $20 |
3251 Prospect St., NW (bet. 33rd St. & Wisconsin Ave.), 202-337-2424
■ In the "heart of Georgetown", where "parking is difficult" and prices are high, trendies find a "tasty", "cheap" alternative to nearby Cafe Milano at this modish Thai; its "beautiful", secluded patio is enticing and the help "aims to please", but the kitchen tends to play it cool "even when you beg for fire."

Bangkok Garden S | 19 | 14 | 19 | $17 |
4906 St. Elmo Ave. (Old Georgetown Rd.), Bethesda, MD, 301-951-0670
☑ One of the first Thai restaurants in Bethesda with a "wide variety of dishes", "good specials" and a kitchen that doesn't stint on spice; it may "need a face-lift", but it's "friendly", "reasonably priced" and delights most.

Bangkok St. Grill & Noodles (CLOSED) | 19 | 16 | 17 | $16 |
5872 Leesburg Pike, Falls Church, VA, 703-379-6707
☑ "Cleaner than the streets of Bangkok", yet striving to replicate that milieu, this Duangrat's sib brings Thai street food and its "bustling", tropical atmosphere to Falls Church; the roster of "affordable", spicy noodle dishes, snacks and soups encourages "experimenting", but some say it's "not as good a value as Duangrat's" or Rabieng.

Barcelona S | ▽ | 16 | 15 | 16 | $26 |
815 King St. (bet. Alfred & Columbus Sts.), Alexandria, VA, 703-548-1670
☑ "As in Spain", where pals gather over tapas and drinks, this "lively" King Street spot is favored for "munching" and "well-spiked sangria" with a crowd; but it will have to be your call whether entrees are "authentic" or "average."

Barolo | - | - | - | E |
223 Pennsylvania Ave., SE (bet. 2nd & 3rd Sts.), 202-547-5011
Upper-level dining describes both the style and the townhouse setting of this latest Roberto Donna (Galileo) venture; here, his compatriot, Enzio Fargione, matches Piedmontese wines with that region's rich cuisine, with mostly first-rate results; Hilltoppers observing budget limitations frequent Donna's casual spaghetteria downstairs.

BD's Mongolian BBQ S | - | - | - | I |
7201 Wisconsin Ave. (bet. Bethesda Ave. & Willow Ln.), Bethesda, MD, 301-657-1080
In a setting almost as raucous as the combos on other people's plates, this young Bethesda entry in the all-you-can-eat, design-your-own-dish Mongolian BBQ game adds a few Jewish grandmother (matzo ball soup) and western touches (chile) to the familiar formula; eager eaters take a trip to the soup and salad bar but still save room for dessert.

Washington, D.C. | F | D | S | C |

BeDuCi S | 20 | 18 | 20 | $34 |
2100 P St., NW (21st St.), 202-223-3824

◪ "Undiscovered"? – not really, although this Dupont Circle Mediterranean's "warm welcome" and "cozy atmosphere" can make it seem so, especially while watching the street scene from the glassed-in terrace; the food, like the service, "can be excellent", but may also reflect "better intentions than what they produce" for "high prices."

Belmont Kitchen S | 17 | 15 | 16 | $23 |
2400 18th St., NW (Belmont Rd.), 202-667-1200

■ Like an "old flame", this Adams Morgan American "rekindles" one's interest with time-tested charms – a laid-back brunch out on the area's best people-watching patio or a "quaint" dinner inside; "funky" and very "'60s", it's "still chugging along" with new owners.

Benjarong S | 22 | 21 | 20 | $19 |
Wintergreen Plaza, 855-C Rockville Pike (Edmonston Rd.), Rockville, MD, 301-424-5533

■ This "roomy" Rockville Thai's "pretty", "serene" interior provides a "nice contrast to its lively, fiery food" and "cheap" tab; not only does it "take you seriously if you like it hot", it treats you well.

Bertolini's S | 15 | 17 | 15 | $21 |
801 Pennsylvania Ave., NW (9th St.), 202-638-2140
White Flint Mall, 11301 Rockville Pike (Nicholson Ln.), Bethesda, MD, 301-984-0004

◪ With their "easy locations", these "Americanized" Italians "catch the crowds", and while few would choose them for a "night out", many use them for a "respectable" salad, pasta or "yummy" gelato; at the Pennsylvania Avenue branch, you can "rub shoulders with DC power brokers" while you wait (and sometimes wait) to be served.

Bertucci's S | 17 | 15 | 16 | $16 |
1218-20 Connecticut Ave., NW (Jefferson Pl.), 202-463-7733
GWU Bldg., 2000 Pennsylvania Ave. (bet. 20th & 21st Sts.), 202-296-2600
6208 Multiplex Dr. (bet. Old Braddock Rd. & Rte. 28), Centreville, VA, 703-803-9300
7516 Fair Knoll Dr. (off Fair Lakes Pkwy.), Fairfax, VA, 703-815-1800
13195 Parcher Ave. (bet. Elden St. & Worldgate Dr.), Herndon, VA, 703-787-6500
7421 Sudley Rd. (Nicholson St.), Manassas, VA, 703-893-5200
6525 Frontier Dr. (Franconia Rd.), Springfield, VA, 703-313-6700
8027 Leesburg Pike (off Rte. 495), Tysons Corner, VA, 703-893-5200

◪ Pros praise these "kid-savvy", "decent value" pizza, salad and pasta places that serve "no-nonsense" pies made with fresh ingredients, mostly in malls; however, while cons' complaints range from "no personality" to "limp" pasta and "untrained" help, the big question is "with their huge wood-burning" ovens, why is the pizza "so cold?"

Washington, D.C.

| | F | D | S | C |

BET on Jazz Restaurant S | - | - | - | E |
730 11th St., NW (bet. G & H Sts.), 202-393-0975
Snazzy art deco dining and great jazz – what a combo; Black Entertainment Television's smashing new supper clubby restaurant and state-of-the-art sound stage near the Convention Center is upbeat and, like its new wave Caribbean cooking, attuned to '90s tastes; there's 'edible art' on the plate, beautiful people at the gate, and wonderful music pulling it all together.

Bilbo Baggins S | 18 | 18 | 17 | $22 |
208 Queen St. (Lee St.), Alexandria, VA, 703-683-0300
◪ Hearty "raisin bread is the best part" of this "cozy Sunday brunch place"; another way to enjoy this popular Old Town standby is to "come for the good wine list and stay for dessert"; its "pub" atmosphere, salads and soups have "held up", but the "quirky" American menu, like the service, can be "unpredictable" and a bit "passé."

Bistro S | 18 | 19 | 19 | $27 |
Washington Monarch Hotel, 2401 M St., NW (24th St.), 202-457-5020
◪ The "charming" hidden courtyard and "airy", etched-glass-and-dark-wood interior of this cosmopolitan West End hotel dining room are "classy" meeting places; while its "inventive" Contemporary American food and service are sometimes "inconsistent" (reflecting periodic "management changes"), celeb sightings at its "excellent" Sunday brunch are a constant and desserts are "works of art."

Bistro Bistro S | 18 | 17 | 17 | $23 |
4301 N. Fairfax Dr. (Glebe Rd.), Ballston, VA, 703-522-1800
Villages at Shirlington, 4021 S. 28th St. (Hwy. 395), Arlington, VA, 703-379-0300
Reston Town Ctr., 1811 Liberty St. (bet. Dulles Toll Rd. & Reston Pkwy.), Reston, VA, 703-834-6300 ◐
◪ With their strategic suburban locations, "nouvelle" comfort food (white chile and veal meat loaf) and "faux elegance", these high-energy bistros "serve a great purpose" as surrogates for bulldozed neighborhood bars; but crowds, noise, sheer size and the resultant "ups and downs" in food and service lead some to "grab a bite before a movie", but not "to linger."

Bistro Francais ◐S | 21 | 18 | 19 | $29 |
3128 M St., NW (bet. 31st St. & Wisconsin Ave.), 202-338-3830
■ "Paris on M Street" is prized for its "lunch bargains" and "early-bird prix fixe specials"; however, it's not until "late night" (when the bars close and the chefs pile in for steak tartare and frites) that this Georgetown bistro truly feels "très français", with an "authentically brusque" staff serving up "reliable" fare in "Left Bank" surroundings.

Washington, D.C. | F | D | S | C |

Bistro 123 ▽ | 24 | 21 | 24 | $28 |
246 Maple Ave. E. (bet. Center & Glyndon Sts.), Vienna, VA, 703-938-4379
■ This "delightful successor" to what was Pierre and Madeleine's brings "affordable" French bistro fare to Vienna's main drag; new owners spruced up the shopping strip premises and added "casual" choices to the classic menu.

Bistrot Lepic S | 24 | 18 | 22 | $38 |
1736 Wisconsin Ave., NW (S St.), 202-333-0111
■ "Very Gallic", "right down to the smoke", "tight seating" and "solid" French Provençal food, this Upper Georgetown storefront charms what is left of that neighborhood's Old Guard, and nearly everyone else; run by a "delightful" couple ("he cooks, she stays out front"), it is considered such "a gem" that one "hesitates to talk it up."

Bleu Rock Inn S | 24 | 25 | 24 | $43 |
Bleu Rock Inn, Rte. 211 (5 mi. west of Hwy. 522N), Washington, VA, 540-987-3190
◪ Overlooking vineyards and rolling hills, this "French-style" Virginia inn with "imaginative", "very good" Contemporary American food and service is best for a "peaceful" Sunday brunch; a popular weekend destination, its "spectacular" surroundings make dining here so "delightful" that missteps ("inconsistent, inexperienced help") are forgiven.

Blue & Gold S | 14 | 18 | 15 | $22 |
3100 Clarendon Blvd. (Highland St.), Arlington, VA, 703-908-4995
◪ Many prefer the cheap "happy hour appetizers" ($2) and "fine" brews in the bar to the "too ambitious", "pricey Cajun menu" at this Clarendon brewpub; it's "loud" and "smoky", but that doesn't mean it's not "fun" for "yuppies."

Blue Ocean S | – | – | – | M |
9440 Main St. (Pickett St.), Fairfax, VA, 703-425-7555
Some of the "best sushi, by far, outside the Virginia Beltway" crow the few who know this Fairfax Japanese and are willing to go out on the deep end about it; while "it's nothing to look at", it's frequented by local Japanese and does an "above-average" job with very fresh fish, tempura and teriyaki.

Blue Plate S | 16 | 16 | 16 | $18 |
2002 P St., NW (bet. New Hampshire Ave. & 20th St.), 202-293-2248
◪ Given its "hip" manners and blue-ribbon "pedigree" (Obelisk and Pizzeria Paradiso cousin), many want this contemporary Dupont Circle "haute diner" "to be better than it is": while many of its updated American classics (grilled cheese, donuts and dessert) "usually succeed", "the word 'diner' doesn't jibe with the prices" and the "spare" atmosphere can seem "chilly."

Blue Point Grill [S] 22 | 18 | 20 | $31

600 Franklin St. (Washington St.), Alexandria, VA, 703-739-0404

■ "Imaginative seafood in forgettable surroundings" is the short of it; the rest of this Alexandrian's story is that "fresh" finfare (from the adjacent Sutton Place Gourmet) is "well presented", albeit slowly, along with congenial California wines, in a saloon-style room and a streetside cafe.

Bob & Edith's Diner ◐ [S] 🚫 16 | 12 | 17 | $10

2310 Columbia Pike (S. Wayne St.), Arlington, VA, 703-920-6103

◪ You won't believe the "long lines" at 2 AM waiting to get into this "greasy, loud and tons o' fun" Arlington "dive"; whether it's the colorful crowd ("many tattoos") or the fact that most "real" diners are defunct, "it's the experience, not the food" or "manic" service, that's the reason most go; still, it's a very "cheap" fill-up.

Bombay Bistro [S] 24 | 14 | 19 | $18

Bell's Corner, 98 W. Montgomery Ave. (Washington St.), Rockville, MD, 301-762-8798

3570 Chain Bridge Rd. (Lee Hwy.), Fairfax, VA, 703-359-5810

■ No "passport" is needed for a "bargain" taste of India at these highly-rated, "dependable but not elegant" suburban natives; patience is advised since they offer "wonderful food and gracious service" in "close quarters" with "no reservations"; take advantage of their vast menu or "great [lunch] buffet" to try "spicy" Southern Indian specialties.

BOMBAY CLUB [S] 25 | 25 | 25 | $36

815 Connecticut Ave., NW (bet. H & I Sts.), 202-659-3727

■ Beltway insiders and "unknowns" alike are "treated like rajas" at this "plush and hushed" Anglo-Indian power-dining room near the White House; a meal here is "elegant", "delicious" and impressive; in short, this place with "top-notch service" "gets everything right", causing one Republican to lament "too bad Clinton likes it."

Bombay Curry Company [S] – | – | – | I

Calvert Shopping Ctr., 3110 Mt. Vernon Ave. (W. Glebe Rd.), Alexandria, VA, 703-836-6363

You'd "be lucky to eat as well in Bombay" as at this relatively unknown Northern Virginia subcontinental, according to write-in enthusiasts; not only does it do an "outstanding" job with familiar favorites and dream up "creative" specials, it's a "bargain" and "friendly" to boot.

Bombay Palace [S] 23 | 21 | 21 | $29

2020 K St., NW (bet. 20th & 21st Sts.), 202-331-4200

◪ This K Street Indian is "not as fancy" as the nearby Bombay Club, but it is brightened by the presence of the "Indian community in regalia", who come for "authentic, spicy" dishes and "courteous" hospitality; however, some foes feel that its "occasional production-line food" diminishes its "good value."

Washington, D.C. | F | D | S | C |

Bread Line | 21 | 13 | 14 | $11 |
1751 Pennsylvania Ave., NW (bet. 17th & 18th Sts.), 202-822-8900
■ Mark Furstenberg's "industrial chic" bakery/cafe near the White House raises "carryout to a new level" with Internationally inspired bread-based meals (empanadas, piadinas), "fabulous soups" and salads, plus "excellent" artisanal loaves; sure you need "strong teeth" and high "tolerance" for lunchtime lines and a "chaotic" atmosphere, but who else could make a "tuna sandwich remarkable"?

B. Smith's S | 20 | 24 | 19 | $29 |
Union Station, 50 Massachusetts Ave., NE (N. Capitol St.), 202-289-6188
☑ Beneath Union Station's "glorious" vaulted space, a "snazzy" crowd of Capitol Hill pols, "homesick Southerners" and tourists waiting for a train dig into "nouvelle" Southern eats at this "elegant" dining spot; its "spirited" supper club vibes complement its highly seasoned cooking and personable help, but there's no unanimity about the food, perhaps reflecting last year's chef change.

Bua S | 21 | 14 | 18 | $20 |
1635 P St., NW (bet. 16th & 17th Sts.), 202-265-0828
☑ "P Street denizens" – an interesting mixture of "class and trash" – supply much of the decor at this neighborhood Thai that's a "reliable standby" for "small portions" of "quick", "affordable", "spicy" fare; but scoping out the street scene from the "outdoor deck" is what really "makes this place."

Bugaboo Creek Steak House S | 13 | 16 | 16 | $19 |
15710 Shady Grove Rd. (Rte. 270), Gaithersburg, MD, 301-548-9200
6820 Commerce Dr. (Backlick Rd.), Springfield, VA, 703-451-3300
☑ Supporters say these "take-the-grandchildren" places with a Canadian Northwest theme have "better props" – "distracting" "animated animals" and talking trees – than other midpriced steakhouses; however, most agree it's no place for gourmet foraging.

Buon Giorno S | 21 | 19 | 23 | $34 |
8003 Norfolk Ave. (Del Rey Ave.), Bethesda, MD, 301-652-1400
☑ For those who were "raised" at this "old-fashioned" – some say "stodgy" – Bethesda Italian, the "well-prepared" fish and pasta are as comforting as the "cocoon-like" surroundings; most patrons are "never disappointed", but there are "no surprises" either.

Burma S | 22 | 10 | 17 | $17 |
740 Sixth St., NW (bet. G & H Sts.), 202-638-1280
■ "Cheap", "exotic" and "delicious" Burmese dining set in a "charming" "upstairs" "dive" that's within scoring distance of the MCI stadium and remains a major "reason to go to Chinatown"; the staff may be "slow", but they are "very knowledgeable about the food."

Washington, D.C.   F | D | S | C

Burrito Brothers ⊘   17 | 8 | 13 | $8
205 Pennsylvania Ave., SE (2nd St.), 202-543-6835
18251 I St., NW (bet. 18th & 19th Sts.), 202-887-8266
1815 M St., NW (bet. 18th & 19th Sts.), 202-785-3309 S
1524 Connecticut Ave., NW (Q St.), 202-332-2308 S
3273 M St., NW (Potomac St.), 202-965-3963 S
2418 18th St., NW (bet. Belmont St. & Columbia Rd.), 202-265-4048
11690 Plaza America Dr. (Sunset Hills Rd.), Reston, VA, 703-478-6394 S

■ Prized for the "amazing amount of food" crammed into one "cheap", "big-as-your-head" wrap, these burrito bars provide "fast, no-frills, no grease, nowhere to sit" (some locations) nourishment; on Capitol Hill, sharing one of their 12-inch "logs" is an intern's "power lunch", though some bean counters retort "filling but tasteless."

Burro ⊘   16 | 10 | 13 | $8
1134 19th St., NW (bet. L & M Sts.), 202-853-5041
1621 Connecticut Ave., NW (bet. Q & R Sts.), 202-483-6861 S
2000 Pennsylvania Ave., NW (20th St.), 202-293-9449 S

◪ Colorful, "clean, fast" Tex-Mex "fuel" stations that compete with "high-profile" Burrito Brothers outlets; you can "fill-up on loose change" at either minichain, but an emphasis on "fresh", low-fat, organic ingredients and a more varied menu is the "good deal" here; however, critics counter that flavor and housekeeping have "slipped" and a decrease in ratings supports this point of view.

Busara S   22 | 22 | 20 | $25
2340 Wisconsin Ave., NW (south of Calvert St.), 202-337-2340
8142 Watson St. (International Dr.), McLean, VA, 703-356-2288

■ These "highly designed" Thais in Tysons Corner and Upper Georgetown offer "exotic drinks" and "high-end fusion cuisine"; among their unexpected attributes are a "garden of Eden" courtyard (DC) and "kid-friendly" (if "overworked") servers (Tysons).

Cactus Cantina S   18 | 16 | 16 | $19
3300 Wisconsin Ave., NW (Macomb St.), 202-686-7222

◪ Cleveland Park families and American U coeds mingle in an atmosphere of festive "mayhem" at this "noisy" neighborhood cantina whose "freshly baked tortillas" and "good margaritas" outclass its south-of-the-border ("Velveeta on tostada") eats; despite seemingly constant expansion, there can be "horrendous waits" for tables.

Cafe Asia S   – | – | – | M
1134 19th St., NW (bet. L & M Sts.), 202-659-2696

Given the popularity of noodle houses for fast, cheap dining, don't be surprised if this "diverse" Dupont Circle Pan-Asian is "rushed" at lunch; its "sushi happy hour ($1 a piece)" is "crowded" too, but don't let that keep you from exploring the "wide selection" of Far Eastern foods.

31

Washington, D.C. F | D | S | C

Cafe Atlantico S   23 | 23 | 20 | $30
405 Eighth St., NW (bet. D & E Sts.), 202-393-0812
■ Don't be so dazzled by the "visual attractions" of this "trendy" Penn Quarter Nuevo Latino that you ignore its "intriguing" menu featuring food that's as "spirited" as the "stunning" multilevel setting, the cosmopolitan staff and clientele; be prepared, however, for a "helter-skelter" atmosphere, especially late at night, when a few feel "din-din not worth the din."

Cafe Berlin S   19 | 17 | 19 | $25
322 Massachusetts Ave., NE (bet. 3rd & 4th Sts.), 202-543-7656
■ Celebrate spring and asparagus along with Senate staffers who frequent the side patio of this "solid" German standby on the Hill, or opt for "brats" and the "largest mugs of beer in town"; for a "leisurely" lunch, there are also bargain soup-and-sandwich combos.

Cafe Bethesda S   23 | 19 | 20 | $38
5027 Wilson Ln. (bet. Arlington & Old Georgetown Rds.), Bethesda, MD, 301-657-3383
■ A "serious evening out" at this "intimate" Contemporary American "oasis in frantic Bethesda Restaurant-land" is like dining in "someone's lovely home", with mostly "excellent" cooking and "never rushed" vibes; however, some find it "crowded" and say "Downtown prices" make it a "better deal at lunch."

Cafe Dalat S   23 | 9 | 20 | $15
3143 Wilson Blvd. (Highland St.), Arlington, VA, 703-276-0935
■ This Clarendon Vietnamese may be "painfully plain", but it features "excellent" fare and is "a real bargain-hunter's treasure"; among its many virtues are the "good vegetarian options", "happy hosts" and a "Mom burns incense outside the door" verisimilitude to its counterpart back home.

Cafe Deluxe S   19 | 18 | 18 | $23
3228 Wisconsin Ave., NW (Macomb St.), 202-686-2233
■ Cleveland Park would welcome the slightest "whiff of Paris", so it's hardly surprising that this "trendy", "breezy sidewalk cafe" with its stylish American "comfort food" and deco decor is a smash hit; despite the "noisy" atmosphere and "discouraging long waits", it's family-friendly early in the evening and there's a major Thursday night bar "scene."

Cafe de Paris S   ∇ 24 | 18 | 21 | $30
14252 Baltimore Ave. (Mulberry St.), Laurel, MD, 301-490-8111
■ "Shush" – Laurel bec fins would rather we didn't "tell anyone about this Gallic gem", with its "copious servings" of "traditional" French bistro fare and ability to create a "cozy" atmosphere in a shopping mall; but if the worst that can be said is that it "tries too hard", it won't remain a secret for long.

Cafe Marianna [S] ▽ 20 | 17 | 20 | $24
1201 N. Royal St. (Bashford St.), Alexandria, VA, 703-519-3776
■ This "funky", "romantic" Alexandria hideaway, with its "quirky" collectibles ("anything is for sale"), bakery and indoor/outdoor seating, dishes up "delicious" New Orleans fare and "great desserts"; the "chef-owner has a heart and soul", likewise the "warm and witty staff", which means that you'll come as a customer, leave as a friend.

Cafe Milano ◐ [S] 20 | 19 | 17 | $35
3251 Prospect St., NW (bet. 33rd St. & Wisconsin Ave.), 202-333-6183
◩ Famed for its late-night Euro/celeb "action" and "curt if you're not a regular" attitude, this supercharged Georgetown pastaria can actually produce a "surprisingly good" meal (when not in the midst of "chef changes"); local "hard-haired ladies who lunch" do so on the "delightful" patio where it's "quiet" and relaxed.

Cafe Mileto [S] ▽ 20 | 18 | 20 | $23
Cloppers Mill Village, 18056 Mateny Rd. (Great Seneca Hwy.), Germantown, MD, 301-515-9370
■ "Decent" brick-oven pizza and an "inexpensive lunchtime buffet" bring a taste of Italy to this Germantown strip; the "eager-to-please" management has created a slick-looking yet "comfortable" cafe with an appealing menu of pastas, seafood and veal.

Cafe Mozart [S] 16 | 13 | 16 | $23
1331 H St., NW (bet. 13th & 14th Sts.), 202-347-5732
◩ Defenders of this "kitschy" German deli declare "when you want kraut and draft dark beer, this place is the only game Downtown"; while critics counter the food is only "so-so" and the atmosphere is "dingy", the consensus is the fare is "filling" and will do "in a pinch."

Cafe New Delhi [S] ▽ 22 | 15 | 21 | $18
1041 N. Highland St. (Clarendon Blvd.), Arlington, VA, 703-528-2511
■ "Standout vegetarian choices" and "fiery vindaloos" distinguish this "gracious" Arlington Indian whose simple surroundings are "more attractive" than others in the "cheap eats class"; check out its offbeat menu items.

Cafe Oggi [S] 18 | 17 | 18 | $30
6671 Old Dominion Dr. (bet. Lowell & Whittier Sts.), McLean, VA, 703-442-7360
◩ "Pretty" McLean Italian with a "suburban sensibility" which, in this case, means that seating is "close", the "mirrors distract" and the tuxedoed waiters are "aloof"; while comments on the food vary from "fine" to "easily forgettable", its greying clientele swears that the place is "improving after a slump."

Washington, D.C. F | D | S | C

Cafe on M S ▽ | 17 | 19 | 15 | $29
Westin Hotel, 2350 24th St., NW (M St.), 202-429-0100

◪ Not many surveyors have been to the dining room of this secluded West End hotel since the departure of its former chef, Robert Weidmaier (now at Aquarelle); however, suave appointments and a "stylish" New American menu make it relatively risk-free "for drinks" or a "nice business lunch."

Cafe Parisien Express S 19 | 13 | 15 | $13
4520 Lee Hwy. (bet. Woodrow & Woodstock Sts.), Arlington, VA, 703-525-3332

■ "Paris on the run" sums up this "popular" Northern Virginia "compact cafeteria" whose "no-frills counter service" and plastic plates signal a determination to remain bon marché; from breakfast on, the chalkboard lists homemade, French-accented fast food which, along with "very good pastries" and "personal touches", get a big '*oui*.'

Cafe Promenade S 19 | 22 | 22 | $32
Mayflower Hotel, 1127 Connecticut Ave., NW (bet. L & M Sts.), 202-347-2233

◪ DC's heavy hitters breakfast "as often as possible" in this "airy", skylit Downtown hotel lobby cafe, not to mention doing power lunches and "wonderful afternoon teas"; chef Tino Buggio "earns respect" for "delicious" Mediterranean food served in an "Old Washingtonian" atmosphere, but some balk at paying premium prices to dine in what is perceived as a coffee shop.

Cafe Renaissance S – | – | – | E
163 Glyndon St. (Maple Ave.), Vienna, VA, 703-938-3311

At this candlelit French "hidden" in a Vienna shopping center, Tony Tasbihi and Saeed Abtahi "go out of their way to make your meal an especially pleasant experience"; its clientele appreciates its "old-world charm" and easy parking.

Cafe Roval S – | – | – | M
Potomac Village, 9812 Falls Rd. (River Rd.), Potomac, MD, 301-299-3000

"Suburban Potomac" takes us to task for "overlooking" its "charming" New American bistro with a French accent whose shopping strip locale belies its serious approach to "quality" dining; it's one of those "they know everyone by name" "sleepers" where you can drop in for something special or just a bite.

Cafe Saigon S 21 | 13 | 21 | $18
1135 N. Highland St. (bet. Clarendon & Wilson Blvds.), Arlington, VA, 703-276-7110

■ Visitors to Clarendon's restaurant corridor often miss this "plain but immaculate" Vietnamese, which is frequented by local Asians; for a few bucks, you can get a fast, "light" meal and discover how "tasty" "good spring rolls", "excellent soft-shell crab" and caramel chicken can be.

Cafe Taj [S] ▽ 22 | 20 | 20 | $23

1379 Beverly Rd. (Old Dominion Dr.), McLean, VA, 703-827-0444

■ The "best of everything buffet lunch" in postmodern digs is one reason why savvy McLean diners "love" this "elegant" Indian with a varied menu; others are its "incredible bread basket", a staff that "remembers clientele", and not having to drive to DC for "top-quality" subcontinental cuisine.

Cajun Bangkok [S] 21 | 12 | 18 | $20

907 King St. (Alfred St.), Alexandria, VA, 703-836-0038

■ In an Alexandria storefront, a Thai chef who formerly cooked in Creole kitchens offers a "quirky combo [menu] that works", meaning it moves from *meong kom* (a Thai wrap) to "good étouffée"; like many "marriages", the food has its ups and downs – still, if you "like it hot, come here."

California Pizza Kitchen [S] 17 | 13 | 16 | $16

1260 Connecticut Ave. (N St.), 202-331-4020
Chevy Chase Pavilion, 5345 Wisconsin Ave., NW (Military Rd.), 202-363-6650
Montgomery Mall, 7101 Democracy Blvd. (Westlake Dr.), Bethesda, MD, 301-469-5090
700 King St. (S. Washington St.), Alexandria, VA, 703-706-0404
1201 S. Hayes St. (12th St.), Arlington, VA, 703-412-4900
Tysons Corner Ctr., 7939-L Tysons Corner Ctr. (Rte. 7), McLean, VA, 703-761-1473

◪ This "high-traffic" Cal-Ital chain upscales everyday dining with a dab of "quality" and "creative" flair; while most applaud their "different" but "dependable" pizzas, pastas and salads, as well as the "kid-friendly" help, critics counter these "cookie cutters" are "too bright" and "noisy" and feature some "bizarre combinations" – "all they need is Pepto-Bismol pizza."

California Tortilla [S] 20 | 13 | 18 | $10

4862 Cordell Ave. (bet. Norfolk & Woodmont Aves.), Bethesda, MD, 301-654-8226

■ "Wrap it up and take in the neighborhood scene" at the "best of [Bethesda's] healthy burrito" shops – a "friendly mom-and-pop" eat-in/carry-out that's willing to roll an "overstuffed" meal "your way"; for "what it is" – fast, fresh food with a huge "hot sauce selection" – you can't "beat the price."

Calvert Grille [S] 16 | 11 | 17 | $16

Calvert Apts., 3106 Mt. Vernon Ave. (bet. Commonwealth Ave. & Glebe Rd.), Alexandria, VA, 703-836-8425

■ How do Don and Lynn Abrams turn "average grub" and "strip mall space" into a "congenial" Del Ray "neighborhood eatery"? – with updated American comfort food, a "good beer selection", a toy-filled "kids' room" and "cheap" prices; "blue collars", button-down shirts – you'll see 'em all here.

Washington, D.C.

| F | D | S | C |

Canton Cafe ◐ S
▽ | 19 | 19 | 16 | $17

Twinbrook Shopping Ctr., 2007 Viers Mill Rd. (Twinbrook Pkwy.), Rockville, MD, 301-309-3888

■ Few Cantonese restaurants offer a cheaper or more comprehensive menu than this bright Rockville storefront; it lists everything from BBQ duck and dim sum to "exotic" innards, but some say "service is lacking" – ditto decor.

CAPITAL GRILLE S
24 | 24 | 23 | $43

601 Pennsylvania Ave., NW (6th St.), 202-737-6200

■ "Beefy, like much of its clientele", this "swank" "red meat and cigar" palace is "close to the Capitol" in more ways than one: its "power lunch roundup" lassoes "every lobbyist and top dog in the biz" for some of DC's "best steaks, lobster" and cosseting; at such times, if you're not a "regular", service can be "abrupt."

Capital Wrapps
17 | 10 | 15 | $10

4733 Bethesda Ave. (bet. Wisconsin & Woodmont Aves.), Bethesda, MD, 301-654-0262

■ A Bethesda pit stop that tweaks the tortilla-based, meal-on-the-run formula with "healthy", "novelty" wraps and "creative" drinks like the "best banana-date shakes"; despite having a "cafeteria-like decor", its patio is a "nice thought" on a lovely day.

Capitol City Brewing Co. S
14 | 16 | 16 | $18

Postal Sq., 2 Massachusetts Ave. (1st St.), 202-842-2337
1100 New York Ave., NW (11th St.), 202-628-2222
7735 Old Georgetown Rd. (Fairmont Ave.), Bethesda, MD, 301-652-2282
2700 S. Quincy St. (28th St.), Shirlington, VA, 703-578-3888

◪ These massive, "noisy" brewpubs are lunchtime "lawyer magnets", with "hyper" happy hours where "weekend Lotharios" prowl; most advise "stick to the burgers" and signature "soft pretzels", since the food takes a backseat to the seasonal microbrews and merriment.

Caravan Grill S
▽ | 16 | 11 | 17 | $18

1825 18th St., NW (bet. S & T Sts.), 202-518-0444

■ "When you're really hungry", the generous buffet of "tasty Persian delights" at this Adams Morgan East enclave is a "great" deal – especially when you factor in one of the area's nicest courtyards; if the "bargain" buffet dishes (a bit "oily" for a few) don't appeal, try the kebab menu.

CARLYLE GRAND CAFE S
23 | 21 | 21 | $26

4000 S. 28th St. (Quincy St.), Shirlington, VA, 703-931-0777

■ Shirlington's "shining star", this "designer" American with "well-executed" food, "team" service and "neo-deco decor" is "enjoyable and professional", despite the fact that a "no-reservations" policy means it's "always packed" and "noisy"; it's a please-everyone place that "earns all the accolades" and remains a surprisingly good value.

CASHION'S EAT PLACE [S]

F	D	S	C
25	21	21	$35

1819 Columbia Rd., NW (bet. Biltmore & Mintwood Sts.), 202-797-1819

■ At award-winning Ann Cashion's "refreshingly different" urban American bistro in Adams Morgan, you "don't have to dress up for great food" and "cosmopolitan" surroundings; they make everyone – from the President and parents with "teenagers in grunge clothes" to solo diners seated at the "happening" bar or sidewalk cafe – feel like "moving right in."

Cedar Knoll Inn [S]

F	D	S	C
17	19	17	$26

9030 Lucia Ln. (Vernon View Dr.), Alexandria, VA, 703-799-1501

◩ The view "overlooking the Potomac is lovely" and the porch is "romantic", but surveyors say the Mediterranean-American food is only "average"; that's too bad – the setting is so "wonderful", one would "like to like" this "homey" South Alexandria "holiday dinner" staple more.

Cesco

F	D	S	C
23	19	18	$38

4871 Cordell Ave. (Norfolk Ave.), Bethesda, MD, 301-654-8333

◩ At Bethesda's "best newcomer", eating Francesco Ricchi's native Tuscan cuisine is "like being back in Italia", with "wonderfully simple" risottos, pastas, roasts and grills; however, start-up glitches are reflected in reports of "inconsistent" food and "service that needs work."

C.F. Folks ⊘

F	D	S	C
23	9	17	$12

1225 19th St., NW (bet. M & N Sts.), 202-293-0162

■ Proclaimed a "national lunchtime treasure" by everyone from bikers to bankers and boldface names, this "dingy" Dupont Circle counter/carry-out dishes up "big time cooking" for small bucks; it's presided over by "DC's own 'Soup Nazi'", whose "insults come free" with the sandwiches and world-inspired blue plates; N.B. it serves weekday lunches only and closes at 3 PM.

Chardonnay [S]

F	D	S	C
▽ 19	18	18	$33

Doubletree Park Terrace Hotel, 1515 Rhode Island Ave., NW (Scott Circle), 202-232-7000

◩ There's an "undiscovered" air about this "lovely" Downtown hotel restaurant that belies its easy-to-reach location off Scott Circle; admittedly, its Contemporary American kitchen and staff can be "uneven" (the former showing "occasional flashes of brilliance"), yet it has a congenial courtyard for romantics and a winsome wine list for oenophiles.

Charley's Place [S]

F	D	S	C
15	15	16	$21

6903 Old Dominion (Rte. 123), McLean, VA, 703-893-1034

◩ Sooner or later, *le tout* McLean does time at this "standby" for a business lunch, meeting friends or "dinner with the kids"; no one really cares that the "middle-aged American" food is "forgettable", the decor "tired" and the service "average" – it's their place.

Washington, D.C. |F|D|S|C|

Charlie Chiang's Grande Cafe S |–|–|–|I|
631 H St., NW (bet. 6th & 7th Sts.), 202-216-9696
One of Chinatown's best bargains, this handsome flagship of a well-established local chain features a big Cantonese buffet spread; but if all-you-can-eat grazing is not your style, "order from the menu" of Szechuan and other regional fare.

Chart House S |19|21|19|$30|
1 Cameron St. (bet. King & Union Sts.), Alexandria, VA, 703-684-5080

■ Of course, you're "paying for the view", and some question whether the Chesapeake seafood and steak are worth serious money and long waits; while pros praise the "reliable" fare, singling out the "great mud pie", foes warn it's got "that franchise feeling" and say stick to brunch.

CHEESECAKE FACTORY ●S |21|18|18|$21|
Chevy Chase Pavilion, 5345 Wisconsin Ave., NW (bet. Jennifer St. & Western Ave.), 202-364-0500
White Flint Mall, 11301 Rockville Pike (Nicholson Ln.), Rockville, MD, 301-770-0999

■ There are no just-in-time arrivals at these Big Food factories – with "no reservations", "humongous" servings and an "overwhelming" California menu (most of it "consistently good"), near "unbearable" noise and waits are routine; adherents avoid the "department store at Christmas" frenzy and bypass the "beeper hall" for the bar, where they "get served right away."

Chicken Out S |17|12|15|$10|
4866 Massachusetts Ave., NW (49th St.), 202-364-8646
4839 Bethesda Ave. (Wisconsin Ave.), Bethesda, MD, 301-907-8646
Cabin John Mall, 11325 Seven Locks Rd. (Tuckerman Rd.), Cabin John, MD, 301-299-8646
15780 Shady Grove Rd. (Gaither Rd.), Gaithersburg, MD, 301-921-9119
245 Kentlands Blvd. (Great Seneca Hwy.), Gaithersburg, MD, 301-975-0100
10116-B River Rd. (Falls Rd.), Potomac, MD, 301-299-8585
1560 Rockville Pike (opp. Congressional Plaza), Rockville, MD, 301-230-2020
1443-A Chain Bridge Rd. (Laughlin St.), McLean, VA, 703-917-8646
2946-L Chain Bridge Rd. (Hunter Mill Rd.), Oakton, VA, 703-319-8646
4648 Plaza America Dr. (Sunrise Valley), Reston, VA, 703-834-1100

■ Most suburbanites swear these recently hatched "high-end" chicken take-out shops are indispensable for everything from a "quick dinner" to "Thanksgiving" help; their "homestyle cooking", "fabulous mashed potatoes" and "decent" prices "beat Boston Market"; the few who "chicken out" from shopping here call the fare "bland and boring."

Washington, D.C.   F | D | S | C

Chicken Place S   ▽ 18 | 10 | 17 | $12
11201 Grandview Ave. (Reedie Dr.), Wheaton, MD, 301-946-1212
■ Head for this simple Wheaton spot for "great cheap meals" that feature "excellent" rotisserie-roasted chicken and "good Peruvian" sides; your food will be politely served in an atmosphere with "no pretensions" and "no decor"; "plan to be out late" if you want to take in the lively music and dancing scene too.

China Canteen S   ▽ 20 | 11 | 21 | $18
808 Hungerford Dr. (Ivy League Ln.), Rockville, MD, 301-424-1606
■ "Don't let the [lack of] decor scare you away" from one of Rockville's "best", most "authentic" Chinese with "good prices"; it's run by "very nice" people who patiently explain the interesting "homestyle dishes" and "unusual" specials.

Chris'   ▽ 17 | 11 | 19 | $19
201 E. Diamond Ave. (bet. Park & Summit Aves.), Gaithersburg, MD, 301-869-6116
■ When folks in Gaithersburg have "had a bad day", they amble over to this "comfortable", "relaxing", fairly priced "meat-and-potato paradise" for "sizable steaks and chops"; rumor has it that it's "too local" for the yups.

"Ciao baby" Cucina   19 | 20 | 17 | $26
Washington Sq., 1736 L St., NW (bet. Connecticut Ave. & 18th St.), 202-331-1500
◪ The "lawyer crowd" mobs this Farragut Square Italian's $12 lunch buffet and there is fierce "competition" for happy hour bar seats, where "free food" vies with a "30-40s" scene; although critics snipe that there's "lots of decor, but few stellar dishes", most concede that "it's a great place when style and price are more important than quality."

Cities   19 | 22 | 17 | $31
2424 18th St., NW (Columbia Rd.), 202-328-7194
◪ An "impressive remodeling" transformed this Adams Morgan International into a "beautiful" backdrop for the "Euro-trendy" and "suburban wanna-bes trying to feel urbane"; "food and decor themes change" and the kitchen is equally changeable but "when it's good, it's good"; regulars hope "their next 'city' will be a place with decent service."

CITRONELLE S   24 | 23 | 23 | $48
(aka Michel Richard's Citronelle)
Latham Hotel, 3000 M St., NW (30th St.), 202-625-2150
◪ This posh Georgetown dining room is the "place to see the who's who of DC", and now that superchef Michel Richard is permanently "at home" in its kitchen, it is equally a place for "exquisite food" and expense-account pampering; given its spectacular multimillion dollar new look and its cutting-edge Cal-French cuisine, its already excellent ratings (which predated the redo) should soar and win over doubters who dub it "overpriced."

Washington, D.C.   F | D | S | C

CITY LIGHTS OF CHINA S   24 | 13 | 18 | $19
1731 Connecticut Ave., NW (bet. R & S Sts.), 202-265-6688
■ "Lines are long", "tables are too close", waiters "snatch the dishes" and the "bathroom decor" ain't much, yet this "great source" of "delicious", "inexpensive" Chinese food is packed; late hours and a convenient Dupont Circle location mean crowds – consequently many "speed dial" for delivery, especially since its new regime (winter '98) limits lingering.

Clyde's S   18 | 21 | 19 | $23
Georgetown Park Mall, 3236 M St., NW (Wisconsin Ave.), 202-333-9180
70 Wisconsin Circle (bet. Western & Wisconsin Aves.), Chevy Chase, MD, 301-951-9600
1700 N. Beauregard St. (Seminary Rd.), Alexandria, VA, 703-820-8300
Reston Town Ctr., 11905 Market St. (Reston Pkwy.), Reston, VA, 703-787-6601 ◐
■ Nearly 1,500 surveyors give these affordable American brasseries "an A for effort", citing "imaginative preparations" of "tavern" fare, farm-fresh ingredients, "alert" servers, late hours and "classy", comfortable, "any occasion" settings; of course, "occasional" stumbles happen – these spots are some of the biggest and busiest in town; still, "all things considered, surprisingly good."

Coco Loco   19 | 21 | 17 | $29
817 Seventh St., NW (bet. H & I Sts.), 202-289-2626
◪ "Think Rio Carnival" to get a handle on this South American's late-night "eat, drink, then rumba" scene; it's fueled by wicked Brazilian drinks and *churrascaria* (an all-you-can-eat "meat fest") and when it revs up, forget conversation; however, some revelers recommend that this Penn Quarter party-place ditch its "too-trendy-for-you" attitude and work on consistency in the kitchen.

Coeur De Lion S   25 | 25 | 25 | $44
Henley Park Hotel, 926 Massachusetts Ave., NW (10th St.), 202-638-5200
■ This "elegant" hotel dining room is formal enough "for a special occasion", yet so "romantic", "you feel like kissing" or dancing the night away; service is "exceptional" and the New American food doesn't lag far behind; blame (or bless) its offbeat Downtown location for keeping it "little known."

Connaught Place S   25 | 20 | 24 | $24
10425 North St. (bet. Rte. 236W & University Dr.), Fairfax, VA, 703-352-5959
■ "Hidden" behind lace curtains in Fairfax City (although it could be in "Delhi or London"), this small, "delightful neighborhood" subcontinental proves that you don't need a "glamorous" address to produce "first-rate" food; here, Indian standards are "subtly seasoned", "not greasy" and served by people who "care about you."

Washington, D.C. F | D | S | C

Coppi's S 20 | 19 | 17 | $23
1414 U St., NW (bet. 14th & 15th Sts.), 202-319-7773
Coppi's Vignorelli S
3421 Connecticut Ave. (bet. Macomb & Porter Sts.), 202-244-6437

◪ These "high-energy", neighborhood-oriented Italian sibs use their wood-burning ovens in "imaginative" ways; yet, at both the "dressy pizza" parlor on U Street, and the full-menu "authentic Ligurian" on Connecticut Avenue, food quality "varies", the pace is "hectic" and the "service could use some help"; however, the "Nutella calzone is divine."

Cottonwood Cafe S 20 | 20 | 19 | $26
4844 Cordell Ave. (bet. Old Georgetown Rd. & Wisconsin Ave.), Bethesda, MD, 301-656-4844
Cottonwood Ranch S
Cloppers Mill Village, 18050 Mateny Rd. (Great Seneca Hwy.), Germantown, MD, 301-515-1003

◪ Comments on these suburban cowboy cantinas are separated by the Continental Divide: pros (mostly young) go for the mingling, the tongue-tingling Southwestern fare and eyeing the "personable" help, while naysayers beg for "asbestos" plates, one "plain" menu item and earplugs; both contingents find them handy for an upscale "business lunch."

Crisfield S 20 | 9 | 17 | $27
8012 Georgia Ave. (East-West Hwy. & Railroad St.), Silver Spring, MD, 301-589-1306

◪ The fresh, "basic seafood" – most of it fried – and the "personalities" that made this Silver Spring fishhouse an "institution" can still be "experienced", though it grows more chancy, "expensive" and "tacky" with time; "sit at the bar and order oysters" or an Old Maryland specialty, "chew the fat" with the help and "forget the cinder block walls."

Crisfield at Lee Plaza S 17 | 13 | 16 | $26
Lee Plaza, 8606 Colesville Rd. (Georgia Ave.), Silver Spring, MD, 301-588-1572

◪ Separately owned and operated, this Silver Spring shopping center spawn lacks the "original" Chesapeake seafooder's nostalgic charm; it may be "prettier", but the majority maintains the food is "not up to the original", with the possible exception of "great crab salad and crab cakes."

Crisp & Juicy S 22 | 6 | 13 | $10
Sunshine Sq., 1331-G Rockville Pike (Congressional Plaza), Rockville, MD, 301-251-8833
Leisure World Plaza, 3800 International Dr. (Georgia Ave.), Silver Spring, MD, 301-598-3333
Lee Hts., 4520 Lee Hwy. (Lorcom Ln.), Arlington, VA, 703-243-4222

■ These aptly named Peruvians "have perfected chicken roasting", spicy saucing and terrific ethnic sides at "cheap" prices; there's "no atmosphere", which makes "takeout" the preferred option.

Washington, D.C. | F | D | S | C |

Crystal Thai S | 23 | 17 | 21 | $18 |
Arlington Forest Shopping Ctr., 4819 Arlington Blvd. (Park Dr.), Arlington, VA, 703-522-1311
■ In a simple Arlington setting that evokes "Hemingway's clean, well-lighted place", this "once-a-week" Thai offers "speedy, pleasant service" of "delicious, inexpensive" food like seafood and curries.

Da Domenico | 20 | 17 | 20 | $31 |
1992 Chain Bridge Rd. (Rte. 123), Tysons Corner, VA, 703-790-9000
◪ An opera-loving padrone envelopes Tysons Corner "high-techies" with a warm "Italian embrace" and "abundant portions" of "hearty classics" at this "'50s in New Jersey" step back in time; even those who find the ambiance "hokey" and menu dated say the staff "always makes you smile."

Daily Grill S | 17 | 19 | 17 | $23 |
1200 18th St., NW (M St.), 202-822-5282
Tysons Galleria, 2001 International Dr. (Rte. 123), Tysons Corner, VA, 703-288-5100
◪ Young Connecticut Avenue strivers brave "long waits" at lunchtime to stoke up on the "endless menu" at this big, bustling American, and after work they drop by for martinis at the handsome horseshoe bar; but what some dub "decent, basic" cooking, others call "overpriced diner food", concluding this chain outpost is "nothing special"; N.B. the Tysons Corner branch is new and unrated.

Dante S | 21 | 21 | 19 | $37 |
1148 Walker Rd. (Colvin Run Rd.), Great Falls, VA, 703-759-3131
■ This "lovely", antiques-filled Victorian cossets Great Falls residents with its "European" manner, raises their "cholesterol levels" with "delicious" Northern Italian food, and charges accordingly; locals find it easier to overlook the "high prices" because the owners are "always there."

Dave and Busters ●S | 12 | 16 | 13 | $18 |
White Flint Mall, 11301 Rockville Pike (Nicholson Ln.), Rockville, MD, 301-230-5151
◪ Nobody goes to this "loud", "cavernous", high-tech playground in White Flint for the food; still, after hours of "sensory overload" ("too loud for my teenage son"), you may need to brace yourself with the "faddish menu" of bar snacks and "typical chain-type food", which is enlivened by "tableside magic", but not by the "mayhem."

DC Coast | – | – | – | E |
1401 K St., NW (14th St.), 202-216-5988
Airy, mirrored, polished and dramatically chic, this long-heralded Downtown newcomer looks every inch the power center it was designed to be; its art deco style matches its smooth personnel profile and, with the much-missed Jeff Tunks (ex River Club) turning out multiregional New American cuisine, it's also fulfilling its food destination destiny.

Washington, D.C. | F | D | S | C |

Dean & DeLuca Cafe | 19 | 14 | 13 | $13 |
3276 M St., NW (33rd St.), 202-342-2500 S
1299 Pennsylvania Ave., NW (bet. E & 13th Sts.), 202-628-8155
1919 Pennsylvania Ave., NW (bet. I & 19th Sts.), 202-296-4327
◪ A "great, post-shopping recovery zone" in Georgetown offering primo "people-watching", counter-served, market-fresh salads, sandwiches "on impeccable bread" and sweets; its "New York style" is appreciated, but not the "Tokyo prices" and "grumpy" manners – the same goes for its midday snackeries Downtown.

Delhi Dhaba S | 19 | 7 | 14 | $11 |
7236 Woodmont Ave. (bet. Bethesda Ave. & Elm St.), Bethesda, MD, 301-718-0008
2424 Wilson Blvd. (bet. Barton St. & Clarendon Blvd.), Arlington, VA, 703-524-0008
■ Offering "amazing", cheap, fast subcontinental eats "complemented" by "zany" and "annoying" Indo/Pak TV, this "dreary" Arlington "cafeteria/truck stop" (or *dhaba*) is much like its counterpart in India; the Bethesda outlet "has moved upmarket" with a full-service dining room (and a stab at decor), while the Courthouse self-serve sib boasts a slick setting; all do "spicy" home cooking, eat-in or carry-out.

Del Ray Garden & Grill S | ▽ 21 | 16 | 21 | $18 |
4918 Del Ray Ave. (bet. Cordell Ave. & Old Georgetown Rd.), Bethesda, MD, 301-986-0606
■ Indochina's "French influence" pervades this "pretty, little" Bethesda spot with "sophisticated", "beautifully prepared" Vietnamese dishes that come as a "pleasant surprise" (or seem "bland") to those who associate more assertively spiced food with the country; other pleasantries include "personable servers", a tiny garden and across-the-street public parking.

District ChopHouse & Brewery S | 19 | 22 | 20 | $28 |
509 Seventh St., NW (bet. E & F Sts.), 202-347-3434
◪ This classy Penn Quarter restoration "captures the chophouse mood" with "great" on-site microbrews, a "pizza to prime rib" menu, billiards and a "jumpin'" bar scene; the effect is somewhat marred by a "s-l-o-w" kitchen, but it's "near MCI" (Sports Arena) and the Shakespeare Theater and makes a "great addition to the area."

Dolcetto S | 16 | 18 | 15 | $31 |
3201 New Mexico Ave. (bet. Cathedral & Nebraska Aves.), 202-966-0500
◪ Sure, in warm weather it's "very nice" to dine on this newcomer's terrace, and it feels like a "romantic grotto" inside; but while this Northern Italian bears Roberto Donna's (Galileo) pedigree, the food is "not there yet" and the service, "while enthusiastic", "needs improvement"; nonetheless, its Northwest DC patrons hope it keeps "evolving nicely", though it "could go either way."

Washington, D.C.   F | D | S | C

Donatello ◐ S   20 | 17 | 21 | $31
2514 L St., NW (bet. Pennsylvania Ave. & 25th St.), 202-333-1485
■ Set in "quaint" West End quarters, this "underrated", "comfy" Italian's "consistent handling of the basics" provides a reality check on the Milano moderns; but while its pre-theater specials remain a Kennedy Center patron's "best call" and diners "don't have to plan a month ahead" to get in, it can be "cramped", "noisy" and "rushed."

DUANGRAT'S S   25 | 21 | 22 | $25
5878 Leesburg Pike (Glen Forest Rd.), Falls Church, VA, 703-820-5775
■ This *Survey's* top Thai provides an "elegant" Northern Virginia backdrop for "skillfully seasoned" food; to say that its "brilliant" specials and "gracious" waitresses (in traditional dress) "make French food seem boring and Italian waiters seem rude" may overstate matters, but still, this place will "impress the boss" for a fraction of the cost of a comparable meal Downtown.

Dusit S   23 | 16 | 20 | $17
2404 University Blvd. W. (Georgia Ave.), Wheaton, MD, 301-949-4140
■ With dozens of under $9 dishes, it's not surprising that this Wheaton Thai is a "regular dining out spot" for local foodies; family-run and "friendly", its "minimalist" setting is prettified with pastels and neon lights, and most think its kitchen "shines."

Dynasty ◐ S   ▽ 20 | 15 | 18 | $17
11123 Viers Mill Rd. (Reedie Dr.), Wheaton, MD, 301-942-3070
■ "Really late" diners can join Wheaton's Chinese residents for Hong Kong treats at this unfancy Cantonese address; its regulars tout "some very good dishes" (like braised duck or salted shrimp), but if you're not one, stick to the "daily Chinese specials" or you'll think you've hit a "greasy spoon."

Eat First S   20 | 7 | 15 | $13
728 Seventh St., NW (bet. G & H Sts.), 202-347-0936
■ Few local ethnics capture the adventurous spirit of "third world" dining as completely as this Chinatown Cantonese; it's just steps from the glitzy MCI Center, yet its "hole-in-the-wall" setting, "excellent" Hong Kong–style duck and noodle soups and "cheapie" prices seem a continent away.

Ecco Cafe S   20 | 17 | 18 | $21
220 N. Lee St. (Cameron St.), Alexandria, VA, 703-684-0321
■ When Alexandria's old guard, mayor and local celebs want Italian food, Virginia-style, they opt for the "abundant portions" of pasta, "unique" pizzas and "familiar faces inside" this popular, "crowded" and "noisy" gathering place; Diana Damewood's exuberant personality (and eclectic decorative taste) pervades her bistro, and service suffers when she's not there.

Washington, D.C.   F | D | S | C

El Catalan   21 | 25 | 17 | $37
1319 F St., NW (bet. 13th & 14th Sts.), 202-628-2299
◪ "Barcelona meets DC" at this "dazzling" evocation of Iberian rusticity, which was instantly annexed upon opening by Downtown VIPs; chef-owner Yannick Cam's "expertise" is reflected both in the refined barroom tapas and the dining room entrees; now that he has directed his attention here, early "kinks" – "inconsistent" dishes served so slowly diners suspect they're "individually shipped" from Spain – should smooth out.

El Gavilan S   ▽ 16 | 10 | 16 | $15
8805 Flower Ave. (Pine Branch Rd.), Silver Spring, MD, 301-587-4197
■ This "lively", "inexpensive" Silver Spring eatery's many Salvadoran customers evidence its authenticity, yet the staff is equally "friendly" and "attentive" to outsiders; surveyors say "try the Salvadoran specials", a "hefty" pork dish or "great" ribs, and for the full cultural experience stick around for the weekend "entertainment."

El Pollo Rico S⊉   24 | 5 | 15 | $8
2541 Ennalls Ave. (Viers Mill Rd.), Wheaton, MD, 301-942-4419
2915-2917 N. Washington Blvd. (10th St.), Arlington, VA, 703-522-3220
7031 Brookfield Plaza Rd. (Amherst Ave.), Springfield, VA, 703-866-1286
■ "Wall-to-wall" rotisserie chickens and their enticing smells are all these "fast, friendly" chicken shacks have in the way of atmosphere, but "frugal folks" don't mind a bit since they're probably doing takeout and definitely paying chicken feed for "moist and flavorful" birds marinated with a "delicious" secret seasoning and Peruvian sides.

El Tamarindo S   17 | 9 | 15 | $14
1785 Florida Ave., NW (bet. 18th & U Sts.), 202-328-3660 ☽
7331 Georgia Ave., NW (Fessenden Rd.), 202-291-0525
4910 Wisconsin Ave., NW (42nd St.), 202-244-8888 ☽
◪ "Late hours" (3 AM) and "great", "potent" margaritas are the attractions at these low-rent Salvadorans popular with Adams Morgan barhoppers, movie-goers and all-night crammers; food is "cheap and plentiful", if "a bit greasy", and it helps if you speak Spanish.

Elysium S   ▽ 26 | 25 | 24 | $42
Morrison House Hotel, 116 S. Alfred St. (bet. King & Prince Sts.), Alexandria, VA, 703-838-8000
◪ "Very Old Town (in a good way)", this "elegant" hotel dining room would feel "stuffy" if the staff weren't so "nice"; an orchestrated prix fixe Contemporary American dinner here is so "relaxing", it's "more [like] therapy" than going out to eat; tea and brunch are equally "delightful" and unrushed.

Evans Farm Inn [S] 13 20 16 $28

1696 Chain Bridge Rd. (Rte.123), McLean, VA, 703-356-8000
◪ "McLean's country heritage" survives in this colonial mansion's traditional furnishings, "beautiful" grounds (duck pond and children's zoo) and American "farmhouse" menu; but not for long – it plans to close by the millenium; so hurry up and schedule those "receptions, office parties" and family gatherings for which it's well known.

Evening Star Cafe [S] 17 18 15 $23

2000 Mt. Vernon Ave. (Howell St.), Alexandria, VA, 703-549-5051
◪ As its name suggests, this Southern-accented American in Del Ray is heralding the neighborhood's comeback; a "funky" lounge and game room have quickly made it a "local hangout"; though capable of good vittles, a number find the food "too spotty" and service "inexperienced."

Faccia Luna Pizzeria [S] 21 16 17 $16

2400 Wisconsin Ave., NW (Calvert St.), 202-337-3132
2909 Wilson Blvd. (Filmore St.), Arlington, VA, 703-276-3099
■ These congenial "pizza and get-together places" bring back your college days with "high-ranking" crusty pies with "great toppings" and microbrews; the "casual and cozy atmosphere" also attracts kids early in the day, followed by dating couples and wearers of backwards baseball caps.

Fadó Irish Pub [S] – – – M

808 Seventh St., NW (bet. H & I Sts.), 202-789-0066
In an Old Country fantasy pub setting near the MCI Center, this recent Gaelic import gives New Irish cooking and hospitality a good name; go for updated versions of shepherd's pie and *boxty* (potato crêpes) all washed down with Irish malt and happy hour/post-game bonhomie.

Faryab Afghan Cuisine 23 17 19 $22

4917 Cordell Ave. (bet. Norfolk Ave. & Old Georgetown Rd.), Bethesda, MD, 301-951-3484
■ This softly lit Bethesda Afghani occupies a "welcome" dining middle ground with its mildly spiced, moderately priced Middle Eastern food and "pleasant" (when not "too crowded") atmosphere; for local mavens the "superb" pumpkin stew, "heavenly" *aushak* (ravioli) and "aromatic rice" are almost "like having [their beloved but defunct] Kabul West back again."

Fedora Cafe [S] – – – M

8521 Leesburg Pike (bet. Dulles Access Rd. & Rte. 123), Tysons Corner, VA, 703-556-0100
Fueling Tysons Corner's high-tech hub requires decent food and a dressed down but upscale atmosphere, as exemplified by this polished wood and etched glass Cal-Italian; it does a "nice business lunch", even better desserts, and turns into a lively singles-mingles spot with live jazz several nights a week.

Washington, D.C. | F | D | S | C |

Felix ☒ | 20 | 20 | 17 | $31 |
2406 18th St., NW (Belmont Rd.), 202-483-3549
■ An unlikely combination of "great" martinis, Manhattan SoHo chic and homemade chicken soup is earning this Adams Morgan Eclectic a following among trendies; its enterprising young chef, Davis Scribner, cooks everything from his mother's Friday night brisket to "creative" cuisine; it's all "very NY" (for DC), including "pushy" waiters, a "dramatic" setting and after-dinner club scene.

Fellini | ▽ 20 | 19 | 18 | $29 |
1800 M St. (18th St.), 202-785-1177
■ This glitzy Italian-Mediterranean cafe, a tribute to director Federico Fellini, is "nicely laid out" (in Gary's former M Street space), with "far-apart tables" that are "great for business" meals, but sometimes without the smooth service that greases deals; still, the food that's "good is very good", and a "generous happy hour buffet" segues into a "party."

Filomena Ristorante ☒ | 21 | 20 | 19 | $32 |
1063 Wisconsin Ave., NW (bet. K & M Sts.), 202-338-8800
◪ With "pasta mamas" making noodles in the window, Xmas in July decor, "gigantic" helpings and "overwhelming" noise, virtually everything about this Italian "production number" in Georgetown is over-the-top and extra-sized; tourists "love it", so do celebs, but gastronomes are less impressed: "heavy", "slow", "tired."

Fiorentino's ☒ | – | – | – | M |
Olney Town Ctr., 18101 Town Center Dr. (Rte. 108), Olney, MD, 301-570-8226
Rosa and Richard Schinella share their love of Italian food and wine in this casual yet candlelit "shopping plaza restaurant" in Olney; he runs the front of the house, she's in the kitchen – together they produce an ambitious six-course *pranzo* (tasting menu) that comes with a gratis glass of wine, or help diners compose lighter, "homemade tasting" meals from the extensive menu.

Firehook Bakery & Coffeehouse ☒ | 24 | 15 | 18 | $9 |
1909 Q St., NW (19th St.), 202-588-9296
917 17th St. (bet. I & K Sts.), 202-429-2253
3411 Connecticut Ave., NW (bet. Macomb & Newark Sts.), 202-362-2253
214 N. Fayette St. (bet. Cameron & Queen Sts.), Alexandria, VA, 703-519-8020
■ "Splendid" specialty breads like "habit-forming" focaccia, "hearty" sandwiches and "TDF" (to-die-for) sweets turn snacks at these bakery/cafes into "memorable lunches", with a quality-to-price ratio that makes them this *Survey's* No. 1 Bang for the Buck; despite occasionally "inept but lovable" service, they're "cozy retreats", with "more seating" in Cleveland Park's delightful garden and modish backroom.

Washington, D.C.   F | D | S | C

Florida Ave. Grill   20 | 11 | 17 | $12
1100 Florida Ave., NW (11th St.), 202-265-1586
■ Its Northwest DC neighborhood has changed (and not for the better), but this Southern diner relic keeps on doing its thing – treating everyone like an "insider", filling their bellies and nurturing their souls; it's "where the famous dress down and sneak off to pig out" on great, "greasy" stuff like "pig's feet for breakfast – hallelujah."

Food Factory S   20 | 6 | 13 | $9
8145-G Baltimore Ave. (University Blvd.), College Park, MD, 301-345-8888
4221 N. Fairfax Dr. (Glebe Rd.), Arlington, VA, 703-527-2279
1116 Herndon Pkwy. (Elden St.), Herndon, VA, 703-435-3333
■ "Highly spiced, belly-busting plates of food" are dished up at these Pakistani kebab-and-curry houses, where the pace at lunch is "fast and furious" and the "no-frills" cafeteria atmosphere "doesn't encourage lingering"; but no one's complaining – "they keep the prices low and the food great."

Foong Lin   20 | 15 | 20 | $19
7710 Norfolk Ave. (Fairmont Ave.), Bethesda, MD, 301-656-3427
■ At tony Bethesda's family Chinese, the "Hunan chicken is addictive, parking is a pain" and when it's "busy things get slow"; still, it uses "high-quality" ingredients, does an "above-average" job with standards and "accommodates" menu "variations" with a smile; in short, it's "reliable", but you "won't get ecstatic."

Fortune S   22 | 13 | 17 | $18
Glen Forest Shopping Ctr., 5900 Leesburg Pike (Glen Forest Dr.), Falls Church, VA, 703-998-8888
N. Point Village Ctr., 1428 Reston Pkwy. (bet. Baron Cameron Rd. & Rte. 7), Reston, VA, 703-318-8898 ☾
■ These Northern Virginians, known for "excellent" dim sum served in an "appropriately crazed Hong Kong–style" (think "crowded" and "noisy"), also produce some of the area's "best" Chinese seafood; but be prepared for language barriers, and when there are no "entertaining" Asian wedding parties, or bumper-to-bumper weekend rolling carts, these banquet halls have all the charm of a "shopping club."

FOUR & TWENTY BLACKBIRDS S   26 | 22 | 24 | $35
Rte. 522 (Rte. 647), Flint Hill, VA, 540-675-1111
■ "Take the back roads" to this "gratifying" example of Virginia small-town rusticity for "superb country dining" and "attentive" hospitality; the setting may be "bucolic", but the "scrumptious" Contemporary American cooking, which relies on top-flight regional ingredients, and the power couple clientele are all quite urbane.

Washington, D.C. | F | D | S | C |

Four Rivers S | 17 | 10 | 16 | $16 |
184 Rollins Ave. (E. Jefferson St.), Rockville, MD, 301-230-2900
◪ This "shabby" Rockville storefront and its "Asian community" clientele can seem forbiddingly "authentic" if you can't read the "Chinese language menu" and don't ask for help; most (but not all) servers will point you to "spicy, flavorful and cheap" Szechuan and vegetarian specialties – however, a few naysayers warn that even with guidance, the food's "gone downhill."

Fran O'Brien's Steak House S | 19 | 16 | 19 | $35 |
Capitol Hilton Hotel, 1001 16th St., NW (L St.), 202-783-2599
■ Fine for strong "drinks and political gossip" and being "able to talk at lunch", this "dark", sports-themed carnivore ("not a veggie to be found") near the White House has "tasty" steaks and ex-Redskin Fran O'Brien's friendliness "makes every meal a treat"; but in the final tally he "finishes behind the big names" like Morton's, Ruth's Chris, Sam & Harry's and The Palm.

Full Kee ◐ S ⊄ | 21 | 7 | 15 | $13 |
509 H St., NW (bet. 5th & 6th Sts.), 202-371-2233
■ "Fabulous Cantonese noodle and dumpling soups" are one of the keys to a "cheap, good" meal here, and finding someone to "interrogate" about the "exotic" specialties is another ("English not spoken by most staff"); the "grungy" surroundings discourage finicky eaters, but with the rapid gentrification of Chinatown, one hopes such colorful "dumps", with their late hours and "rock-bottom" prices, will manage to survive.

Full Key ◐ S | 21 | 8 | 14 | $17 |
Wheaton Manor Shopping Ctr., 2227 University Blvd. W. (Georgia Ave.), Wheaton, MD, 301-933-8388
◪ On many Sinophiles' lists of "crummy but good" places to eat, this Wheaton Cantonese is best liked for "soup meals" and barbecue meats; however, even if you "know what to order" (try the clams in black bean sauce), "communication problems" and an "uneven" kitchen send some diners scurrying elsewhere.

Gabriel S | 23 | 20 | 21 | $31 |
Radisson-Barcelo Washington Hotel, 2121 P St., NW (bet. 21st & 22nd Sts.), 202-956-6690
■ "Spanish touches" and "warm" surroundings energize some of DC's "best" brunches, "incredible" lunch spreads and "happy hour tapas deals" (Wednesday–Friday) at this "civilized" hotel dining room off Dupont Circle; when the "inventive" Contemporary Latin kitchen and "friendly" staff are clicking, such as on Sunday when the "whole roasted pig is a sight to behold", very few aren't "wowed."

Washington, D.C. | F | D | S | C |

Gadsby's Tavern S | 18 | 24 | 21 | $28 |
138 N. Royal St. (Cameron St.), Alexandria, VA, 703-548-1288

An Old Town tavern recreating the food, drink and history of the colonial era that delights some "history buffs" and "out-of-town guests", as well as locals who take advantage of the lovely "outdoor seating" for Sunday brunch; however, most say its hokey ("they'll park your horse") authenticity and mostly "ho-hum" fare make it a "go once" experience.

Galaxy S | ▽ 21 | 15 | 21 | $32 |
Tower Sq. Ctr., 155 Hillwood Ave. (Annadale Rd.), Falls Church, VA, 703-534-5450

Unlike the new wave of glitzy Asian restaurants, this recycled, "'50s-style cafeteria" in the heart of Falls Church provides little visual stimulation, but the "staff will take you on a gastronomic tour of Vietnam" that evokes their homeland's pungent tastes and smells; P.S. on weekends the restaurant becomes a club that's a "dancer's delight."

GALILEO S | 26 | 23 | 23 | $52 |
1110 21st St. (bet. L & M Sts.), 202-293-7191

"The Italian of choice" for "wonderful" food and wine in a star-studded setting; Roberto Donna, his "creative" executive chef Todd Gray and a "knowledgeable" staff "maintain standards" that win this "classy" Downtown restaurant national acclaim; go for a "fantastic" chef's tasting meal in the kitchen to understand why, even with "occasional lapses" and "pricey" tabs, it's "the most fun in town."

Generous George's S | 17 | 14 | 16 | $14 |
3006 Duke St. (Cranberry Rd.), Alexandria, VA, 703-370-4303
7031 Little River Rd. (John Marr Dr.), Annandale, VA, 703-941-9600
Concord Shopping Ctr., 6131 Backlick Rd. (Commerce St.), Springfield, VA, 703-451-7111

"Generous" doesn't even begin to cover the "two meals in one dish", "gargantuan" pastas piled on pizzas at these "zany", "loud", pink pizza joints that are ideal "for large and unruly families with young kids"; as for decor, George plainly goes "overboard" at every garage sale in Northern Virginia, and one or two fastidious types think it's time to "steam clean" these spots.

George Starke's Head Hog BBQ S | 18 | 11 | 16 | $16 |
11014 Rockville Pike (bet. Nicolson Ln. & Security Blvd.), Rockville, MD, 301-881-7195

In early '98, ex-Redskin George Starke pulled up stakes and moved his pit crew and "pigskin" memorabilia to this "commercial" rec-room; here, the "hard man" scores "a field goal, not a touchdown", with "good BBQ" and "pretty fine ribs for the money"; fans say the "surroundings are stark", but it's the "friendliest place in town."

Washington, D.C. | F | D | S | C |

Georgetown Seafood Grill S | 20 | 18 | 19 | $28 |
1200 19th St., NW (bet. M & N Sts.), 202-530-4430
■ While this Georgetown transplant lost its "neighborhood feel" when it relocated to "sleek" office space below Dupont Circle, it remains a "haven for seafood in a city with few" "reasonably" priced fish houses; at lunch, in an area where briefcase dining rooms are at a premium, the "excellent" raw bar, "incredible" crab cakes and grilled fish are the standouts.

GEORGIA BROWN'S S | 23 | 23 | 21 | $32 |
950 15th St., NW (bet. I & K Sts.), 202-393-4499
◪ "Visually stunning" and lined with "lawyers and pols" who revel in its "huge portions" of "nouvelle" Southern cooking and "boisterous" bonhomie, this Downtown crowd-pleaser feels "truly" DC; sure, it's "too noisy for conversation" and sometimes serves "heavy" food that requires a "nap after lunch", but it's a surefire bet for spotting "dignitaries" and has a "spectacular" Sunday gospel brunch.

Geppetto S | 18 | 16 | 16 | $19 |
Wildwood Shopping Ctr., 10257 Old Georgetown Rd. (Democracy Blvd.), Bethesda, MD, 301-493-9230
◪ Dubbed Bethesda's "Pepperoni HQ" due to its overloaded deep-dish pizza and "garlicky" thin-crust pies (the white version "excels"), this "family dining" mainstay also does salads and "heart-healthy" entrees; the "comfortable", "cheerful" atmosphere and outdoor seating make it ideal for neighborhood lunch meetings and post-movie snacks, but a few are put off by service that's "slow when busy."

Geranio S | 22 | 20 | 23 | $30 |
722 King St. (bet. Columbus & Washington Sts.), Alexandria, VA, 703-548-0088
◪ Year after year, Alexandria's gentry enjoys the pleasures of this Italian's "solid" cooking, "romantic" townhouse setting and "sensitive" coddling by an "attentive", well-drilled staff; lively, even noisy when busy, its "old-fashioned" ambiance is most appealing when you're sitting "by the fireplace" on a "rainy night."

GERARD'S PLACE | 27 | 22 | 24 | $55 |
915 15th St., NW (bet. I & K Sts.), 202-737-4445
■ With star chefs Jean-Louis Palladin (of the Watergate) and Jean-Pierre Goyenvalle (Le Lion D'Or) gone from the DC scene, attention is focused on Gerard Pangaud's "subtle" but "stellar" and "worth every dime" French on McPherson Square; his cooking is showcased in this "small, intimate dining room", with the "elegant" touches and "impeccable" service that make a "power lunch or romantic meal"; lately, he's been in and out (attending to his Georgetown bistro, Vintage), but it hardly seems to matter since surveyors say it's "always at least excellent."

Washington, D.C.　　　　F D S C

Germaine's S (CLOSED)　　21 | 17 | 20 | $32
2400 Wisconsin Ave., NW (Calvert St.), 202-965-1185
◪ Germaine Swanson's legendary charm powers her Upper Georgetown dining room, perking up the "'70s" decor and invigorating her "beautifully presented" Pan-Asian dishes; it remains a "favorite haunt" of that era's intelligentsia, and is worth visiting to view the famous "fine" photographs "lining the wall"; the unseduced find it "tired" and "overrated, but I did see Alan Greenspan there."

Golden Palace S　　18 | 14 | 16 | $18
720 Seventh St., NW (bet. G & H Sts.), 202-783-1225
◪ Daylong "dim sum is the draw", along with its proximity to the MCI Center, at this Chinatown Cantonese, whose "dated" opulence and some Americanized menu offerings belie its low prices and "authentic" food; but, as in many Chinese restaurants with a native clientele, English is not always spoken, so you may have trouble finding out what's good.

Goldoni S　　25 | 23 | 22 | $48
1120 20th St., NW (bet. L & M Sts.), 202-293-1511
■ A fall '98 move to larger business center digs, with an all-day dining bar and more formal dining room, will outdate the above decor rating but provide a new setting for Fabrizio Aielli's "inventive" Venetian-inspired cuisine and the charms of his host-wife Ingrid; despite the "high cost of admission", a move closer to the action is unlikely to break its stride.

Good Fortune ●S　　23 | 14 | 17 | $17
2646 University Blvd. (bet. Georgia Ave. & Viers Mill Rd.), Wheaton, MD, 301-929-8818
■ Hit Wheaton's best Cantonese "before noon on weekends" or you'll join the "great line of Asian diners" waiting for "excellent dim sum"; there's also a "huge" bilingual menu, but don't expect guidance because service can be "minimal."

Greenfield Churrascaria S　　– | – | – | M
1801 Rockville Pike (Randolph Rd.), Rockville, MD, 301-881-3397
Carnivores will have a field day at this sprawling, all-you-can-eat Brazilian on Rockville Pike, where the *churrascaria* game is played by simple rules: for a set price ($9.95 at lunch, $18.95 at dinner), diners help themselves to the salad-and-side-dish buffet, while roving waiters stop tableside to slice slabs of BBQ meats.

Greenwood's at Cleveland Park S　　▽ 25 | 21 | 16 | $31
3529 Connecticut Ave., NW (Porter St.), 202-833-6572
■ In spring '98, fans of Carole Greenwood's "fresh, seasonal" American food put their money where their mouths were by backing (and packing) her "dramatic-looking" new Cleveland Park venue; early reports are very "promising", but since everything is "painstakingly" prepared to her exacting standards, pacing is "slow."

Washington, D.C.   F | D | S | C

Grillfish   19 | 18 | 17 | $26
1200 New Hampshire Ave., NW (M St.), 202-331-7310

◪ "One fish, two fish, we grill good fish and that's all" could be the motto of this "funky" fish house and "Gen X people-watching" perch near the West End; apparently, serving "basic" "fish without fuss" (but with a choice of sauces) in a "*Twilight Zone*", "candles everywhere" environment is "very in"; still, some decibel-challenged trendies are irked by the "really lousy acoustics caused by the hip decor."

Grill from Ipanema S   19 | 17 | 17 | $25
1858 Columbia Rd., NW (Belmont Rd.), 202-986-0757

◪ You're in Adams Morgan, but pretend it's Rio with a couple of "tart, refreshing" and deadly caipirinhas and characteristically "spicy" meat or fish dishes at this spirited, "cleverly named" Brazilian cafe; black lights, "helpful" waiters and a little imagination can turn dinner into a "friendly adventure", which can include "hit-or-miss" food.

Gulf Coast Kitchen S   14 | 15 | 16 | $18
7750 Woodmont Ave. (bet. Cheltenham Dr. & Old Georgetown Rd.), Bethesda, MD, 301-652-6278

◪ Despite some "positive" attempts to be taken seriously as a Southern restaurant, this Delta roadhouse with a "fun", "beach hut atmosphere" and rooftop deck can't help getting used as a Bethesda "young-and-single" scene; sandwiches and Louisiana eats please some lunchers and parents with kids, but "good visuals, poor victuals" is the majority call.

Haad Thai S   22 | 17 | 19 | $18
1100 New York Ave., NW (bet. 11th & H Sts.), 202-682-1111

■ It's no surprise that this Downtown Thai is "always crowded" with briefcase types longing for a vacation, since a mural and simple touches establish a tropical scene that's "like eating on a Pacific island at sunset"; the "excellent", "refined" food is presented like "artwork", the "fast" service can "handle large crowds" and prices are "reasonable."

Haandi S   24 | 18 | 21 | $22
4904 Fairmont Ave. (Old Georgetown Rd.), Bethesda, MD, 301-718-0121
Falls Plaza Shopping Ctr., 1222 N. Broad St. (Rte. 7), Falls Church, VA, 703-533-3501

■ These moderately priced "faves" serve some of the area's best Northern Indian food in "tasteful" surroundings; many learned to "like Indian food" with their "solicitous" aid, and despite the appeal of cheaper, Southern Indians (like Bombay Bistro) and elegant Anglo-Indians (Bombay Club), Haandi's "distinctive curries" and tandooris remain a "measure" of excellence – hence, it can be "hard to get in."

Hard Rock Cafe ☾ [S] 14 | 20 | 15 | $18
999 E St., NW (10th St.), 202-737-7625
◩ Despite being lauded as the "best of the celebrity chains", with "decent" burgers and salads and a "handy" location near the Ford Theater, this "tourist trap's" "special appeal" eludes many; but that doesn't stop a clientele of mostly young daters and "teens on a class trip" from soaking up the beyond "loud", rock memorabilia–filled atmosphere.

Hard Times Cafe [S] 19 | 15 | 17 | $13
Woodley Gardens, 1117 Nelson St. (Rte. 28), Rockville, MD, 301-294-9720 ☾
3028 Wilson Blvd. (Highland St.), Arlington, VA, 703-528-2233 ☾
1404 King St. (West St.), Alexandria, VA, 703-683-5340
K-Mart Shopping Ctr., 394 Elden St. (bet. Herndon Pkwy. & Van Buren St.), Herndon, VA, 703-318-8941 ☾
■ When "you've just got to" get down with some "tasty", "trailer park" chile (especially the "great" vegetarian version), a "cold beer" and the "best country jukebox east of Nashville", these "cheap", "fast", "jeans-and-T-shirt" joints which, happily, "haven't had a new thought in years", fit the bill; P.S. regulars "ask for chile dry" to decrease the grease.

Hautam Kebobs [S] ▽ 20 | 15 | 19 | $18
Ritchie Ctr., 785-D Rockville Pike (Wooton Pkwy.), Rockville, MD, 301-838-9222
■ A "pleasant" Persian that uses "good meat" for its properly grilled kebabs, bakes "great bread", makes "tasty salads" and provides tablecloth dining in a "no-atmosphere" Rockville strip mall; yet these efforts to please "just miss" for some folks.

Havana Cafe [S] 20 | 15 | 17 | $20
3401 Clarendon Blvd. (Washington Blvd.), Arlington, VA, 703-524-3611
■ The "delightful courtyard" and "spacious" digs of this Clarendon gathering spot "look like Old Havana"; it's one of the few local sources of "authentic" Cuban food – "Moors and Christians" (black beans and rice), ropa vieja – that even "Castro would feel comfortable with."

Hee Been [S] ▽ 24 | 15 | 20 | $21
6231 Little River Tpke. (Beauregard St.), Annandale, VA, 703-941-3737
■ Geared to "Korean clients" and expats, this popular, "highly recommended" Arlington spot offers a "very well-prepared lunch buffet" and Korean BBQ grilled tableside; the "helpful" staff guides first-timers through the basics, but when faced with an unfamiliar question in English, some "just smile."

Washington, D.C. | F | D | S | C |

Hibiscus Cafe S | 22 | 22 | 17 | $29 |
3401 K St. (34th St.), 202-965-7170
■ This "colorful" K Street Islander works "on a very laid-back schedule", yet when Jimmy and Sharon Banks crank up the reggae and the "fiery" Caribbean food, the "place jumps"; however, a few foes say that the "bill takes the bloom off" this hibiscus.

Hinode S | 19 | 18 | 19 | $21 |
4914 Hampden Ln. (Arlington Blvd.), Bethesda, MD, 301-654-0908
134 Congressional Ln. (bet. Jefferson St. & Rockville Pike), Rockville, MD, 301-816-2190
■ Suburban Japanese duo that delivers "fresh sushi", "terrific tempura" and "bargain" bento box meals in a "calm, yet child-friendly" atmosphere – all "without costing a mint"; P.S. you can get a "video and sushi to go in one stop" at the Bethesda location, which is next to Rocky's Video.

Hisago S | ▽ 22 | 20 | 21 | $37 |
Washington Harbour, 3050 K St., NW (bet. 30th & 31st Sts.), 202-944-4181
◪ A "window seat" at this Washington Harbour Japanese "commands a good view" of the Potomac and complements the "very fresh", "beautiful sushi" and "attentive" help; but since it's "overpriced", when it's not filled with "tourists" and "expense-account" types, it can be a "morgue."

Hogate's S | 12 | 14 | 14 | $26 |
800 Water St., SW (bet. Maine Ave. & 9th St.), 202-484-6300
◪ Steady "tour bus" traffic seems to be what keeps this Maine Avenue seafooder afloat, because not even "civil servants" will put up with "mass" feeding, "warehouse seating" and "cattle call" treatment for the sake of a "complimentary rum bun" and a "great" river view.

Hollywood East ●S | ▽ 21 | 10 | 17 | $15 |
2312 Price Ave. (Elkins St.), Wheaton, MD, 301-942-8282
■ In the unadorned "Hong Kong atmosphere" of a Wheaton storefront, this "family" operation exemplifies low-budget ethnic dining at its best, where "non-Chinese speakers [can] try authentic dishes"; while even "simple" standards from the "extensive" menu have "complex flavors", the audacious advise "don't miss" the "adventurous" blackboard specials.

Houston's S | 19 | 17 | 18 | $21 |
1065 Wisconsin Ave., NW (bet. K & M Sts.), 202-338-7760
7715 Woodmont Ave. (bet. Cheltenham Dr. &
Old Georgetown Rd.), Bethesda, MD, 301-656-9755
12256 Rockville Pike (Montrose Rd.), Rockville, MD, 301-468-3535
■ It seems like the "beeper never goes off" when you're waiting to get into these "superchains" that are popular for good reason: they "consistently" serve some of the "best, fast" "saloon food" in a "dark, clubby" atmosphere.

Washington, D.C. F | D | S | C

Hunan Chinatown S   20 | 14 | 17 | $19
624 H St., NW (bet. 6th & 7th Sts.), 202-783-5858
◼ Although it's "missing the old spark", "vaguely upscale decor", "decent" manners and a "better-than-average job with the classics" (lemon chicken) mark this old-timer as one of the "best of the dwindling number of Chinatown Chinese" left standing after the MCI Center redevelopment.

Hunan Lion S   20 | 19 | 19 | $20
2070 Chain Bridge Rd. (Old Courthouse Rd.), Vienna, VA, 703-734-9828

Hunan Lion II S
18140 The Galleria (near Tysons II), Tysons Corner, VA, 703-883-1938
◼ Northern Virginia's "haute" Chinese is a "high-end" setting for a Tysons Corner business lunch, with "good quality" food and "special occasion" service; it operates independently from Tysons Galleria Lion II, though both attract a cosmopolitan clientele ("this is where General Tso gets his chicken").

Hunan Number One ◐ S   21 | 15 | 17 | $18
3033 Wilson Blvd. (Garfield St.), Arlington, VA, 703-528-1177
◼ This "very basic" but "very good" Arlington Chinese is made-to-order for a family dim sum feast – parents pile up the small plates, while "kids love the lobster tank"; it's also "great for the late-night Chinese munchies" ("Peking duck to go") and the staff is "fun."

Hunan Palace   ▽ 19 | 13 | 17 | $17
Shady Grove Ctr., 9011 Gaither Rd. (Shady Grove Rd.), Gaithersburg, MD, 301-977-8600
◼ While it's best to visit this comfortable Gaithersburg restaurant specializing in Taiwanese and Shanghai cooking with someone who "speaks Chinese" and "knows what to order", you can manage with the bilingual English/Chinese menu and "helpful" staff.

Hunter's Inn S   16 | 18 | 17 | $27
917 Quince Orchard Rd. (Great Seneca Hwy.), Gaithersburg, MD, 301-527-1400
10123 River Rd. (Falls Rd.), Potomac, MD, 301-299-9300
◼ These "classy" hunt club settings in Kentlands and Potomac provide "predictable" Traditional American fare; a few find them "nice additions", but others opine the "food does not match the expectations."

Ichiban S   19 | 15 | 17 | $22
637 N. Frederick Ave. (near Lake Forest Mall), Gaithersburg, MD, 301-670-0560
◼ Now that Gaithersburg has developed a varied restaurant scene, this commodious Korean-Japanese "crossbreed" seems less novel; still, it offers "quality sushi", a "good value buffet" and "fun to grill at your table" Korean BBQ.

Il Borgo [S] | 23 | 20 | 21 | $34 |

1381-A Beverly Rd. (bet. Elm St. & Old Dominion Dr.), McLean, VA, 703-893-1400

■ Vittorio Testa, McLean's "friendliest chef", "greets" every guest and his "delicious", "very rich" Italian food, like the setting, epitomizes fancy dining "'70s-style"; it ain't cheap, but some tony eaters call it their "fave place in the 'burbs."

Il Cigno [S] ▽ | 21 | 19 | 21 | $29 |

Lake Anne Plaza, 1617 Washington Plaza (N. Shore Dr.), Reston, VA, 703-471-0121

■ "Summertime" dining on an "umbrella-covered terrace" overlooking Reston's "beautiful" Lake Anne is this Italian's claim to fame; the food is "basic", but it's the memory of "sitting outside in the sunshine" that stays with surveyors.

Il Pizzico | 23 | 16 | 20 | $24 |

Suburban Park, 15209 Frederick Rd. (Guide Dr.), Rockville, MD, 301-309-0610

■ Offering the "appeal of a family-owned business" and very "good Italian cooking" keeps this Rockville trattoria humming; toss in "fair prices" and "gracious service" and it's clear why it's "worth the trek"; "no reservations" means it's best to "go early" (or late) on weekend nights.

Il Radicchio | 18 | 15 | 16 | $19 |

223 Pennsylvania Ave. (C St.), 202-547-5114
1509 17th St., NW (bet. P & Q Sts.), 202-986-2627
1211 Wisconsin Ave. (M St.), 202-337-2627 [S]
1801 Clarendon Blvd. (Rhodes St.), Arlington, VA, 703-276-2627

■ These handy, "innovative" "corner spaghetti houses" featuring "mix-'n'-match pastas and sauces" and salads are "where real Washingtonians" ("movers and shakers" included) go when they're "too tired" to cook; the staff can be "distracted" when busy, but the atmosphere is "upbeat" and for "high-quality" dining they're downright "cheap."

Il Ritrovo | 20 | 17 | 21 | $31 |

4838 Rugby Ave. (bet. Auburn & Woodmont Aves.), Bethesda, MD, 301-986-1447

■ "When it's good", this endearing but uneven Mediterranean with "great paella" and "beautiful" desserts makes firm friends; tucked away on a quiet side street in Bethesda Triangle, it's "managed *con amore*" by a "charming" couple who are determined "to please."

I Matti [S] | 23 | 19 | 19 | $32 |

2436 18th St., NW (bet. Belmont & Columbia Rds.), 202-462-8844

■ Don't let "too many beautiful people" ("including the staff") and the "hip environment" keep you from appreciating this Adams Morgan trattoria's real strength – "excellent", "authentic" food; some find Roberto Donna and Co.'s "Italian country cooking" here more "rewarding" and "accessibly priced" than his high-end fare at Galileo.

Washington, D.C.　　　　　　　　F | D | S | C

Indigo S　　　　　　　　▽ 25 | 22 | 23 | $45
*774 Walker Rd. (Georgetown Pike), Great Falls, VA,
703-759-4650*
■ "New and needs time" is the word on this "pricey" New American in Great Falls that's weathering chef, staff and "concept" changes; at present, it offers "interesting" fare in a stylish, blue-tinted space, with a patio on the Village commons; given the scarcity of upscale dining in this posh purlieu, file it under 'P' for "potential."

Inn at Glen Echo S　　　　　19 | 20 | 19 | $30
*6119 Tulane Ave. (bet. Cabin John Pkwy. & MacArthur Blvd.),
Glen Echo, MD, 301-229-2280*
◪ Since it's "very pleasant" for an "away-from-it-all" brunch on the "rustic" deck, Sunday jazz in the "cozy" bar or a "long Saturday lunch with old friends" in one of the "quaint" dining rooms, most can overlook the fact that this converted roadhouse's "straightforward" American food and service have as many "ups and downs as the carousel" in nearby Glen Echo Amusement Park.

INN AT LITTLE WASHINGTON S　　29 | 29 | 29 | $96
*Inn at Little Washington, Main & Middle Sts., Washington, VA,
540-675-3800*
■ "Nearly perfect" scores make this the *Survey*'s No. 1 rated restaurant across-the-board, as well as the "ultimate" Virginia country destination; chef/co-owner Patrick O'Connell's "spectacular" Contemporary American food, "opulent" appointments and the staff's constant "attention to detail" leave surveyors sighing "nirvana" that's "worth every penny"; N.B. try to reserve a chef's table in the state-of-the-art, multimillion dollar kitchen.

Ireland's Four Courts ●S　　　– | – | – | M
*2051 Wilson Blvd. (N. Courthouse Rd.), Arlington, VA,
703-525-3600*
Write-ins hoist a "pint of Guinness" to the "best Irish pub and pub grub" in the Arlington area; it captures the Gaelic spirit with music, beer and shepherd's pie served in "cozy" fern bar surroundings and out on the sidewalk cafe.

I RICCHI　　　　　　　　25 | 23 | 23 | $45
1220 19th St., NW (bet. M & N Sts.), 202-835-0459
◪ This "top-notch" classic Tuscan that's now Christianne Ricchi's place (you'll find Francesco Ricchi, her ex-husband, at Cesco) "pampers" its Dupont Circle darlings, impresses their "important clients" and produces "fantastic" breads, grills, pastas and "peasant" specialties in a "special-occasion" atmosphere; but some stress that "service is better if you're a regular."

Washington, D.C. | F | D | S | C |

Isabella | 17 | 20 | 18 | $31 |
809 15th St., NW (bet. H & I Sts.), 202-408-9500
◪ The "snazzy", fit for a "pasha" decor of this Downtown Mediterranean is the backdrop for major lunch and happy-hour networking and chef Caroline Broder's (ex Cafe Milano, Coco Pazzo) "bistro-style" fare – think "chicken frites"; N.B. spring '98's lowered prices, menu and staff changes are not fully reflected in the above ratings.

Ivy's Place S | 18 | 11 | 17 | $18 |
3520 Connecticut Ave., NW (Porter St.), 202-363-7802
7929 Norfolk Ave. (Cordell Ave.), Bethesda, MD, 301-656-9225
◪ "Easy neighborhood" Thai and Indonesian eateries that are near the Uptown movie theater in Cleveland Park and in Bethesda, with "ear-ringing" spicing, "grad student" pricing and scant atmosphere; although the "quality of the food is uneven", specialties like curries are done well.

JALEO S | 23 | 21 | 19 | $26 |
480 Seventh St., NW (E St.), 202-628-7949
■ The "atmosphere is electric" at this pioneering Penn Quarter trendsetter that "despite popularity, crowding" and "waits" just "keeps getting better"; most find it "impossible to get bored" with its Spanish tapas concept, which allows for the "pleasure" of sharing "great food" and offers "flexible" dining before or after MCI Center events.

Jasmine Cafe S | ▽ 23 | 18 | 20 | $22 |
Lake Anne, 1633-A Washington Plaza, Reston, VA, 703-471-9114
◪ Reston's unsung "gem" is burnished by "great outdoor seating in summer" on Lake Anne's Washington Plaza; the "creative" Contemporary American cuisine is strong on the "imaginative use of ingredients", but a meal indoors is merely cozy and sometimes "disappointing."

Jean-Michel S | 23 | 19 | 21 | $38 |
Wildwood Shopping Ctr., 10223 Old Georgetown Rd. (Democracy Blvd.), Bethesda, MD, 301-564-4910
◪ "K Street memories" are evoked at this "formal" French Bethesda suburban transplant that caters to "an older crowd" that appreciates the "expert hand in the kitchen", the "attentive service" and the "comfortable room"; while a few critics carp about the "not too exciting" food, most are happy to have a "Downtown" tradition "around the corner."

Jefferson Restaurant S | 24 | 24 | 25 | $43 |
Jefferson Hotel, 1200 16th St., NW (M St.), 202-833-6206
◪ One of DC's legendary places to "whisper" secrets, this highly "civilized" hotel dining room near the White House is a premier choice for off-the-record meetings; its "impeccable" service is a signature, as are "warm scones from the oven" served at one of the "best high teas in town", but its usually "excellent" New American kitchen has had periodic chef changes, which have resulted in some "uneven" meals.

Washington, D.C.   F | D | S | C

Jerry Seafood   ▽ 27 | 13 | 23 | $30
9364 Lanham Severn Rd. (1½ mi. west of Rte. 495, exit 20A), Seabrook, MD, 301-577-0333

■ "Get 'the Bomb'", the "best", most "stupendous" 10-oz. crab cake around, at this old-time Seabrook seafooder with an "institutional setting"; the truth is "you can't go wrong" with any of the "very fresh seafood" choices recommended by the "deferential", "call you hon" waitresses or Jerry Gainey himself, a man who "would die if he didn't please."

Jin-Ga S   ▽ 21 | 23 | 22 | $33
1250 24th St., NW (bet. M & N Sts.), 202-785-5319

■ A meal at this West End "luxury" Japanese-Korean features "costumed" staffers and "authentic" Asian fare that's played out against a "serene", sophisticated backdrop; while it could use "more ventilation" and "English"-speaking help, it's hard not to applaud an $8.95 lunch.

Jockey Club S   24 | 25 | 25 | $50
Westin Fairfax, 2100 Massachusetts Ave., NW (21st St.), 202-659-8000

■ Nancy Reagan's chicken salad is always on the menu at DC's version of the "21 Club", a long-standing bastion of old money and power and a "pampering oasis for grown-ups"; this "model of civility" boasts "top-flight" Continental cuisine that some say is "predictable", but most consider it "worth a visit", if only for "history's sake"; N.B. its hotel affiliation switch from the Ritz-Carlton to the Westin Fairfax may cost it some cachet.

John Harvard's Brew House ●S   15 | 16 | 16 | $20
1299 Pennsylvania Ave., NW (bet. E & 13th Sts.), 202-783-2739

◪ Even though many advise "don't go for the food", the "clubby" booths at this Downtown Ivy League brewpub are in demand at lunch, happy hour and for "beers and burgers after a softball game"; it's "loud but fun" and as for decor, one devotee declares "I love feeling like I'm in a copper vat."

J. Paul's ●S   18 | 18 | 18 | $22
3218 M St., NW (bet. Potomac St. & Wisconsin Ave.), 202-333-3450

◪ A "quintessential pub" that's "loud, crowded" and open to the passing parade in Georgetown (there's a branch in Baltimore's Inner Harbor too); the "all-American fare" is secondary to "entertaining" tourists and the "bar scene."

Kabul Caravan S   ▽ 22 | 23 | 20 | $23
Colonial Shopping Ctr., 1725 Wilson Blvd. (bet. Quinn & Rhodes Sts.), Arlington, VA, 703-522-8394

■ Flickering candles and "exotic" decorations give this Arlington strip mall storefront an "unexpected" air of mystery, which is heightened by its "delightfully complex" Afghan food, including a "unique way with vegetables"; "friendly" service and reasonable prices are added pluses.

Washington, D.C. | F | D | S | C |

Kawasaki ▽ | 26 | 19 | 23 | $36 |
1140 19th St., NW (bet. L & M Sts.), 202-466-3798
■ This *kappo* (authentic) Japanese may be better known in Asian offices than in Downtown DC, but those who seek out its "basement location" find "very fresh sushi"; if you're feeling flush and adventurous, sidle up to the sushi bar and say *'omikase'*, meaning your meal will be the chef's choice.

Kazan | 23 | 20 | 24 | $27 |
McLean Shopping Ctr., 6813 Redmond Dr. (Bridge Rd.), McLean, VA, 703-734-1960
■ "Trust the daily specials" and the "very good doner kebab" at this "honest" Ottoman in McLean to learn why Turkish cooking impresses gastronomes; the "warm, family welcome" from the owner helps obliterate the "'70s decor."

King Street Blues S | 17 | 19 | 18 | $17 |
112 N. St. Asaph St. (King St.), Alexandria, VA, 703-836-8800
◪ The "kids' happy hour" never ends at this campy "vertical diner" in Old Town where "meat loaf, garlic mashed" and the rest of the "cheap", "bad for you but good" Southern-accented dishes play second fiddle to "good music"; if food matters, go for brunch.

KINKEAD'S S | 28 | 23 | 25 | $44 |
Red Lion Row, 2000 Pennsylvania Ave., NW (I St., bet. 20th & 21st Sts.), 202-296-7700
■ Nearly 1,500 respondents rate Bob Kinkead's very '90s American bistro No. 2 for food and popularity in this *Survey*; his "brilliant innovation" – serving a "spectacular" seafood-oriented menu with "awesome choices" in handsome, "not too formal" settings – revolutionized DC "power" dining; "knowledgeable" service, an "excellent wine list" and "great jazz" are other reasons why most people feel "lucky" to "get in."

Kramerbooks & | 16 | 14 | 14 | $18 |
Afterwords Cafe ●S
1517 Connecticut Ave., NW (bet. Dupont Circle & Q St.), 202-387-1462
◪ A Dupont Circle pioneer in the pairing of books, coffee and singles ("hasn't everybody in DC met a date" at this "NY [Greenwich] Village" clone?); while its American kitchen comes up with some "weird combos" and the staff has been known to serve "whine", it's still "one of the best lazy Sunday [and after midnight] hangouts" for "people-watching."

Krupin's S | 18 | 11 | 15 | $18 |
4620 Wisconsin Ave., NW (Chesapeake St.), 202-686-1989
◪ Mel Krupin doesn't change ("be careful" or he'll "yell at you"), but fortunately neither do his high standards; despite its "seedy" appearance, this Northwester remains the "best" local source of a "decent pastrami sandwich" and other "delicious" "Jewish soul food" in a "deli-challenged" town.

Washington, D.C.   F | D | S | C

La Bergerie   25 | 23 | 24 | $43
218 N. Lee St. (bet. Cameron & Queen Sts.), Alexandria, VA, 703-683-1007
■ "Steady as she goes" is the maxim of this "top-notch", "Basque-accented" French, whose "old-world decor" (some say "dated"), "delicious" duck confit and "great soufflés" are essential for celebrating Alexandria's "special occasions"; the French waiters "fuss over" their pets, but the operation is far too "professional" to slight newcomers.

La Brasserie S   21 | 19 | 19 | $32
239 Massachusetts Ave., NE (bet. 2nd & 3rd Sts.), 202-546-9154
■ "In good weather", this "very Hill-ish" French bistro's sun-splashed terrace is the place for "spotting politicos" over a "romantic business lunch"; however, while some feel it's "past its prime", with "traditional" food and "worn" decor, the majority maintains that a "solid and simple" meal here can be enough "like Paris" to make the effort worthwhile.

La Chaumiere ●   23 | 22 | 22 | $37
2813 M St., NW (bet. 28th & 29th Sts.), 202-338-1784
■ Flanked by Georgetown's trendsetting eateries, Tahoga and Vintage, this country French "hideaway" upholds its Norman legacy with "well-prepared" specialties like "filling" cassoulet (Thursdays), a surprisingly "great" wine list and a "cozy fireplace" guaranteed to "warm" up a "cold" day; it's a "Washington old-guard institution with egalitarian service."

La Colline   24 | 20 | 22 | $39
400 N. Capitol St., NW (bet. D & E Sts.), 202-737-0400
■ From breakfast on, Robert Greault's "very discreet" French bistro "seldom disappoints" for a "fine", "reasonably priced" business meal on Capitol Hill or as a "perfect" venue for a "fund-raiser"; yet, despite accolades for his "elegant" food, a few find the place "boring", "done in" by the "stodgy" surroundings and "too many politicians."

La Costa de Sol/Las Tapas S   ▽ 20 | 18 | 19 | $30
710 King St. (bet. Columbus & Washington Sts.), Alexandria, VA, 703-836-4000
■ "Classic Spanish dishes" are served both in the modish Old Town Las Tapas bar and its more formal upstairs dining space, La Costa de Sol; however, many favor the bar because it's "the cheaper route", adding that the "surprisingly empty" dining room isn't helped by bright lights and loud music.

La Cote d'Or Cafe S   22 | 21 | 21 | $37
6876 Lee Hwy. (bet. Washington Blvd. & Westmoreland St.), Arlington, VA, 703-538-3033
■ Located "in the middle of nowhere", this "sweet and cozy" Arlington bistro brings "enjoyable" French dining within suburban reach; but while locals laud its salads, veal and "fantastic desserts", dissenters dis its "uneven food" and "Downtown prices" – "after all, this is Falls Church."

La Dolce Vita [S] ▽ 23 15 18 $24
10824 Lee Hwy. (bet. Main St. & Rte. 123), Fairfax, VA, 703-385-1530
◩ Don't "pass by" this "excellent find in a shack setting" in Fairfax – not that its "outstanding" pizza and "good quality" pastas and entrees are any "secret"; in fact, the amusingly painted premises are already way "too small" to handle the "crowds", making it advisable to go off-hours for a stab at "intimate dining."

LAFAYETTE [S] 25 27 24 $46
Hay-Adams Hotel, 800 16th St., NW (H St.), 202-638-2570
■ "Just sitting" in this "consummate, inside the Beltway" dining room with the "best view of the White House" would "make you feel important", even if it weren't wonderfully "elegant", with "first-rate" New American food and "attentive" service; best known for power breakfasts and lunches, its "old-world charm" is also endearing at tea.

La Ferme [S] 22 24 22 $44
7107 Brookville Rd. (East-West Hwy. & Western Ave.), Chevy Chase, MD, 301-986-5255
◩ A feeling of visiting a "French country home" pervades this "pretty", pastoral Chevy Chase place, adding luster to its "good", "basic", if "uninspired", food; for its "older crowd" clientele, the "comfort factor" looms large: it's "not cramped" and the staff "treats customers like family."

La Fourchette [S] 21 18 19 $29
2429 18th St., NW (bet. Columbia Rd. & Kalorama St.), 202-332-3077
■ "Artsy" types "smoking Gauloises" and scarfing "basic" bistro fare at sidewalk tables or in "funky" rooms – that's "Parisian life" Adams Morgan–style at this long-running cafe; here, "ambiance" rules and prices are "reasonable", which helps most overlook the slightly "run-down" decor.

La Lomita [S] 20 13 20 $17
1330 Pennsylvania Ave., SE (G St.), 202-546-3109
◩ It doesn't seem to matter whether this "cheerful, cheap" Capitol Hill dive serves "delicious Tex-Mex with margaritas to match" – "after a few margaritas, it's all good"; come with a crowd 'cause it's "too loud for couples."

La Madeleine French Bakery [S] 17 18 14 $15
3000 M St. (30th St., NW), 202-337-6975
7607 Old Georgetown Rd. (Commerce St.), Bethesda, MD, 301-215-9142
11858 Rockville Pike (Montrose Rd.), Rockville, MD, 301-984-2270
500 King St. (Pitt St.), Alexandria, VA, 703-739-2853
Bailey's Crossroads, 5861 Crossroads Ctr. (Columbia & Leesburg Pikes), Falls Church, VA, 703-379-5551
(Continues)

Washington, D.C. | F | D | S | C |

La Madeleine French Bakery (Cont.)
1833 Fountain Dr. (bet. Baron Cameron Rd. & Reston Pkwy.), Reston, VA, 703-707-0704
1915-C Chain Bridge Rd. (Rte. 7), Tysons Corner, VA, 703-827-8833

◪ "French food à la Howard Johnson's" or "a useful concept, well realized" – it depends on how you slice it: most "like" these "convenient" cafe/bakeries, with their faux farmhouse atmosphere and quick, "hybrid" eats, "despite themselves"; however, critics counter that the food is "mediocre", the "cafeteria-style service is for the birds" and the "high school kids trying to speak with a French accent" provide more amusement than help.

La Miche | 23 | 20 | 22 | $38 |
7905 Norfolk Ave. (bet. Old Georgetown Rd. & Wisconsin Ave.), Bethesda, MD, 301-986-0707

■ "Bethesda is blessed" with this "totally reliable" country French "home away from home", an "attractive" place that "understands" the "pre- and post-parenting yuppies" that frequent it; although it has a "limited menu" and isn't cheap, it's "always enjoyable", particulary for private events.

Landini Brothers | 21 | 18 | 20 | $29 |
115 King St. (Union St.), Alexandria, VA, 703-836-8404 S
Hilton Hotel, 901 N. Stuart St. (Glebe Rd.), Ballston, VA, 703-243-1222

◪ At this "dark" Old Town place with "*Godfather*" ambiance, local movers and shakers hit the bar, then head to the back to chow down on calamari, "homemade" pasta and other Northern Italian fare; the newer Ballston branch is not nearly as "clubby" (or "touristy"), but that doesn't discourage traffic.

La Panetteria S | 17 | 16 | 18 | $23 |
4921 Cordell Ave. (bet. Norfolk Ave. & Old Georgetown Rd.), Bethesda, MD, 301-951-6433

◪ Although there's "better Italian food elsewhere" in Bethesda, this old-fashioned, "family Italian" has its niche – it's a "good place for kids", garden seating or a "romantic corner" table for two and also offers a "real value early-bird" prix fixe; a "try hard" ethic has kept it in business for years.

La Provence | 24 | 20 | 21 | $38 |
Vienna Shopping Ctr., 144 W. Maple Ave. (bet. Center St. & Courthouse Rd.), Vienna, VA, 703-242-3777

◪ This French "gem" in Vienna prettifies its "strip mall" surroundings and provides suburbanites with close-to-home haute dining; Marie and Keo Kountakoun (ex Le Paradis) earn kudos for "delicious" "Provençal cooking", but surveyors say success has its price, since it's "a little rushed", "noisy" and "erratic."

Las Placitas [S] 21 | 12 | 20 | $16

18-28 Columbia Rd. (18th St.), 202-745-3751 ◐
517 Eighth St., SE (bet. E & G Sts.), 202-543-3700

■ "When God created the great neighborhood joint, he created" the prototype for these Salvadoran "havens" in Adams Morgan and "near the Marine barracks" on Capitol Hill; while not perfect, much that they offer is "good" – "good value, good staff", good hours and most of all, "unusually good" food that goes beyond Latin standards to seafood specials, "wonderful steak" and "magic margaritas."

La Tomate [S] 17 | 17 | 17 | $27

1701 Connecticut Ave., NW (bet. R & S Sts.), 202-667-5505

◪ Those who can't understand why this Dupont Circle Italian "is so popular" simply haven't had "fun" "people-watching" on its "pretty patio" or taken advantage of the "privacy" of its "cozy" nooks; while it's a "neighborhood haunt", regulars admit the "overpriced" food is mostly "fair and clichéd" and advise sticking to salads and pasta.

L'AUBERGE CHEZ FRANCOIS [S] 27 | 28 | 27 | $50

332 Springfield Rd. (2 mi. north of Georgetown Pike), Great Falls, VA, 703-759-3800

■ There is "no more enjoyable place for a celebration" than this rustic French farmhouse in Great Falls, our DC surveyors' perennial favorite restaurant; lovingly managed by the Haeringer family in the "European" manner, its "hearty" Alsatian food is "plentiful, delicious" and gives "full value"; the "unique setting" down a "winding" country road is "less formal than you'd expect", with an utterly "magical" garden.

L'AUBERGE PROVENCALE [S] 27 | 27 | 26 | $64

L'Auberge Provencale, Rte. 340 (Rte. 50), White Post, VA, 540-837-1375

■ This "romantic getaway" near Virginia's horse country featuring a "creative, herb-enhanced [five-course] menu" and an "interesting wine list" makes "you think you're in a French Provençal hotel"; most find the effect "charming" and say "it's up there with the best."

Lauriol Plaza ◐ [S] 20 | 16 | 18 | $22

1801 18th St., NW (S St.), 202-387-0035

◪ "If you want to experience true neighborhood restaurant life" at this "packed" "Dupont Circle/Adams Morgan classic", sit out on the "great people-watching patio" fortified with a "strong margarita" or sangria and wearing shades; while the Mexican-Spanish food draws mixed reviews, with pros praising the "consistent" fare ("great fajitas" and "earthy salsa") and critics calling it "mediocre", the consensus is it's "good for drinks and crowds."

Washington, D.C. F | D | S | C

Lavandou S 23 | 16 | 20 | $34
3321 Connecticut Ave., NW (bet. Macomb & Newark Sts.), 202-966-3002
☑ "Gallic spirit" suffuses this Cleveland Park bistro with "homey" country French fare and "good buy early-bird menus"; however, its post-*Survey* revamp may improve "cramped" quarters and "slipping" food.

LEBANESE TAVERNA S 23 | 18 | 20 | $24
2641 Connecticut Ave. (bet. Calvert St. & Woodley Rd.), 202-265-8681
5900 Washington Blvd. (McKinley Rd.), Arlington, VA, 703-241-8681
■ There are two types of people who eat at these "dependable", child-"friendly" Mediterranean villas: those who "love" "flavorful" Lebanese food and those who will by the end of the meal; the latter are advised to "bring friends, order *meze*" (appetizers) and "be adventurous"; P.S. put yourself in the hands of the "handsome" waiters because, when not made "cranky" by conventioneers, they "care."

Le Bon Cafe ⌿ 21 | 15 | 13 | $13
210 Second St., SE (bet. C St. & Pennsylvania Ave.), 202-547-7200
☑ The "lines are ridiculously long", the "staff is slow" and it's "not always open when you need it" (in the evening); nevertheless, this pocket-sized "piece of Paris on Capitol Hill", with its "wonderful sandwiches", "fresh salads", breakfast goodies and "sunny" outdoor seats is awfully "nice to have" in "Hillites" territory, and even a necessity – its "French roast fuels the Library of Congress."

Legal Sea Food S 19 | 17 | 18 | $30
2020 K St., NW (bet. 20th & 21st Sts.), 202-496-1111
Tyson Galleria, 2001 International Dr. (Rte. 123), Tysons Corner, VA, 703-827-8900
☑ While pros praise the "good clam chowder" and lab-tested raw bar fare at these Massachusetts-based fish houses, foes feel they don't measure up to the "Boston standard", citing seafood that's "prosaic", "overpriced" and "slow" in arriving at the table; still, their "power corridor" locations keep them busy as "corporate dining rooms" and happy hour hunting grounds (VA).

Le Gaulois 24 | 21 | 21 | $31
1106 King St. (bet. Fayette & Henry Sts.), Alexandria, VA, 703-739-9494
☑ For many, a meal at this Gallic stronghold in Alexandria is "as French [dining] should be", with "reasonably priced", "hearty" fare that's served without "pretense" in a "country cottage" setting; but even when it occasionally falls short ("crowded", "noisy"), it satisfies – after all, "who else still does quenelles?"

Washington, D.C. | F | D | S | C |

Le Paradis | 22 | 18 | 21 | $33 |
Festival Shopping Ctr., 347 Muddy Branch Rd. (bet. Clopper Rd. & Great Seneca Hwy.), Gaithersburg, MD, 301-208-9493

While it may be true that "suburbanites are pitifully grateful for decent food" and willing to overlook "strip mall neon signs", "modest" premises and city prices for "good French food and feel", give this "great, little" Gaithersburg outpost credit; it's survived management and kitchen changes (reflected in a lower food rating) and remains one of the area's "only good" restaurants.

Le Petit Mistral | ▽ 24 | 18 | 24 | $30 |
6710 Old Dominion Dr. (Chain Bridge Rd.), McLean, VA, 703-748-4888

It can be an ill wind – but in this case when Congressional gift restrictions blew this "promising" French off Capitol Hill, it wound up "knocking 'em out" in McLean; locals are delighted to have its maestro, Joseph Alonzo, back "doing what he does best" – orchestrating "a lovely range of classic" and modern dishes in a pretty storefront.

Le Refuge | 23 | 19 | 20 | $33 |
127 N. Washington St. (bet. Cameron & King Sts.), Alexandria, VA, 703-548-4661

A chalkboard menu and French posters lend this "smoky" Old Town "dive" the "romantic" air of a Parisian Left Bank cafe; "good, solid" bistro food (like bouillabaisse) and Gallic "arrogance" complete the picture, but for a few, "too cozy" seating turns "charming and quaint into cluttered."

Le Rivage S | 21 | 22 | 21 | $34 |
1000 Water St., SW (bet. Maine Ave. & 9th St.), 202-488-8111

Arena Stage–goers would be lost without this French stalwart's "summer outdoor deck", "lovely river view", "reliable" seafood, "reasonable prices" and even the sometimes "rushed" service that gets them out by curtain time; a few critics call it "predictable", but for others it's a "pearl amongst the waterfront tourist traps."

Les Halles ●S | 21 | 18 | 18 | $33 |
1201 Pennsylvania Ave., NW (12th St.), 202-347-6848

At this beefed-up French brasserie, a quintessential "steak, red wine and cigar" place with "archetypal French waiters" ("rude") and Downtown's "best" frites, lunchtime is a "lawyers' convention" and eating "takes awhile"; although heavy traffic has resulted in "disappointments", they seldom occur when seated outdoors, watching Pennsylvania Avenue pass by.

Washington, D.C. | F | D | S | C |

LESPINASSE | 27 | 28 | 26 | $75 |
Sheraton Carlton Hotel, 923 16th St., NW (K St.), 202-879-6900
■ "Elegance personified", this "exquisite", "impeccable" Contemporary French showpiece in a hotel near the White House is the ultimate indulgence when someone else "pays" and the site of DC's most "dazzling" (some say "ostentatious") "VIP business" lunch; but given its NY prices, many expect it to "walk on water" – and it merely glides; N.B. it sailed back from its summer '98 vacation with a new French chef, Sandro Gamba (who trained with France's Alain Ducasse), and a lower tab.

Levante's S | – | – | – | M |
7262 Woodmont Ave. (Elm St.), Bethesda, MD, 301-657-2441
Jammed from day one, this splashy Euro import brings Levantine cuisine – an amalgam of Eastern Mediterranean brick-oven pizzas, pita-wrapped sandwiches, salads, grills and *meze* – to a high-style, open-to-the-street format in the heart of Bethesda; while it's casual dining, the word is it's overseen with attitude to the nth degree.

Le Vieux Logis | 23 | 21 | 22 | $41 |
7925 Old Georgetown Rd. (Auburn Ave.), Bethesda, MD, 301-652-6816
◪ An eye-catching outdoor mural draws attention to one of Bethesda's lesser-known "gems", an "old-fashioned" French filled with nooks, knickknacks and some well-known names; its discriminating "older crowd" ("they can afford it") gets "very personal" attention (they "remember my name") and "wonderful food"; however, a few critics counter "it's crowded" and "overpriced for what it provides."

Lewie's S | ▽ 17 | 15 | 16 | $17 |
6845 Reed St. (bet. Bethesda & Woodmond Aves.), Bethesda, MD, 301-652-1600
◪ A virtual Puns-R-Us in Bethesda, this cafe/bar/boutique/nightclub complex ensconced in an industrial chic setting offers an eclectic mix of Cal-Ital pasta and sandwiches with cutesy names like Lewie XV (roast beef); "live music" and "great" (big) desserts make it a "nice place to hang out on a lazy afternoon" or head for as an after-dinner destination; if only the staff acted "less like bored college kids."

Listrani's S | 16 | 14 | 17 | $21 |
5100 MacArthur Blvd., NW (Dana Pl.), 202-363-0619
◪ Supporters say this "reliable neighborhood Italian" MacArthur Boulevard "joint" with salads, pizza and pasta is "cheap" and "good for kids"; while foes "can't understand its popularity" because the food is only "average" and the "interior is tacky", they speculate that "neighbors keep it going because there's nowhere else" nearby.

Washington, D.C.   F | D | S | C

Little Fountain Cafe S   – | – | – | M
2339 18th St., NW (Belmont Rd.), 202-462-8100
You'd expect to find this kind of "quiet", "intimate" bistro with an "always-changing, always-fresh" International menu and "owners who really care" in Paris or Rome; this one gets a little "lost among the Adams Morgan array" and deserves to be found.

Little Viet Garden S   21 | 15 | 17 | $18
3012 Wilson Blvd. (Garfield Rd.), Arlington, VA, 703-522-9686
◼ On summer nights, with the sparkling "little lights" and "pretty palm trees" on the "wonderful outdoor terrace" obscuring the not-so-scenic dumpster and "adjoining parking lot", this "crowded" Vietnamese "takes you out of Arlington" to a "romantic" place; its familiar menu has enough "faves" (spring rolls, noodle dishes, grilled pork) to keep customers happy, notwithstanding "inconsistent" cooking, "sketchy service" and a "dark", "weird" interior.

Los Chorros S   20 | 12 | 19 | $16
8401 Snouffer's School Rd. (Center Way), Gaithersburg, MD, 301-840-5894
2420 Blue Ridge Ave. (Georgia Ave.), Wheaton, MD, 301-933-1066
◼ "Go for the Salvadoran entrees" ("good papusas" and seafood) at these "unusually crowded" Central Americans or it may be "hard to see why" people are virtually "pushing and shoving" to get into these eateries with "cheap" prices and a "welcoming staff"; while they're "holes-in-the-wall" to begin with, some say Wheaton's remodeling wasn't exactly an improvement.

Louisiana Express Co. S   21 | 9 | 15 | $15
4921 Bethesda Ave. (Arlington Rd.), Bethesda, MD, 301-652-6945
◼ In Bethesda, as in Louisiana's bayou country, the best "cheap", "hot and spicy" Cajun-Creole eats are found in bare-bones dives similar to this "zero-decor" luncheonette, which offers "incredible" catfish, po' boys, beignets and steaming café au lait; but "don't go if you're in a hurry" – it's fast food served slow.

Lucia's Italian Deli S   – | – | – | I
2409 University Blvd. (Elkin Rd.), Wheaton, MD, 301-949-2112
With just a few tables, chairs, a counter and some shelves, this Wheaton deli doesn't look like much, but it's where the neighborhood goes for "heavenly pastries"; "delicious" homemade pizza and substantial subs are also a "great bargain."

Luigino [S] 21 | 19 | 18 | $32

1100 New York Ave., NW (bet. H & 12th Sts.), 202-371-0595

◪ An "urbane" Italian in a Convention Center "neighborhood where stylish cuisine is still hard to find", with "wonderful", rustic specialty soups, stews and pastas; while the "sleek" space can be a bit "cold at dinner", it warms up for a "good business lunch", but since "everything's cooked to order", pacing (and sometimes "quality") can be "erratic."

Luna Grill & Diner [S] 18 | 16 | 17 | $16

1301 Connecticut Ave., NW (N St.), 202-835-2280
4024 28th St. S. (Quincy St.), Arlington, VA, 703-379-7173

◪ "Hectic and eclectic", like its Dupont Circle 'hood, this "convenient", "funky diner" dishes up "amazingly cheap", "basic" American fare and it's usually mobbed; "daily green plate specials" (for vegetarians), "great mashed potatoes" and "don't miss sweet potato fries" hearten "herbivores and carnivores alike"; now if only the staff would "wake up"; N.B. the Arlington branch is new and unrated.

Maggiano's Little Italy [S] 20 | 19 | 19 | $24

Tyson Galleria, 1790-M International Dr. (Rte. 123), Tysons Corner, VA, 703-356-9000
5333 Wisconsin Ave. (Western Ave.), 202-966-5500

◪ Supporters say the bigger your "gang", the more they'll like this "dark", mall-based Southern Italian's "must-share" format of "tremendous portions" of garlicky "grandmother's" food; but foes feel it's a "noisy", "crowded" "factory" with only "ok" fare and suggest solo diners are better off heading for its adjacent Corner Bakery and Cafe (and its 'round-the-Beltway clones) for "express service."

Majestic [S] – | – | – | M

2922 Annandale Rd. (bet. Arlington Blvd. & Jefferson Ave.), Annandale, VA, 703-538-8888

This large, though hardly majestic, Falls Church Chinese-Vietnamese features a comprehensive multiregional menu and "exotic" preparations of local seafood; it's been so successful in developing a diverse clientele that it canned its nightclub to focus on the food.

MAKOTO [S] 27 | 24 | 27 | $44

4822 MacArthur Blvd., NW (Reservoir Rd.), 202-298-6866

■ "Exquisite little things just keep coming" during a "stunning set dinner" at this "sauna-sized" (four tables and 10 sushi bar seats) Palisades Japanese; one of this *Survey*'s top-rated spots, a meal here is an "aesthetically pleasing experience" that's reputedly "as good as all but the best in Japan" and for "one quarter of the price."

Malibu Grill [S] | – | – | – | M

5715 Columbia Pike (Rte. 7), Falls Church, VA, 703-379-0587

It doesn't take long for Falls Church families to learn the drill at this mammoth, all-you-can-eat Brazilian: turn the table tag to green to summon "gauchos" brandishing swords of sizzling meats, then hit the buffet to sample rib-busting "specialties" and salads; on weekends, hundreds defy the food police at its bargain $9.95 brunch ($5.95 for kids).

M & S Grill ◐[S] | – | – | – | M

600 13th St., NW (F St.), 202-347-1500

Like its power-full, seafood-centered brethren, McCormick & Schmick's, this handsome, spirited evocation of an Edwardian chophouse on a prime Downtown corner was overbooked from day one; in high-backed booths, curtained alcoves or at the massive bar, suits and tourist T-shirts chow down on a roster of seafood, steaks, salads, trendily rubbed grills and assorted libations worthy of Diamond Jim Brady.

Mango Mike's [S] | 18 | 16 | 17 | $20

4111 Duke St. (bet. Jordan St. & Quaker Ln.), Alexandria, VA, 703-823-1166

◪ You "half expect Jimmy Buffett" to be scoping out "Duke Street traffic" from this West Alexandria watering hole's front porch or sitting inside soaking up its "Key West" funk; decorated like a Caribbean-themed "junior prom", it features "pepper hot" Island cooking and a "steel drum brunch" and rates an 'A' for "atmosphere", but not for putting it "all together."

Mare e Monti [S] | ▽ 20 | 13 | 17 | $21

Free State Mall, 15554-B Annapolis Rd. (Hwy. 197), Bowie, MD, 301-262-9179

■ Like a "jewel in a very plain setting", a meal at this "remarkable" (for Bowie) Italian is heightened by its location in an undistinguished mall; in an area dominated by pizza joints and chains, it's an "unlikely spot" for homemade pastas like *timballo* (lasagna made with crêpes) and Abruzzi regional dishes you won't often find at high-dollar dineries Downtown.

Mark, The ◐[S] | – | – | – | I

401 Seventh St., NW (bet. D & E Sts.), 202-783-3133

On the mark with a smart, sophisticated, multiplex layout, a prime Penn Quarter address (just steps away from the Folger Shakespeare Theater and Downtown office suites) and Alison Swope's (ex Santa Fe East, New Heights) skillful fusion of eclectic ingredients and cooking techniques, this fledgling New American bistro has done its homework; calling it "promising" covers all bets.

Washington, D.C. | F | D | S | C |

Market St. Bar & Grill S | 22 | 20 | 20 | $31 |
Hyatt Hotel, 1800 President St. (Market St.), Reston, VA, 703-709-6262

An "airy", attractive "grown-up place for lunch" or "excellent martinis" "hidden" in Reston Town Center, this "helpful" hostelry's "pairing" of Contemporary American "cuisine and jazz brings urbanity to suburbia"; while it leaves a few things to be desired – it can be "noisy" and "pricey" – don't miss its "something for everyone" brunch.

Martin's Tavern S | 17 | 19 | 18 | $23 |
1264 Wisconsin Ave., NW (N St.), 202-333-7370

"Four generations of Martins" have preserved this "landmark" Georgetown saloon's "1946 time warp" aura, straightforward American menu and tradition of outspoken (some say "surly") staff; today, a mix of early settlers and young strivers follow in the Roosevelts' and the Kennedys' footsteps for "late-night pub fare", "shad roe in spring" and the "best early-morning breakfast in town."

Matuba | 23 | 14 | 20 | $21 |
4918 Cordell Ave. (Old Georgetown Rd.), Bethesda, MD, 301-652-7449
2915 Columbia Pike (Walter Reed St.), Arlington, VA, 703-521-2811

"Tightly packed" like their "fresh", "affordable" sushi, these "modest" Japanese workhorses play to suburban families with constant "good deals", sushi with unfamiliar twists (bagel rolls), off-menu specials and raw fish–teriyaki combos for the "can't decide" brigade; that being said, making customers feel like they're "going home for sushi" is their stock-in-trade.

Max's of Washington | – | – | – | E |
1725 F St. (bet. 17th & 18th Sts.), 202-842-0070

Gleaming wood, etched glass, soft lighting, Western accents and a discreetly designated 'Presidential entrance' signal the transformation of this close to the White House address (formerly Maison Blanc) into a suave steakhouse with a handsome horseshoe bar; Gerard Pain (La Chaumiere), a seasoned pro, is hedging his menu bets with lobster salad and latkes, along with traditional meat and seafood dishes.

McCormick & Schmick's S | 22 | 22 | 21 | $33 |
1652 K St., NW (bet. 16th & 17th Sts.), 202-861-2233
11920 Democracy Dr. (Library St.), Reston, VA, 703-481-6600

With their Victorian splendor (paneled booths and "private" snuggeries), corporate cordiality and "fresh fish", these Downtown and Reston "power spots" are "first choice" sites for doing deals, "family meals", happy hour and late-night snacking on $1.95 plates; however, while some say this "high-end" operation "handles crowds with aplomb", others claim diners can be "lost in the shuffle."

Washington, D.C. | F | D | S | C |

Meadowlark Inn S | ▽ | 18 | 20 | 21 | $26 |
Rte. 107/Fisher Ave. (bet. Rte. 109/Ogden Rd. & Cattail Rd.), Poolesville, MD, 301-428-8900
☑ This "retro" stage set for a "Sunday dinner" in the country, with its "back to the '60s" American food, prices and downright "pleasant" help, caps a "nice drive" to Poolesville; but while it works for "retirement parties" and nostalgia buffs, the rest yawn "boring, but it doesn't offend."

Mediterranee S | 21 | 17 | 22 | $29 |
3520 Lee Hwy. (Monroe St.), Arlington, VA, 703-527-7276
☑ It's "off the beaten path" in Arlington, but on target when it comes to Pan-Mediterranean cooking that includes "excellent couscous" served by a "friendly" staff; however, its location and "too close tables" lead some to conclude it's "promising but expensive for what is provided."

Mehak S | - | - | - | I |
7716 Lee Hwy. (Rte. 7), Falls Church, VA, 703-573-8118
The "Lee Highway crowd" tipped us off about this "delicious cheap Indian" in their part of town; its "hearty" standards are priced and "spiced just right" for once-a-week dining; while the food is flavorful and the service is "friendly", you're certainly not paying for decor.

MELROSE S | 26 | 25 | 25 | $47 |
Park Hyatt Hotel, M & 24th Sts., NW, 202-955-3899
■ One of DC's top "creative" Contemporary Americans, this hotel dining room has an "understated elegance" that makes it a "quiet oasis" and "escape from the city" right in the heart of the West End; with "excellent" food, well-chosen wines, "gracious" service and luxurious appointments like fine art and a "cascading fountain" on the "romantic" terrace, it's a "little pricey but perfect for a special occasion."

Memphis Bar-B-Q Co. S | 15 | 14 | 15 | $15 |
Ballston Commons, 4238 Wilson Blvd. (Glebe Rd.), Arlington, VA, 703-875-9883
11804 Baron Cameron Rd. (bet. Reston & Towne Ctr. Pkwys.), Reston, VA, 703-435-5118
13067-H Lee Jackson Hwy. (Stringfellow Rd.), Fairfax, VA, 703-449-0500
☑ Folks from Memphis "don't get too excited" about the 'cue at these kitschy mall-based "barns"; as for the rest of the populus, their divergent views range from "good basic barbecue" to "mixes the worst of BBQ with T.G.I. Friday's."

Mendocino Grille & Wine Bar S | 22 | 21 | 21 | $39 |
2917 M St., NW (bet. 29th & 30th Sts.), 202-333-2912
☑ "California on M Street", this young Contemporary American brings a West Coast sensibility and "a great wine list" to Georgetown; while it's "innovative", hungry diners complain that there's "not enough" of its "beautifully presented food" on their plates.

Washington, D.C. | F | D | S | C |

Meskerem ◐ S | 22 | 20 | 19 | $21 |
2434 18th St., NW (Columbia Rd.), 202-462-4100

■ It's "fun" to "sit on a tuffet" and "eat with your hands" at this Adams Morgan Ethiopian, but it's "not for everyone"; even if you're not squeamish about unfamiliar foods, the cooking can be "uneven", the service "iffy" and the decor downstairs like being in "someone's rec room."

Metro Center Grille S | 17 | 16 | 18 | $25 |
Marriott at Metro Ctr., 775 12th St., NW (bet. H & J Sts.), 202-737-2200

■ While this near the Convention Center Contemporary American hotel dining room "is better than most for a quiet biz lunch", many opt for the "best buffet lunch in town" offered in the "great" clubby bar downstairs; perhaps that's because apart from tables spaced for "privacy", upstairs is "all grill, no charm" or because some dishes like duck salad are "utterly great", but others are duds.

Metro 29 ◐ S | 16 | 15 | 16 | $14 |
4711 Lee Hwy. (Glebe Rd.), Arlington, VA, 703-528-2464

■ Although critics credit the "long weekend lines" outside this neo-"classic diner" in Arlington to the fact that the area has "no breakfast places", others disagree; its "gorilla-sized portions" of "excellent French toast" and other morning treats, not to mention its "late" hours and "rich desserts", have them enthusing "eat a lot, don't pay much, have fun."

Mezza 9 S | – | – | – | M |
Hyatt Arlington, 1325 Wilson Blvd. (Nash St.), Arlington, VA, 703-276-8999

This recently transformed Mediterranean-themed setting, with its myriad make-a-meal-of-appetizers possibilities and creative, eclectic entrees, is bound to surprise tourists expecting routine Arlington hotel fare; it already has nearby canyon dwellers and worker bees buzzing.

Mike Baker's 10th St. Grill ▽ | 16 | 16 | 19 | $22 |
518 10th St. (bet. E & F Sts.), 202-347-6333

■ Mike Baker, a "legendary" DC barkeeper, brings his "personal touch" to this rookie Downtown venture; its historic space (opposite Ford Theatre) is now a "perfect dive bar", with a more formal dining room offering "good" American fare; "it's too early to tell", but patrons seem "happy."

Mike's American Grill S | 21 | 20 | 19 | $22 |
6210 Backlick Rd. (Old Keene Mill Rd.), Springfield, VA, 703-644-7100

■ The "'burb formula works" at this "handsome", "youth-oriented", "all-American" bistro in Springfield, filling the "monster" space with "big bar action" and keeping the kitchen hopping with orders for burgers and "great" blackened prime rib; the biggest problem is that it's "nearly always full", causing "vicious waits" and unremitting din.

Mi Rancho [S] 20 | 17 | 20 | $19

19725 Germantown Rd. (Middlebrook Rd.), Germantown, MD, 301-515-7480
8701 Ramsey Ave. (Fiddler Ln.), Silver Spring, MD, 301-588-4872

■ These "well-managed", "family-friendly" Latins offer an "unpretentious", "less expensive and less mobbed" rendition of the Tex-Mex recipe popularized by Rio Grande Cafe; besides "good" fajitas, "authentic" dishes include carne asada; P.S. Silver Spring sports a "nice patio."

Miss Saigon [S] 19 | 15 | 18 | $21

3057 M St. (Thomas Jefferson St.), 202-333-5545

◪ If you "like its style" – "delicate" Vietnamese staples, "good wines", "affordable" prices and lots of "fake plants" – you'll "take this [Georgetown] restaurant over the Andrew Lloyd Webber show"; however, mixed with mostly "good" reviews are reports of "shrimp frozen longer than an Iranian asset" and having to order by phone "before I get there because it's slow at lunch."

Miyagi ▽ 25 | 16 | 21 | $22

6719 Curran St. (Old Dominion Dr.), McLean, VA, 703-893-0116

■ Happily, for McLean's ardent sushi fiends, this "serene", bento box–sized retreat with the "freshest" selections and a "limited menu" of cooked foods remains largely undiscovered; its only flaw seems to be that it could use another "very friendly" server; N.B. post-*Survey*, its popular sushi chef has moved on.

Moby Dick ⊄ 23 | 7 | 14 | $11

1070 31st St., NW (bet. K & M Sts.), 202-333-4400 [S]
7027 Wisconsin Ave. (Leland St.), Bethesda, MD, 301-654-1838 [S]
Buchanan Mall, 2103 S. Jefferson Davis Hwy. (23rd St.), Crystal City, VA, 703-413-5100
6864 Old Dominion Dr. (Rte. 123), Tysons Corner, VA, 703-448-8448 [S]

■ These masters of the Persian art of grilling kebabs earn "no awards for decor", but for what they do – "wonderful, healthy, economical fast food" – they're tops, producing some of the most "tender" meats, "fragrant" rice and "freshly baked bread" this side of their namesake cafe in Tehran; P.S. "surroundings are drab", so "take out, don't cram in."

Mongolian Grill [S] 18 | 12 | 15 | $17

7710 Wisconsin Ave. (bet. Cheltenham Ave. & Old Georgetown Rd.), Bethesda, MD, 301-654-8811

◪ Fans of this Bethesda youngster's "build your own stir-fry" gimmick say it's "conceptually appealing" 'cause it lets you "control your calories" or opt for "utter gluttony"; however, foes feel that it has its limitations – "cafeteria-like", "slow" and a bit "expensive" for self-serve food; if you go, "follow their recipes" and bring the kids.

Washington, D.C. F | D | S | C

Monocle 15 | 16 | 18 | $31
107 D St., NE (1st St.), 202-546-4488
You'll spot more "senators than on the Capitol floor" at this "geographically advantaged" men's club (the closest Hill restaurant on the Senate-side), not to mention "Supreme Court justices" and "uptight" Hill staffers; it's also "menuically challenged" because its "average" American fare "hasn't changed" in years, but since no one "comes for the food", "who cares?"

Monroe's S 19 | 20 | 20 | $24
1603 Commonwealth Ave. (Monroe Ave.), Alexandria, VA, 703-548-5792
"A great outdoor patio", "wine jugs on the table" and a menu of Italian "comfort foods" strike a neighborly note at this shiny Del Ray trattoria; although it maintains the "kid-friendly", "low-key tradition" that distinguishes its nearby kin, the Calvert Grille, it still "needs polishing" – the "food is inconsistent, but when it's good, it's great."

Montgomery's Grille S 14 | 16 | 16 | $21
7200 Wisconsin Ave. (Bethesda Ave.), Bethesda, MD, 301-654-3595
This all-purpose Bethesda American is a "Tuesday night restaurant when you don't feel like cooking", a meeting place where "there's always a table at lunch" and a Thursday and Friday night "noisy" mob scene when you're just "looking"; since the food is only "ok" and "service is spotty", its long hours and decent parking are the draws.

MORRISON-CLARK INN S 26 | 26 | 25 | $43
Morrison-Clark Inn, 1015 L St., NW (bet. 11th St. & Massachusetts Ave.), 202-898-1200
"A lovely restaurant with class, charm and the wonderful cooking" of Susan Lindeborg, one of the area's top chefs, who "imaginatively" "updates" "everyday" American food; while the "setting is elegant and refined", its "very professional" staff puts boldface names, "foreign visitors" and just-folks at ease; now that the nearby MCI Center is revitalizing what was an "out-of-the-way" neighborhood, its only "negative" becomes another plus.

MORTON'S OF CHICAGO S 26 | 22 | 23 | $49
3251 Prospect St., NW (Wisconsin Ave.), 202-342-6258
Washington Sq., 1050 Connecticut Ave., NW (L St.), 202-955-5997
Fairfax Sq., 8075 Leesburg Pike (Aline Rd.), Tysons Corner, VA, 703-883-0800
"Check your belt at the door" of these "macho" beefhouses and dig into a "steak as big as a house cat" and a baked potato that's the "size of Idaho"; sure, the "cigar smoke", the "hustle", the "chatty waiters" and the bill are all "a bit much", but isn't that the point? N.B. they serve lobster, veggie platters and chocolate soufflés too.

Washington, D.C. | F | D | S | C |

Mr. K's S | 23 | 23 | 23 | $40 |
2121 K St., NW (bet. 21st & 22nd Sts.), 202-331-8868
◪ "The fanciest Chinese restaurant on earth" is what surveyors say about this K Street "white glove" Asian, which "wows" the "expense-account set" with "elegant" fare served with "French flair" in "quiet", "luxurious" rooms; however, wallet-watchers wail the experience is "a version of Chinese torture called 'overpriced small portions'."

Mrs. Simpson's S | 20 | 21 | 21 | $33 |
2915 Connecticut Ave., NW (Cathedral Ave.), 202-332-8300
◪ This Woodley Park memorial to the romantic Windsor-Simpson legend is probably too "cute" for Wallis to "have dined here", but that doesn't mean that your "visiting aunt" won't be enthralled; its "sweet" interior and terrace and "creative" American dishes are especially delightful on "rainy afternoons" or at brunch.

Mr. Yung's S | 18 | 11 | 17 | $18 |
740 Sixth St., NW (bet. G & H Sts.), 202-628-1098
◪ The Yung clan's "consistent" Cantonese storefront gets a shot in the arm from nearby MCI Arena "pre-game" traffic, supplementing its sporadic "tour bus" clientele; but don't let that deter you from trying its "wonderful dim sum."

Music City Roadhouse S | 15 | 17 | 15 | $18 |
1050 30th St., NW (bet. K & M Sts.), 202-337-4444
◪ This "honky-tonk" may be in Georgetown, but rural Tennessee is its spiritual home; it's a "cool hangout", serving beers good ole boy–style (with a "paper bag and a pickle"); go for a "cheap" Southern fat fix with a large group and don't miss its "fun gospel brunch."

Mykonos | 19 | 17 | 20 | $25 |
1835 K St., NW (19th St.), 202-331-0370
121 Congressional Ln. (Rockville Pike), Rockville, MD, 301-770-5999
◪ K Street briefcase toters take a "quick trip to the Aegean" at this "refreshing" Ionian enclave; while its staples won't be confused with your Greek "grandma's cooking", they offer "good lunch value"; the "delightful" owners and (sometimes "cranky") Greek waiters lend an air of authenticity; N.B. the Rockville branch is new and unrated.

Nam's S | 20 | 14 | 19 | $19 |
4928 Cordell Ave. (bet. Old Georgetown Rd. & Woodmont Ave.), Bethesda, MD, 301-652-2635
11220 Georgia Ave. (University Blvd.), Wheaton, MD, 301-933-2525
■ "It's amazing what they do with a few noodles", some seafood, shrimp (and the "sweetest" smiles) at these "easy on the wallet" Vietnamese; while the Bethesda outlet is more "upscale", Wheaton's "low-grade" "looks don't matter when the food is so good."

Washington, D.C. | F | D | S | C |

Nam Viet ⓢ | 23 | 14 | 20 | $20 |
3419 Connecticut Ave. (bet. Macomb & Porter Sts.), 202-237-1015
1127 N. Hudson St. (Wilson Blvd.), Arlington, VA, 703-522-7110
■ While this Clarendon Vietnam veteran seems "far from the madding crowd", especially when dining beneath its "romantic" patio lights, its "hugely crowded", "hectic" Cleveland Park sibling is blessed for bringing Arlington "excellence" to a busy part of town; go for pho (noodle soups), "crispy fish" and "anything grilled", at "close to the price you'd pay in Vietnam."

NEW HEIGHTS ⓢ | 25 | 23 | 23 | $43 |
2317 Calvert St., NW (Connecticut Ave.), 202-234-4110
■ "Wonderfully seductive" and "original", this Contemporary American "pushes the creative envelope" with "gorgeous presentations", drawing a steady, discriminating clientele that "never tires of trying something new"; its second-story space, overlooking Rock Creek Park, is awash with art and "when the trees are in bloom" is "magical", but service, while "phenomenally nice", is a bit "slow."

Nizam's ⓢ | 21 | 19 | 22 | $30 |
Village Green Shopping Ctr., 523 Maple Ave. W. (Rte. 123), Vienna, VA, 703-938-8948
■ "Doner kebab nights (Tuesdays and weekends) are the best" time to experience this lively Ottoman bazaar scene in Vienna, especially when owner Nizam Ozgur is on hand; but while the atmosphere is "intimate" and "warm", attempts to introduce newcomers to the authentic "Turkish delights" that draw expats here can be "intimidating."

NORA | 26 | 24 | 24 | $47 |
2132 Florida Ave., NW (bet. Connecticut & Massachusetts Aves.), 202-462-5143
■ "DC's best combo of romance, fine food and unstuffy elegance", spiked with "guaranteed celebrity" sightings, is found at this "original" New American set in a "charming" carriage house near Dupont Circle; chef-owner Nora Pouillon practically invented market-driven menus featuring "natural" ingredients and her staff is "knowledgeable" too.

Normandie Farm ⓢ | – | – | – | E |
10710 Falls Rd. (River Rd.), Potomac, MD, 301-983-8838
Whether for a "special occasion" (receptions, anniversaries) or "lunch with the girls", this "cozy" Potomac "country inn setting" is a "favorite" for Old Marylanders; affectionately known as the "Popover Palace", customers "return for good [Continental] meals" highlighted by heaping baskets of those "great, golden, hot" rolls.

Washington, D.C.

| F | D | S | C |

Nulbom ◐ S | - | - | - | I |
4870 Boiling Brook Pkwy. (Nicholson Ln.), Rockville, MD, 301-468-2930
This ordinary-looking restaurant and nightclub in an out-of-the-way Rockville strip caters to local Asians and gives Westerners a chance to sample "good Korean food [and sushi] at reasonable prices"; just don't expect much more from the staff than smiles.

OBELISK | 27 | 23 | 25 | $53 |
2029 P St., NW (bet. 20th & 21st Sts.), 202-872-1180
■ "Refined, understated and excellent" food makes Peter Pastan's "delightful little jewel box" off Dupont Circle this *Survey*'s top Italian; though the "prix fixe menu is limited", everything's "pure, simple, handmade" and hence "close to perfection"; since many maintain it's the "best high-end value in town", it's become a "favorite for spoiling friends."

Occidental Grill S | 22 | 23 | 21 | $39 |
Willard Complex, 14th St. & Pennsylvania Ave., 202-783-1475
◧ It looks like an Old "Washington restaurant should", "classy" and "gentlemen's clubby", with photos of fabled movers and shakers lining the walls and "power" types at its tables; however, while loyalists laud the "good", "dependable" American fare like grilled fish, chopped salads and burgers, the food isn't always "as good as you'd expect" at this "legendary" Downtown location.

Old Angler's Inn S | 23 | 24 | 21 | $49 |
10801 MacArthur Blvd. (1 mi. past Clara Barton Pkwy.), Potomac, MD, 301-365-2425
◧ Go for a "romantic" "drink by the fireplace in winter" or a starlit dinner on the "wonderful patio" outside (it's a bit "claustrophobic" upstairs) and discover why this "quaint" C&O canal setting is made-to-order for getting engaged, "cheating on your spouse" or making amends; much of its "expensive" Contemporary American cooking seems to weather periodic chef changes.

Old Brogue Irish ◐ S | 16 | 17 | 19 | $20 |
760 Walker Rd. (Georgetown Pike), Great Falls, VA, 703-759-3309
■ This rollicking Irish snug with "Guinness on tap", Irish bands and "decent" pub food is *the* "place to be" in Great Falls on St. Patrick's Day; while it's more a place to have "fun in" than to be "fed in", everyday eating is enhanced by a "blazing" fire and a "lovely" all-year-round patio overlooking the village green.

Washington, D.C. F | D | S | C

Old Ebbitt Grill ◐ S 19 | 22 | 20 | $28
675 15th St., NW (bet. F & G Sts.), 202-347-4801
■ "Deservedly mobbed", this handsome Downtown "institution" is virtually a White House "annex" filled with a "who's who" of "journalists" and "wide-eyed out-of-towners" who find that its "celebratory" mood, "polished" manners, long hours and "serious" all-American food fit any occasion; it's "quintessentially DC" and "considering the quality", "you get your money's worth."

Olde Towne Tavern & Brewing Co. ◐ S 16 | 19 | 19 | $22
227 E. Diamond Ave. (N. Summit Ave.), Gaithersburg, MD, 301-948-4200
◾ Depending on the time of day, this spiffy restoration operates as an "upgraded college hangout", a happening live music scene or a business backdrop with ambitious American saloon food; although it's a toss-up whether the "beer is better than the vittles", or vice versa, the "atmosphere" is better than both.

Old Europe S 18 | 17 | 18 | $28
2434 Wisconsin Ave., NW (Calvert St.), 202-333-7600
◾ Supporters say it's "always Oktoberfest" at this "authentic" Glover Park German with "excellent brats and beer"; but while admirers admit it's "a little shopworn as befits a [50-year-old] classic", critics call the menu and decor "tired" and the "oompah" atmosphere "hokey."

Old Glory BBQ ◐ S 19 | 16 | 17 | $19
3139 M St., NW (bet. 31st St. & Wisconsin Ave.), 202-337-3406
◾ "Elvis kitsch" like "Graceland nachos" and "White Lightning" vodka drinks, along with "solid BBQ" are served up at this "smoky", "rowdy" in-town pit; still, it's a "cool" way to be under 25 "in Georgetown and not spend much money."

Old Hickory Grill S ▽ 22 | 9 | 18 | $19
15240 Old Columbia Pike (Rte. 198), Burtonsville, MD, 301-421-0204
■ The "best ribs", "great mashed potatoes and onion rings" and "delicious cornbread and biscuits" lure loyalists to this Burtonsville American; the "unpretentious" decor may leave something to be desired, but the "price is right."

Olney Ale House S 19 | 17 | 18 | $16
2000 Sandspring Rd. (Doctor Bird Rd.), Olney, MD, 301-774-6708
◾ Bikers and Olney theatergoers have kept this countrified hippie throwback "true unto itself" for nearly 25 years; now strivers from nearby developments are drawn to its "cozy" fireplace and such "down-home" Americana as "super stew"; some say that the "staff is a little too casual", but "atmosphere and beer" bring boosters back.

On the Border [S] — | — | — | I

1488 Rockville Pike (bet. Knowles & Templeton), Rockville, MD, 301-881-9257
Spectrum Ctr., 11880 Spectrum Ctr., Reston, VA, 703-904-1240
8027 Leesburg Pike (Gallows Rd.), Tysons Corner, VA, 703-893-4395

These big-as-Texas cantinas around the Beltway follow the familiar formula of "great fajitas" and killer margaritas, although their "good value" menu extends into less familiar territory like *carne guisado*; but, as you'd expect, with an ever-changing, fresh-faced crew, they are "still working out the bugs" when it comes to service.

Oodles Noodles 21 | 15 | 17 | $16

1120 19th St., NW (bet. L & M Sts.), 202-293-3138
4907 Cordell Ave. (bet. Norfolk & Old Georgetown Rds.), Bethesda, MD, 301-986-8833 [S]

■ "Bright flavors in a very large bowl" are the focus at these "fast"-paced, "well-priced", "something for everyone" noodle houses; "noise", "too close together tables" and Bethesda's "parking nightmare" don't prevent them from "putting the 'ood' in 'good'" "Asian comfort food" and being "very popular."

Oriental Star [S] 19 | 16 | 23 | $22

3221 Brook St. (Quaker Ln.), Alexandria, VA, 703-370-4100

■ In '90s Northern Virginia, your basic "neighborhood joint with good food" is likely to be a budget Asian, like this one hidden in a North Alexandria shopping strip; pros praise the "consistent quality" of its Thai cooking, the "cheap" ($6.75) Chinese buffet brunch and "pleasant staff."

Original Pancake House [S] — | — | — | I

Discovery Bldg., 7700 Wisconsin Ave. (Old Georgetown Rd.), Bethesda, MD, 301-986-0285
12224 Rockville Pike (bet. Randolph Rd. & Rolling Ave.), Rockville, MD, 301-468-0886

Famished families are stacked up at the doors of these "cheap" and cheerful Montgomery County eateries waiting for a chance to dig into the "best crêpes this side of the Atlantic", hotcakes with "ultrafresh" fruit sauces and a "terrific variety" of early-morning munchies; their major flaw is that they're "crowded" and hard to get into.

Outback Steakhouse [S] 19 | 15 | 18 | $22

7720 Woodmont Ave. (bet. Old Georgetown Rd. & Wisconsin Ave.), Bethesda, MD, 301-913-0176
Hilltop Plaza, 6868 Race Track Rd. (Rte. 450), Bowie, MD, 301-464-5800
Germantown Sq., 12609 Wisteria Dr. (Great Seneca Hwy.), Germantown, MD, 301-353-9499
Aspen Manor Shopping Ctr., 13703 Georgia Ave. (Connecticut Ave.), Silver Spring, MD, 301-933-4385

(Continues)

Washington, D.C. F D S C

Outback Steakhouse (Cont.)
Beacon Mall, 6804 Richmond Hwy. (Rte. 1), Alexandria, VA, 703-768-1063
Arlington Forest Shopping Ctr., 4821 N. First St. (Park Dr.), Arlington, VA, 703-527-0063
Colonnade, 5702 Union Mill Rd. (Rte. 29), Clifton, VA, 703-818-0804
Twinbrooke Shopping Ctr., 9579-B Braddock Rd. (Twinbrooke Dr.), Fairfax, VA, 703-978-6283
Elden Plaza, 150 Elden St. (Herndon Pkwy.), Herndon, VA, 703-318-0999
Backlick Ctr., 6651 Backlick Rd. (Old Keene Mill Rd.), Springfield, VA, 703-912-7531
Potomac Run Plaza, 46300 Potomac Run Plaza (Rte. 7), Sterling, VA, 703-406-3377
Giant Shopping Ctr., 315 Maple Ave. E. (Glyndon St.), Vienna, VA, 703-242-0460
Potomac Festival, 14580 Potomac Mills Rd. (Bixby Rd.), Woodbridge, VA, 703-490-5336

◼ It's easy to beef about these matey meateries ("the Alka-Seltzer chain"), but "if you steer around" the faux "Aussie trappings", you can get a "decent steak at a very decent price", along with a salad and fried, highly seasoned sides, served in a "baseball caps encouraged" atmosphere; unfortunately, smoke, noise, hyperfriendly helpers, limited hours and long "waits" are also part of the package.

Oval Room 23 | 22 | 22 | $41
800 Connecticut Ave., NW (H St.), 202-463-8700
◼ You'll spot "former presidents" and other boldface "pols" at this "casually elegant" New American on the K Street corridor that's "great for business lunches" and "pre-concert" romance; it's "run in the first-class fashion" you'd expect from the talents behind Bombay Club and 701, yet despite its "creative" food, it's something of a "sleeper."

PALM, THE S 24 | 20 | 22 | $46
1225 19th St., NW (bet. M & N Sts.), 202-293-9091
◼ This Dupont Circle "macho" meathouse is not for the "weak of heart" (or slim of purse) – in "true NY tradition" it combines a "crusty clientele" with "delightfully surly" waiters and "awesome portions" of "top-rate" steak and lobster; but the atmosphere can be "a little too DC insider" for a relaxing meal – if you "can't find your congressman at night", chances are he's here with his "cardiologist."

Panjshir 23 | 13 | 20 | $19
924 Broad St. (West St.), Falls Church, VA, 703-536-4566 S
224 W. Maple Ave. (Rte. 123), Vienna, VA, 703-281-4183
◼ "Fine Afghan food" is served in a "quaint" atmosphere at these Northern Virginia stalwarts; "cheap" and "consistent", they're "vegetarian paradises" that please "timid guests" ("not too spicy"), yet have regulars raving about the "variety of tastes in one dish."

Washington, D.C. | F | D | S | C |

Paolo's S | 20 | 19 | 18 | $25 |
1303 Wisconsin Ave., NW (N St.), 202-333-7353 ☾
Reston Town Ctr., 11898 Market St. (Fountain St.), Reston, VA, 703-318-8920
☑ So maybe the pastas, pizzas and salads at these Cal-Itals "with pizazz" are "not even pseudo-Italian", they're "tasty" and "much better than one should expect" from an overworked "yuppie" chain with some of the longest hours and hottest locations in the area; while these "pretty" "people-watching" paradises "try hard to be hip", they succeed in being very "popular" and "way too loud."

Paradise S | ▽ 21 | 17 | 18 | $24 |
7141 Wisconsin Ave. (Montgomery Ave.), Bethesda, MD, 301-907-7500
■ Recently revamped Bethesda restaurant that serves as an unofficial Iranian community center, vouching for the authenticity and quality of its "generous" (and very busy) lunch and dinner buffets and "hospitality"; it offers a "wonderful", reasonably priced opportunity for "sampling Persian dishes", especially now that it looks "much nicer" (brighter, more open and airy).

Pariolo S | 19 | 18 | 17 | $31 |
4800 Elm St. (Wisconsin Ave.), Bethesda, MD, 301-951-8600
☑ An "umpteenth change of ownership" (in '97) left Bethesda sharply divided on this popular, good-looking Italian; everyone praises its "menu pricing" (all pastas are one price, appetizers another), but there's simply no consensus about the food ("good veal and pasta" vs. "disappointing" fare), the service ("smooth" vs. "slow") or even its trendy downstairs cigar lounge; perhaps the key word is "chaotic."

Parkway Deli S | 20 | 11 | 18 | $14 |
Rock Creek Shopping Ctr., 8317 Grubb Rd. (bet. Connecticut Ave. & 16th St.), Silver Spring, MD, 301-587-1427
☑ This Silver Spring "Saturday breakfast must" brings a "bit of the old country" (via NYC) to the "new country" with the "best potato latkes in the world", "great kosher hot dogs", "eat-with-a fork" matzo ball soup and "big" corned beef sandwiches, all "practically thrown" on the table; P.S. its "pickle bar rocks."

Pasha Cafe S | 23 | 16 | 22 | $21 |
Cherrydale Shopping Ctr., 2109 N. Pollard St. (Military Rd.), Arlington, VA, 703-528-2126
■ "Fond memories of Egypt" pervade this "cute", little Cherrydale spot whose affordable, "accessible" food is full of "delightful" surprises; order a round of starters and discover "distinctive flavors" in seemingly familiar dishes like lentils and hummus; N.B. new owners promise the reverie will continue.

83

Washington, D.C.   F D S C

Pasta Plus S   23 | 14 | 20 | $22
Center Plaza, 209 Gorman Ave. (bet. Rtes. 1 & 198E), Laurel, MD, 301-498-5100
■ "Finding this good [but ordinary-looking] Italian restaurant in a Laurel strip mall is like finding the pearl in an oyster" – only better, because you can keep rediscovering its "reliable", "delicious" Italian specialties; everybody, from its "model" owner to the busboy, "works hard to keep the customer satisfied"; no wonder locals consider it "well worth the waits."

PATISSERIE CAFE DIDIER   26 | 15 | 17 | $17
(nka Xavier & Bruno Patisserie Cafe)
3206 Grace St., NW (bet. K & M Sts.), 202-342-9083
■ Popular and prestigious pâtissier Didier Schoner has sold his boutique cafe/bakery off the C&O canal in Georgetown to bakers Xavier Deshayes and Bruno Feldeisen (ex Four Seasons hotels); they've changed the name and are planning some minor alterations in the appearance of the place, but not its focus on quality desserts, light lunches and tea; the above ratings, earned by the departed Didier, are obsolete, but it looks like these talents will do as well.

Paul Kee ◑ S   ▽ 19 | 9 | 14 | $15
11305-B Georgia Ave. (University Blvd.), Wheaton, MD, 301-933-6886
■ English language menus help circumvent the "communication problem" at this "excellent" Wheaton Cantonese; as the "long lines" of Chinese-speaking customers indicate, this big, plain place is the "real" deal – go for soups, roasted meats and chow foon (noodles); N.B. it's where young second gen Asians go late at night.

Peking Gourmet Inn S   25 | 15 | 20 | $25
Culmore Shopping Ctr., 6029 Leesburg Pike (Glen Carlin St.), Falls Church, VA, 703-671-8088
■ "Awesome Peking duck", "excellent" dumplings and homegrown greens explain why the area's top Chinese restaurant "needs a traffic director" and why its major decorative feature is its "celebrity" photo–filled wall; sure the "decor is a throwback", but the waiters put on a "very entertaining" duck carving show and its "madhouse" mien adds Asian authenticity.

Perry's S   19 | 21 | 15 | $26
1811 Columbia Rd., NW (18th St.), 202-234-6218
◪ The martinis, "beautiful women" and "sushi-on-the-rooftop scene" at this Adams Morgan Eclectic make frogs feel like "hip and trendy" princes; loaded with "attitude" (service can be "a joke") and sporting "too many rules", it has a "high-style" interior which, like the Asian-accented menu, changes often but is always "cool"; P.S. on Sundays, the "drag brunch is anything but."

Washington, D.C. F D S C

Persimmon   - | - | - | M
7003 Wisconsin Ave. (bet. Leland & Walsh Sts.), Bethesda, MD, 301-654-9860
Fresh paint, white tablecloths and enthusiasm transform George Starke's former BBQ joint into this spiffy New American; its young chef-owner Damien Salvatore has an eclectic culinary bent, which includes a nice touch with seafood, plus a flair for presentation; this means that Bethesda diners can enjoy the kind of cuisine popularized by Kinkead's and Tahoga (his alma maters) close to home.

Pesce S   25 | 15 | 20 | $33
2016 P St., NW (bet. Dupont Circle & 20th St.), 202-466-3474
■ One of the town's top seafooders, this "lively" urban bistro off Dupont Circle boasts an "original", "skillfully" executed, daily-changing menu featuring "fish that doesn't get better than this", a "wine list of wonders" and "attentive" help (when not "rushed"); the whitewashed "fish store" setting is in keeping with the "exquisite simplicity" of the concept; the only gripe is too bad it's so "small."

Petitto's S   19 | 18 | 19 | $30
2653 Connecticut Ave., NW (Calvert St.), 202-667-5350
◪ Opera buffs and "romantics" give this "beautiful townhouse" in Woodley Park higher marks than some Italian gastronomes do, which doesn't mean that you won't spend a pleasant evening here, especially if you select a seafood pasta special, then head to the "little treasure" dessert haven downstairs; however, some snipe that "it's showing its age" and a "face-lift" would not be out of line; P.S. Friday is opera night and it's "fabulous."

P.F. Chang's China Bistro S   - | - | - | I
Tysons II Galleria, 1716-M International Dr. (Rte. 123), Tysons Corner, VA, 703-734-8996
In one of Northern Virginia's poshest malls, this Arizona import fuses "gorgeous" decor with Chinese food and "American-style" service and sets it all humming to a vintage rock beat; the resulting runaway hit has everyone from briefcase toters to parents with toddlers complaining that it's too "loud and crowded" while fighting to get in.

Phillips Flagship S   15 | 15 | 14 | $24
900 Water St., SW (9th St.), 202-488-8515
Phillips Seafood Grill S
American Ctr., 8330 Boone Blvd. (bet. Rtes. 7 & 23), Tysons Corner, VA, 703-442-0400
◪ While this "poor ambassador" of Chesapeake seafood services the "tour bus" trade with "massive buffets" and waterfront views, ratings suggest that some surveyors feel, except for "great" crabs, it's past "its prime"; N.B. the Tysons Corner location has an all-you-can-eat menu, instead of a buffet, and no view.

85

Washington, D.C.   F | D | S | C

Pho Cali S ▽ 22 | 13 | 17 | $13
1621 S. Walter Reed Dr. (Rte. 395, Glebe Rd. exit), Arlington, VA, 703-920-9500

◪ Becoming nearly as familiar to bargain-seeking Westerners as to native Vietnamese, meal-in-a-bowl *pho* houses provide "fresh", "healthy", "cheap eats"; what lifts this "accommodating" Arlington "neighborhood place" above the crowd are such Vietnamese specialties as seafood fondue and whole fish; however, we hear that "new management" may not be for the good.

Pho 95 S ▽ 21 | 9 | 18 | $12
Ritchie Shopping Ctr., 595 Rockville Pike (Ritchie Pkwy.), Rockville, MD, 301-294-9391

◼ There's "nothing fancy" (to put it charitably) about this Vietnamese "soup kitchen" or its nearby foe (Pho 75) off Rockville Pike; while this house has a full menu, most stick with its "good", "cheap", filling noodle soups.

Pho 75 S∅ 22 | 8 | 16 | $15
1510 University Blvd. E. (bet. N. Glebe Rd. & Pershing Dr.), Langley Park, MD, 301-434-7844
771 Hungerford Dr. (Jefferson St.), Rockville, MD, 301-434-7844
1711 Wilson Blvd. (Quinn St.), Arlington, VA, 703-525-7355
3103 Graham Rd. (Rte. 50), Falls Church, VA, 703-204-1490

◼ Among the first *pho* restaurants in the area, these are "always packed, and for good reason" – they provide lots of "fresh food that's certainly cheap"; go for "healthy", "steaming hot bowls of noodle soup" – "they should market it as a cold and flu remedy" – served in an "order, don't ask" "school cafeteria ambiance."

Pilin Thai S 22 | 15 | 19 | $17
116 W. Broad St. (Rte. 29), Falls Church, VA, 703-241-5850

◪ An across-the-board rating slide signals that this "once great" Falls Church Thai, while still "as good or better" than many, "could use a boost of flavor"; praise for the "gracious staff", "clean, pretty dining room" and a "regional" menu "worth working one's way through" comes with a caveat that sometimes the low "price is reflected in the dishes."

Pines of Rome S 18 | 11 | 17 | $19
4709 Hampden Ln. (Wisconsin Ave.), Bethesda, MD, 301-657-8775

◪ Italian "family dining", circa the '70s, "endures" in the heart of Bethesda, satisfying periodic cravings for "good white pizza", broiled fish, wine in "jelly jars" and "grimy (like Rome)", "old shoe" familiarity; however, hatchet men (many of whom "go once a week") taunt that it's "committed to the principle 'better to be cheap than good.'"

Washington, D.C. | F | D | S | C |

Pizza de Resistance 🅂 | 16 | 17 | 14 | $19 |
Courthouse Plaza, 2300 Clarendon Blvd. (bet. Barton St. & Courthouse Rd.), Arlington, VA, 703-351-5680

◪ "Very New York", or is it California that inspires this snazzy Courthouse Plaza space with "a little too much attitude" and a "gourmet" pizza menu with "many obscure" options?; though it's a popular "dinner/movie date" site for the young and hungry, some surveyors say this pizza isn't hard to resist 'cause it's "cold" and "looks better than it tastes."

PIZZERIA PARADISO 🅂 | 25 | 17 | 18 | $18 |
2029 P St., NW (bet. 20th & 21st Sts.), 202-223-1245

■ "The epitome of pizza", "best anywhere", "no rivals" – once again, this *Survey*'s top pizza honors go to this whimsically decorated Dupont Circle denizen and its "perfect" pies, which are distinguished by "delicious, fresh toppings" and a "smoky", crispy crust; other pluses include sandwiches, salads and a staff that doesn't panic "even when it's packed", i.e. at peak hours.

Planet Hollywood ◐🅂 | 11 | 20 | 13 | $20 |
1101 Pennsylvania Ave., NW (11th St.), 202-783-7827

◪ Although "only a tourist would admit to eating" at this Downtown American "glitz" palace, plenty of Beltway types "let the kids get their way" or drop by themselves to browse though its "museum quality" Hollywood memorabilia; when you go (and you probably will) remember that food (burgers, salads and such) is "incidental", albeit "expensive", conversation "can't happen" and you'll be routed through the gift shop on the way to the door.

Polly's Cafe ◐🅂 | 17 | 18 | 16 | $16 |
1342 U St., NW (bet. 13th & 14th Sts.), 202-265-8385

◪ It's New U's "funky" *Cheers*, a "dark, subterranean" "neighborhood haunt for starving artists" and such; loyalists like the veggies, burgers and "brunch by the fire", playing "one of the best jukeboxes" and letting the "hard to find" help find them; while foes feel the "food is nondescript" and the "service is distracted", all told it's an "anti-trendy" antidote to the '90s.

Po Siam 🅂   ▽ | 22 | 14 | 20 | $17 |
3807 Mt. Vernon Ave. (Russell Rd.), Alexandria, VA, 703-548-3925

■ This "efficient", "deserving" North Alexandria Thai does things in "traditional" ways, which is why familiar soups (coconut-lemongrass) and noodle dishes (pad Thai) taste so "delicious" here; an "excellent value", it's not widely known outside the neighborhood, but it should be.

Washington, D.C.

| F | D | S | C |

Positano Ⓢ | 19 | 18 | 18 | $28 |
4940 Fairmont Ave. (Old Georgetown Rd.), Bethesda, MD, 301-654-1717

◪ Along with its "romantic grape arbor" and come-back-to-Sorrento feel, this Bethesda "standby" offers "hearty" home cooking; while the less enthused say it may be "hurting from all the Italian competition", insiders instruct: order pasta and "drink wine outside in the warm months" to understand its enduring appeal.

Potowmack Landing Ⓢ | 16 | 21 | 16 | $27 |
Washington Sailing Marina, George Washington Pkwy. (½ mi. south of Nat'l Airport), Alexandria, VA, 703-548-0001

◪ "Terrific" Potomac River and airplane runway views make this site near National Airport a place to take visitors for Sunday brunch or "happy hour"; "jet noise", "generic" American food and up-and-down service explain why it has never taken off as a dining destination.

PRIME RIB | 26 | 24 | 25 | $48 |
2020 K St., NW (bet. 20th & 21st Sts.), 202-466-8811

■ The "retro supper club appeal" of "blonds, booze", crab imperial, "exceptional" prime rib and getting "dressed up" for a "great evening out" keep this Downtown "art deco classic" steakhouse filled with distinguished-looking types, "trophy wives" and late-night revelers; run by real pros who "treat you right", it's been a "quiet place to do [the nation's] business" for years.

Primi Piatti | 21 | 19 | 20 | $36 |
2013 I St., NW (bet. 20th & 21st Sts.), 202-223-3600
8045 Leesburg Pike (Gallows Rd.), Tysons Corner, VA, 703-893-0300

◪ Among the area's most "sophisticated Italian" restaurants, with pasta, "fish and veal chops as good as anywhere" and stylish, open-to-the-street (DC) bistro settings; but lately some feel that they're "not quite what they ought to be" – perhaps they're too "hit or miss" or "NY" wanna-be.

Prince Michel Ⓢ ▽ | 27 | 23 | 26 | $59 |
Rte. 29 S, HCR4, Box 77, Leon, VA, 540-547-9720

◪ Respondents regret that this prestigious winery's restaurant is "too far away" (near Culpeper) for "'favorite'" dining establishment status because its French tasting menu is "magnificent" and the experience is "memorable"; while some carp that the faux garden room "needs work", most say it's a "reserve for very special occasions" place.

Provence Ⓢ | – | – | – | E |
2401 Pennsylvania Ave., NW (L St.), 202-296-1166

In fall '98, this posh Mediterranean villa is slated to shift its focus from Provence to Italy with a new menu, chef and name; meanwhile, despite Yannick Cam's departure, the kitchen is still cooking South of France cuisine.

Washington, D.C. F | D | S | C

Queen Bee S   22 | 13 | 18 | $18
3181 Wilson Blvd. (Washington Blvd.), Arlington, VA, 703-527-3444

◪ Chances are that after you've "tried the rest" of Clarendon's Vietnamese, you'll "keep going back to the 'Bee'"; it sure "doesn't look like much", you'll be "rushed" and the food's "sometimes greasy", but there's an "enticing" menu and many consider it the "best for the price."

Rabieng S   25 | 18 | 21 | $21
Glen Forest Shopping Ctr., 5892 Leesburg Pike (Glen Forest Dr.), Falls Church, VA, 703-671-4222

■ This highly rated "up-country" Thai is a "perfect complement to Duangrat's", its citified sib close by; it's "cheaper" and just "as good", but more of a "quiet" "hideaway" with "graceful", albeit "spotty", service; you'll find "uniquely flavorful" regional dishes like the "chef's specials", just "don't expect to order them less spicy than the menu dictates."

Rainforest Cafe S   13 | 24 | 15 | $18
Tysons Corner Ctr., 7928-L Tysons Corner Ctr. (Rte. 7), Tysons Corner, VA, 703-821-1900

■ "If you must amuse a child through a meal" in the Northern Virginia 'burbs, this is one way to go; in the process, you'll "spend a fortune on nowhere food" (Eclectic, "cutsey-named" sandwiches, salads and such) and endure "unrelenting noise", "humidity", "teenage servers" and gift shop waits; still, the "special effects" – tropical storms, wild beasts and talking trees – are really special.

Raku S   17 | 20 | 16 | $20
1900 Q St., NW (19th St.), 202-265-7258
7240 Woodmont Ave. (Elm St.), Bethesda, MD, 301-718-8681

◪ Give Mark Miller credit for pioneering a "great" Asian diner concept – noodles, skewers and snacks served in heavily trafficked, new wave street cafes; but "erratic" execution is the majority's verdict, with gripes about commissary-cooked, "over-spiced and -priced" food, "uncomfortable seats" and "spotty service."

Ramparts ◐ S   16 | 14 | 16 | $18
1700 Fern St. (Kenwood St.), Alexandria, VA, 703-998-6616

◪ Although the "original charm" of this "homey" Fairlington "neighborhood joint" is in the pubby middle room and bar, its "easy" spirit pervades the newer dining room too; here, "simple" mostly succeeds with "basic American" fare and "half-price burger night on Monday."

Red Hot & Blue S   19 | 15 | 17 | $18
16811 Crabbs Branch Way (Shady Grove Rd.), Gaithersburg, MD, 301-948-7333
677 Main St. (Rte. 216), Laurel, MD, 301-953-1943
(Continues)

Washington, D.C. F | D | S | C

Red Hot & Blue (Cont.)
1600 Wilson Blvd. (Pierce St.), Arlington, VA, 703-276-7427
3014 Wilson Blvd. (Highland St.), Arlington, VA, 703-243-1510
4150 Chain Bridge Rd. (Rte. 123), Fairfax, VA, 703-218-6989
208 Elden St. (Herndon Pkwy.), Herndon, VA, 703-318-7427

Transplanted "Memphis boys" endorse the "great blues and barbecue" ribs, rings and sides at this area chain of Elvis-inspired pits; they're "superfast" (or in "outer space"), good for carryout, and "kid-friendly" to an extreme; but while devotees declare they "know how to pull that pig", others say some of their former spirit is gone – "used to be redder, hotter and bluer" before "commercialization."

RED SAGE S   22 | 25 | 20 | $36
605 14th St., NW (F St.), 202-638-4444

Mark Miller's "Southwestern circus" is enjoying a long run; located near big-name law and lobby palaces, the White House and the Mall, its "upstairs chile bar" "serves the masses", not to mention "celebs and pols", casual bites of "exciting" regional cuisine in "electric" surroundings – even more "spectacular" is the "tumbleweeds-on-acid decor" in the down-under dining room; "if you can handle the spice", the downstairs price and having your waiter occasionally "disappear", by all means, go.

Red Sea ◐ S   19 | 14 | 17 | $20
2463 18th St., NW (Kalorama Rd.), 202-483-5000

"Cheap eats" and outdoor seats on Adams Morgan's hottest stretch keep this Ethiopian "contender" in the ring; this is where those "in the mood" for "spicy finger food" go for a hands-on, laid-back, not for the squeamish, "hole-in-the-wall" experience – preferably with a group.

Red Tomato Cafe   19 | 19 | 18 | $19
2030 M St., NW (21st St.), 202-463-9030
4910 St. Elmo Ave. (bet. Norfolk & Old Georgetown Rds.), Bethesda, MD, 301-652-4499

Bethesda's "cafe society" and DC's loosened-tie types hit these "very inviting" Italians for "fanciful" pizza or pasta, a salad and a "great wind down" on Friday night; their agreeable "ambiance" is achieved with rich tones and "tiles", "low" lights and a sidewalk cafe (M Street); however, critics counter that "service is lacking" from their "formula" and the "food doesn't look as good as the place."

Renato S   20 | 17 | 20 | $30
10120 River Rd. (Potomac Pl.), Potomac, MD, 301-365-1900

This "neighborhood trattoria", one of the "best Italians in the 'burbs", is "great about accommodating regulars" (aka the Potomac Celebrity Crowd) with upscale pastas, veal or seafood; an attractive, subdued space for group dining, it "can handle a larger table" better than it can a stranger.

Washington, D.C. | F | D | S | C |

Rhodeside Grill S | 19 | 17 | 18 | $21 |
1836 Wilson Blvd. (Rhodes St.), Arlington, VA, 703-243-0145
■ With its hip wall mural and "live music", this "relaxed" Arlington watering hole is "trying hard" to please; despite what some call "amateurish service", its affordable New American food fortifies nearby canyon dwellers for the "pickup action" at its "great bar scene", as well as earning foodie raves for an "inspired and well-executed menu."

Ricciuti's S | ▽ 21 | 15 | 20 | $15 |
3308 Olney-Sandy Spring Rd. (Georgia Ave.), Olney, MD, 301-570-3388
■ Olney got lucky when these "wonderful people" (James and Amy Ricciuti) and their brick pizza oven turned the old Olney House into a warm place; since "gourmet pizza" is in short supply here, the "quality" and "freshness" of their pies are "appreciated", as is their desire to keep "improving."

RIO GRANDE CAFE S | 22 | 17 | 18 | $20 |
4919 Fairmont Ave. (Old Georgetown Rd.), Bethesda, MD, 301-656-2981
4301 N. Fairfax Dr. (Glebe Rd.), Arlington, VA, 703-528-3131
Reston Town Ctr., 1827 Library St. (Reston Pkwy.), Reston, VA, 703-904-0703
☑ Since they're "always jam-packed" with loads of kids and a major bar scene (Ballston), it's easy to forget that these "loud" Tex-Mex "warehouses" serve "gut-busting portions" of "very good food"; while foes feel they're "too commercial", the majority maintains that everything tastes "fresh"; "no reservations" means prime-time waits, but once you're seated, the food arrives almost "too fast."

RITZ-CARLTON, THE GRILL S | 24 | 26 | 24 | $45 |
Ritz-Carlton at Pentagon City, 1250 S. Hayes St.
(bet. Army Navy Dr. & 15th St.), Arlington, VA, 703-412-2760
■ The "publicity" surrounding the Linda Tripp/Monica Lewinsky tell-all tea spotlighted this "elegant" Northern VA hotel dining room, long considered a "superb" business lunch setting because of its privacy and hush; "sumptuous" Contemporary American food is enhanced by "beautiful" "English country" decor and "fantastic service"; it's a "great splurge" with "someone you love."

RITZ-CARLTON, THE RESTAURANT S | 25 | 27 | 26 | $48 |
Ritz-Carlton at Tysons II, 1700 Tysons Blvd.
(Galleria Int'l Blvd.), Tysons Corner, VA, 703-506-4300x748
■ "Reverential" "Tysons Corner CEOs" regard this hotel dining room as the "only place, other than their private club, to take important clients" for "impeccable" American-Continental cooking and "reliable Ritz", "white glove" treatment; other acolytes appreciate the "delightful afternoon tea" or the "wonderful" "Friday night seafood and Sunday brunch buffets."

Washington, D.C. | F | D | S | C |

Riverside Grille S | ▽ | 13 | 17 | 17 | $22 |
Washington Harbour, 3050 K St., NW (30th St.),
202-342-3535

◪ One of several Washington Harbour bases for people-watching and seasonal mating, this Italian-accented cafe offers "great" Potomac River views, along with seafood and sundry edibles "at 100 decibels"; "outdoor ambiance" and attractive help are what bring locals "back."

Rock Bottom Brewery S | 14 | 18 | 17 | $19 |
7900 Norfolk Ave. (St. Elmo Ave.), Bethesda, MD,
301-652-1311

◪ "If you want a pick-me-up, hit the Bottom" along with Bethesda twentysomethings "for the scene"; while cons quip this brewpub is "well-named", fans philosophize that the pub "food is heavy, the beer's ok (not great), but we go anyway" – mostly after work; at lunch, waiters are "attentive" and you don't "need earplugs."

Rockland's S | 22 | 12 | 16 | $15 |
2418 Wisconsin Ave., NW (Calvert St.), 202-333-2558
4000 Fairfax Dr. (Quincy St.), Arlington, VA, 703-528-9663

■ This *Survey*'s top-rated American BBQ is "meant to be eaten standing up" at the "no-nonsense", communal counter space in Upper Georgetown; the "down-home aroma" of these "tender and delicious" vittles, their "wonderful" accompaniments and a "wall full of hot sauces for sampling" are so tempting, you'll never make it home; the Arlington branch offers sit-down service at Carpool, a billiards bar, which features the same "heavenly" ribs 'n' things, with "car nostalgia" served on the side.

Roof Terrace Kennedy Center S | 17 | 22 | 18 | $38 |
Kennedy Ctr., 2700 F St. (New Hampshire Ave.),
202-416-8555

◪ "Convenience" counts for Kennedy Center patrons and so do "million-dollar" "Virginia skyline views" and "well-timed service", but this Contemporary American rooftop dining room plays to a "captive, not captivated audience" that complains that it's too "expensive for what you get"; however, given good early reports on its new, post-*Survey* executive chef, now they may be applauding more than its perennially popular Sunday "kitchen" brunch.

Royal Restaurant S | 16 | 11 | 16 | $13 |
703 N. Asaph St. (Madison St.), Alexandria, VA,
703-548-1616

◪ The '50s American "food's not great and the atmosphere is a little tired", but that's just why this long-lived Alexandria "dump" is such a "treasure" – there simply aren't that many vintage "greasy spoons" around, so in the old-time dinery derby, this "place gets points for tackiness", "slipshod service" and a "good", "cheap" weekend breakfast spread.

Washington, D.C. | F | D | S | C |

R.T.'s ◐S | 23 | 14 | 21 | $26 |
3804 Mt. Vernon Ave. (Glebe Rd.), Alexandria, VA, 703-684-6010

■ "Belly up" to cold "beer and cayenne" cookin' at this "tiny" Arlandria bar that's been a longtime "fave for good seafood in a relaxed setting" at a fair price; a number of 'names' have "braved" its surprisingly "seedy" 'hood for "rich" New Orleans fare, "good tunes" and "noisy" camaraderie.

R.T.'s Seafood Kitchen S | 17 | 16 | 17 | $23 |
Courthouse Plaza, 2300 Clarendon Blvd. (bet. Barton St. & Courthouse Rd.), Arlington, VA, 703-841-0100

◪ While the New Orleans cooking and office complex atmosphere at R.T.'s Arlington kin are "nothing to rave about", its "convenient", "close to the theater location" and "easy mall parking" are nothing to sniff at, either; while the "kitchen is inconsistent", with a little luck, you can put together a decent meal – try the "tasty Arcadian shrimp" or something fried.

RUPPERTS | 25 | 20 | 24 | $45 |
1017 Seventh St., NW (bet. L St. & New York Ave.), 202-783-0699

■ Raw "vegetables on the table", "exotic" produce on the plate – the highly "innovative" Contemporary American cooking here "challenges even the sophisticated palate", so "if you have to ask what you're eating, you don't belong here"; while the "menu is limited" and prices are "expensive", its "shockingly good" food, "knowledgeable" servers and "hip urban ambiance" make it an "important" destination for faces and foodies who frequent this "pioneer" in a "marginal, but improving neighborhood."

RUTH'S CHRIS STEAK HOUSE S | 24 | 22 | 23 | $44 |
1801 Connecticut Ave., NW (S St.), 202-797-0033
7315 Wisconsin Ave. (Elm St.), Bethesda, MD, 301-652-7877
2231 Crystal Dr. (23rd St.), Crystal City, VA, 703-979-7275

■ "You get what you pay for" at these "solid" cow palaces: butter-drenched beef, "fancy" New Orleans decor, "extraordinary" courtesy and "fantastic" panoramic airport views at the Crystal City branch; but "in a city of steakhouses", they rank "at the lower end of the top tier" – possibly Ruth's "formula" is a little too "different tasting", "pricey" or "not personally engaging."

Sabang S | 20 | 19 | 21 | $21 |
2504 Ennalls Ave. (Georgia Ave.), Wheaton, MD, 301-942-7859

■ One of the area's "few Indonesians", its "complex flavors" "offer a break from other Eastern cuisines"; rijsttafel, its specialty, consists of a tableful of "spicy" little plates, so bring a crowd along when you test-drive this "friendly" exotic.

Washington, D.C. F D S C

Saigon Crystal S   - | - | - | I
536 S. 23rd St. (Jefferson Davis Hwy.), Arlington, VA, 703-920-3822
This agreeable peach-and-green Arlington cottage features Vu Nguyen's (ex Pho Cali) full-flavored Vietnamese food; although there's an extensive menu, knowledgeable diners who flocked to his former location favor the seasonal seafood specials and server recommendations; when the weather is willing, be sure to take advantage of the porch.

Saigon Gourmet S   22 | 15 | 21 | $22
2635 Connecticut Ave., NW (Calvert St.), 202-265-1360
■ "Fake palm" trees and genuine warmth help this Woodley Park Vietnamese establish a tropical mood, both inside and out on the terrace, that sets off the light, "unexpected blend of flavors" in its food; a "worthwhile" menu and "fabulous service" keep the neighborhood coming "back", even though the "tourist" traffic would ordinarily turn them off.

Saigon Inn S   19 | 15 | 19 | $18
2928 M St. (30th St.), 202-337-5588
2614 Connecticut Ave. (Calvert St.), 202-483-8400
☑ So "cheap", "so tacky" – yet where else in Georgetown (or Woodley Park's Convention-land) can you find a four-dishes-for-$4.50 lunch?; these Vietnamese "try so hard" to provide "fresh" fare that advocates overlook unsophisticated touches like "pictures of food in the window."

Saigonnais S   20 | 16 | 19 | $21
2307 18th St., NW (Belmont Rd.), 202-232-5300
☑ This Vietnamese's "delicate", French-influenced food, "soothing atmosphere" and "lackadaisical service" sharply contrast with the frenetic Adams Morgan street scene outside; while some critics call the menu "uneven", it offers "some interesting dishes not found elsewhere."

Sakana   ▽ 23 | 17 | 20 | $24
2026 P St., NW (bet. 20th & 21st Sts.), 202-887-0900
■ It's easy to pass by this basement Japanese near Dupont Circle without noticing it; yet once inside, you're "in Tokyo" – a "tight, crowded", "traditional" room serving "very inventive sushi and rolls" and "huge appetizers for the price."

Sala Thai S   21 | 13 | 18 | $19
2016 P St., NW (20th St.), 202-872-1144
■ "Killer mai tais" and "fresh, colorful" Thai food, including "tear-producing" curries, are served by "cute waitresses" in a neon-lit "fallout shelter" "convenient" to Dupont Circle; if you think DC power dining doesn't include places like this, go see who turns up for lunch.

Washington, D.C. F | D | S | C

Samadi Sweets 🆂 — | — | — | I
5916 Leesburg Pike (bet. Seven Corners & Skyline St.), Falls Church, VA, 703-578-0606
Write-ins scrambled to tell us about this sweet success story – a Middle Eastern bakery in Bailey's Crossroads blossoming into a restaurant that serves "freshly cooked" Lebanese dishes that taste like they do back home ("falafel that's not a Play-Doh tennis ball"); be sure to leave room for some of the "best pastries in town."

SAM & HARRY'S 24 | 23 | 24 | $45
1200 19th St., NW (bet. M & N Sts.), 202-296-4333
8240 Leesburg Pike (Rte. 123), Tysons Corner, VA, 703-448-0088 🆂
■ This is a "classy", "civilized" steakhouse "for clients, not dates", where ya "gotta love the mashed potatoes", "amazing" beef, "excellent wine list" and its legendary ability to "make customers feel wanted"; the smashing, unrated Tysons Corner complex, consisting of a beefhouse, saloon and drive-by cigar outlet, has become an instant power "mecca" too.

Sam Woo 🆂 ▽ 21 | 15 | 16 | $21
1054 Rockville Pike (Edmonds St.), Rockville, MD, 301-424-0495
◪ Since our last *Survey*, there's a "new owner", but little else has changed at this "upscale" Asian "value" on Rockville Pike; its Japanese and Korean specialties (like cooking BBQ on the tabletop grill) are the "real thing"; if the "slightly confused" help can't help you, strike out on your own and sample the "great lunch buffet."

Santa Fe East 🆂 20 | 22 | 19 | $28
110 Pitt St. (bet. King & Prince Sts.), Alexandria, VA, 703-548-6900
◪ The fountain courtyard, fireplace and "charming" rooms of this historic Old Town building firmly "transport" diners to Old Santa Fe, but its "ambitious" Southwestern menu is "uneven", although "great when it works"; happily, that's often enough to make dining here a "tempting option", especially out on the "pretty, little outdoor patio" on a "warm summer evening" when its "tortoise-like service" is in sync with one's mood.

Savory ▽ 17 | 15 | 14 | $13
7071 Carroll Ave. (Columbia Ave.), Takoma Park, MD, 301-270-2233
■ "Takoma Park loves to hate" this "appealing" coffeehouse and communal living room; not for what it is – a "limited" operation ("hot foods nuked"), with comfortable seating, "comatose waitrons" and "wonderful desserts" – but for what it "isn't" – "a decent full-service restaurant."

Washington, D.C.   F | D | S | C

Sea Catch   22 | 20 | 20 | $37
Canal Sq., 1054 31st St., NW (M St.), 202-337-8855

◪ There's "romantic" summer "dining under the mulberry trees by the C&O canal", or by the fire on a frigid night, on "fine fresh fish", so what's the catch — why does this Georgetowner "never seem crowded"?; possibly because some surveyors say the seafood is "slightly overpriced" and it seems like there's a different "chef a day"; N.B. food lovers are hoping its Louisiana-born incumbent will stay.

SEASONS S   26 | 26 | 26 | $52
Four Seasons Hotel, 2800 Pennsylvania Ave., NW (28th St.), 202-944-2000

◪ An "opulent" and "tranquil" "dream world" setting "overlooking lots of green", and equally "elegant" New American cooking, are the reasons respondents rate this "luxurious" hotel one of DC's "best" dining sites for all seasons; it's a "great place for business meetings", "getting engaged" and "impressing your aunt", plus its Sunday brunch "buffet blitz" will bliss you out.

Sequoia ◐ S   16 | 24 | 16 | $30
3000 K St., NW (Washington Harbour), 202-944-4200

◪ Sweeping Potomac vistas from this "dramatic" Washington Harbour perch should make it "a perfect place to watch the sunset and eat dinner", and it would be, were it not for the "mediocre service" and "ordinary" American food; it's best for a "business lunch" or brunch, but "only the brave attempt" the "busy bar scene" on the outside terrace.

Serbian Crown S   20 | 20 | 19 | $42
1141 Walker Rd. (Colvin Run Rd.), Great Falls, VA, 703-759-4150

◪ This Great Falls candlelit, "old-world" enclave with "strolling musicians" has "few competitors in the race for Imperial Russian kitsch" and is so "romantic that even the worst date looks good"; that being said, opinion is divided: pros pronounce it an "elegant" "taste of Russia" that's "expensive but worth it", but cynics counter the service is "imperious", the food is "disappointing" and it's only "a total success if you drink enough vodka."

Sesto Senso   20 | 18 | 18 | $28
1214 18th St., NW (bet. Jefferson Pl. & M St.), 202-785-9525

◪ Its "loud" "late-night scene" lures a "large Euro crowd", but "successful lawyers" and serious eaters descend upon this Dupont Circle spot at lunch, when you can "taste Italy" in the food, appreciate its "casual" hospitality and see past the "beautiful people" to the rustic brick decor; the anomaly of having a "real" Northern Italian kitchen in a "hot spot" means that it's "often overlooked" as a dining destination — but its expansion will give it room for both.

Washington, D.C. | F | D | S | C |

701 S | 23 | 23 | 23 | $38 |
701 Pennsylvania Ave., NW (7th St.), 202-393-0701

■ "Sexy" and "sophisticated", this "classy" Contemporary American is "the place to go in the Pennsylvania Avenue corridor for a power lunch or a romantic" rendezvous; designed for "adults", it's a "gem with jazz" that also has a "great" vodka and caviar bar and, miraculously, it delivers "luxury without a huge price tag" and with "no attitude."

Seven Seas ●S | 22 | 12 | 17 | $19 |
Federal Plaza, 1776 E. Jefferson St. (bet. Montrose & Rollins Aves.), Rockville, MD, 301-770-5020

■ "Order from the red menu" and take your cue from the "large variety" of live sea critters swimming in the fish tanks at this Rockville Chinese, which is well regarded among Asians for "outstanding" seafood; if the "friendly" server's English falters, try "anything in black bean sauce."

1789 S | 26 | 27 | 26 | $51 |
1226 36th St., NW (Prospect St.), 202-965-1789

■ "Great everything" – "warm, inviting surroundings", "first-class" American regional food and "special guest" treatment for all; its chef, Ris Lacoste (ex Kinkead's), sparked a "renaissance" at this "historic", "romantic" Georgetown residence, putting it in the Top 10 for food, decor and service and causing hundreds of devotees to declare if you "have something to celebrate, do it here!"

Shamshiry S | ▽ 19 | 13 | 16 | $17 |
8607 Westwood Center Dr. (Leesburg Pike), Vienna, VA, 703-448-8883

◪ "No one starves" at this "delightful" Persian in Vienna where the heaping serving of "fabulous" rice that comes with the kebabs is "enough for a meal"; but some surveyors say this gathering spot can be "unfriendly" to outsiders.

Shelly's Woodroast S (CLOSED) | 14 | 19 | 16 | $21 |
Congressional Shopping Ctr., 1699 Rockville Pike (Halpine St.), Rockville, MD, 301-984-3300

◪ This "rustic" Rockville American "theme restaurant" with a "backwoods log cabin" motif serves "wood-roasted" meats and fish that often "smell better than they taste"; it's "cigar-friendly", big-time, with a dedicated stogie room that, like the bar, is "overblown" with smoke.

Silverado S | 20 | 19 | 20 | $20 |
Magruder's Shopping Ctr., 7052 Columbia Pike (Gallows Rd.), Annandale, VA, 703-354-4560

◪ Trend-smart Great American Restaurants, Inc. (Artie's, Carlyle Grand Cafe, Mike's American Grill) alleviates Annandale's "suburban blight" by adding "Southwestern touches" to its "successful" formula – "great prime rib" and "excellent value"; it possibly may be "the weakest [link] in the chain", but it also offers the "best mall food" in the vicinity.

Washington, D.C.　　　　　　　　F | D | S | C

Silver Diner S　　　　　　　14 | 15 | 16 | $14
14550 Baltimore Ave. (Cherry Ln.), Laurel, MD, 301-470-6080 ☻
11806 Rockville Pike (bet. Montrose & Old Georgetown Rds.), Rockville, MD, 301-770-2828 ☻
3200 Wilson Blvd. (bet. Clarendon & Washington Blvds.), Arlington, VA, 703-812-8600
Potomac Mills Mall, 14375 Smoketown Rd. (Gideon Rd.), Dale City, VA, 703-491-7376 ☻
12251 Fair Lakes Pkwy. (W. Ox Rd.), Fairfax, VA, 703-359-5999
8150 Porter Rd. (Gallows Rd.), Fairfax, VA, 703-204-0812 ☻
8101 Fletcher St. (International Dr.), McLean, VA, 703-821-5666 ☻
11951 Killingsworth Ave. (Baron Cameron/Reston Pkwy.), Reston, VA, 703-742-0801 ☻
Springfield Mall, 6592 Franconia Rd. (Loisdale Rd.), Springfield, VA, 703-924-1701 ☻

■ "Nostalgia goes '90s with an updated menu" mixing "greasy spoon" classics with "heart-healthy options" at these "modern recreations of '50s diners"; sure, they're "unpredictable", "slow" and no substitute for the "real" thing, but "late nights", "jukeboxes at every table" and "enough noise" that you don't have to worry about your kids "bothering other customers" are assets.

Skewers/Cafe Luna S　　　　　20 | 15 | 18 | $19
1633 P St., NW (bet. 16th & 17th Sts.), 202-387-7400

■ "Scheherazade would appreciate the Arabian bites" at "bargain" prices served at this upstairs kebab cookery, while locals frequent Cafe Luna downstairs for "homey" Mediterranean fare; while service can be "slow", both eateries act as a Dupont Circle East "neighborhood hangout", hosting "interesting exhibits" and special events.

Song Ho/Pho Tay Ho S　　　　 - | - | - | I
6015 Leesburg Pike (Bailey's Crossroads), Falls Church, VA, 703-578-3037 ⊕
6037 Leesburg Pike (bet. Columbia Pike & Seven Corners), Falls Church, VA, 703-931-5597

These steps-away-from-one-another storefront North Vietnamese in Bailey's Crossroads are well known among their compatriots for uncommon regional dishes; Song Ho, the restaurant, can be a "fun, cheap" adventure if you adhere to its crispy fish with curry noodles; "stick to the noodle dishes" at Pho Tay Ho, the *pho* shop, as well.

Soper's on M　　　　　　　　- | - | - | M
1813 M St., NW (18th St.), 202-463-4590

This business district newcomer's suave, postmodern, sculptured space, with see-and-be-seen (but not overheard) tables and seasoned servers gives the suits that swarm the Daily Grill, next door, an alternative venue; the Caribbean-accented American menu is just different enough, but not too much so – after all, what do you expect from Mike Soper (Union Street Public House), he's a pro.

Washington, D.C. | F | D | S | C |

Sostanza ⓢ ▽ | 19 | 20 | 18 | $43 |
1606 20th St., NW (Q St.), 202-667-0047
■ "The more Vincenzo's changes, the more it stays the same" say surveyors about the recent rebirth of this gourmet "favorite" off Dupont Circle as a Roberto Donna Group Italian steakhouse run by Vince McDonald; the new menu features steak alla Fiorentina plus refined regional fish and pasta dishes served up in a serene space.

Southside 815 ⓢ | 18 | 15 | 17 | $20 |
815 S. Washington St. (bet. Franklin & Green Sts.), Alexandria, VA, 703-836-6222
◪ "Heavy Southern slam-your-arteries-shut food" can be good for the soul; if you're not convinced, dig into the "layered chicken-oyster combo" at this "accommodating", if a bit "uneven", Old Town Dixie dive; "sidewalk dining and fried tomatoes" – what a deal.

Spices ⓢ | 20 | 14 | 17 | $20 |
3333-A Connecticut Ave., NW (bet. Macomb & Newark Sts.), 202-686-3833
◪ Oddly-shaped, "dark" and "cramped", yet a Cleveland Park Pan-Asian "pleaser" when your ethnically-minded group "can't decide on what it wants"; while a few feel it "tries to do too much", the "dizzying array of menu choices" includes "good sushi."

Stardust Restaurant & Lounge | – | – | – | M |
608 Montgomery St. (bet. St. Asaph & Washington Sts.), Alexandria, VA, 703-548-9864
It looks like savvy restaurant talents John Kilkenny and Avery Kincaid (ex R.T.'s) mostly got it right with this appealing new Downtown Alexandria venture; a stylish decor of celestial scapes and cool colors is the backdrop for an Asian-American fusion menu featuring seafood and steak.

Starland Cafe ⓢ | 20 | 18 | 20 | $28 |
5125 MacArthur Blvd., NW (Arizona Ave.), 202-244-9396
■ With few serious restaurants in the Palisades, the success of this "classy" but casual New American "sleeper" was a given; the real "surprise" is that it's mostly so good – an "imaginative yet affordable" bistro menu, "nice patio" dining and live music at brunch make it a "welcome newcomer."

Star of Siam ⓢ | 18 | 13 | 16 | $18 |
1136 19th St., NW (bet. L & M Sts.), 202-785-2838
2446 18th St., NW (bet. Belmont St. & Columbia Rd.), 202-986-4133
◪ Respondents are decidedly divided on whether these stars shine: pros praise the "dependably good" fare, including "velvety", super-charged curries, as well as the "great view of DC" from Adams Morgan's roof, and the cheap outdoor lunch served at the Downtown branch; but critics counter that the food is only "ok" and the "decor is dreary."

Washington, D.C. | F | D | S | C |

Stella's ☒ | 18 | 19 | 18 | $24 |
1725 Duke St. (Diagonal Rd.), Alexandria, VA, 703-519-1946
■ There's plenty of "potential" at this Alexandrian with a "'40s theme", alfresco dining "next to a fountain" and Contemporary American "comfort food"; but some say that it suffers from the "who is the chef now?" syndrome, and while one respondent acknowledges its "friendly staff", another describes "service occasionally provided by the unwilling."

Stone Manor ☒ | ▽ 25 | 26 | 25 | $56 |
5820 Carroll Boyer Rd. (Sumantown Rd.), Middletown, MD, 301-473-5454
■ Few "romantic getaways" in the region match this 18th century restoration outside Frederick; although the Contemporary American prix fixe menu is modish ("green seaweed soup with mussels"), "lovely" period appointments and "beautiful presentations" establish the illusion of "dining in a private home" in an earlier, more "elegant" era.

Straits of Malaya ☒ | 20 | 15 | 17 | $23 |
1836 18th St., NW (T St.), 202-483-1483
■ It's a good thing the "dynamite" "rooftop dining" among the trees serves as a "romantic introduction" to the sweet and hot cuisines of this Adams Morgan Malaysian, because fans feel its interior "needs sprucing up"; while the food can be "inconsistent", much of it is "imaginative" and "tasty."

Sunny Garden ☒ | ▽ 16 | 11 | 16 | $17 |
1302 E. Gude Dr. (S. Law Rd.), Rockville, MD, 301-762-7477
■ Although the fare at this Rockville Taiwanese is still "far better than the storefront dive decor" would lead you to believe, some feel the "magic" is gone; still, you can get "served in seconds", and if you go with a native, benefit from its "special menu and service."

Sushi Chalet ☒ | 17 | 12 | 16 | $18 |
4910 Fairmont Ave. (Old Georgetown Rd.), Bethesda, MD, 301-652-7733
Festival Shopping Ctr., 323 Muddy Branch Rd. (Great Seneca Hwy.), Gaithersburg, MD, 301-945-7373
■ Whether these "Wal-Marts" for sushi are a "great value" or just the great "pretender" is your call: insiders insist that you can "stuff yourself to death" at the "all-you-can-eat sushi bar", supplemented by "hot food" for $6.95 at lunch and $15.95 at dinner; but foes say "fuhgeddaboutit" – "large pieces of rice with little fish" is "no bargain."

SUSHI-KO ☒ | 26 | 15 | 20 | $29 |
2307 Wisconsin Ave., NW (south of Calvert St.), 202-333-4187
■ A post-*Survey* total transformation of DC's "drab" and "dated" "original sushi bar" into a sleek and tasteful retreat, together with the return of Japanese master-chef Tetsuro Takanashi, who first made it the local "gold standard for sushi", can only increase the above food and decor ratings.

Washington, D.C.

| F | D | S | C |

Sushi Sushi S | ▽ 25 | 17 | 21 | $20 |
4915-A Fairmont Ave. (bet. Norfolk Ave. & Old Georgetown Rd.), Bethesda, MD, 301-654-9616

■ In a pristine, pocket-sized, "traditional setting", a "master sushi chef" prepares Bethesda's "freshest" sushi and a few choice appetizer-like dishes; while some say "service can be brusque", prices are reasonable.

Sushi Taro S | – | – | – | E |
1503 17th St., NW (P St.), 202-462-8999

Japanese aficionados alerted our surveyors to this "excellent" Dupont East sushi spot that's as "authentic" as any in the area; it offers "exceptional" sushi ("huge pieces of fish", "best spicy tuna") and a "good broad menu."

Sweetwater Tavern S | 21 | 21 | 21 | $23 |
14250 Sweetwater Ln. (Multiplex Dr.), Centreville, VA, 703-449-1100
3066 Gatehouse Rd. (bet. Gallows Rd. & Rte. 50), Vienna, VA, 703-645-8100

◪ The Great American Restaurant group has struck paydirt with these "fun" "Oktoberfest"-comes-to-cowboy-country-themed brewpubs in Centreville and Merrifield; their please-all American menus, "eager" servers, "well-done" designer digs and high-energy ambiance (no "conversation" possible) mean there are "long waits."

Tabard Inn S | 22 | 22 | 21 | $31 |
Tabard Inn, 1739 N St., NW (bet. 17th & 18th Sts.), 202-833-2668

■ Countless romances have been kindled over "drinks by the fireplace" at this "shabbily" quaint Dupont Circle "institution" where the "late '60s still rule" in the "cozy" dining room and "delightful" garden; while the American food can be "uneven", leading think-tank "liberals" who "hang out" here to wonder whether "it [and they] will regain its former glory", the post-*Survey* arrival of a new chef should help both.

TABERNA DEL ALABARDERO | 25 | 26 | 24 | $46 |
1776 I St., NW (18th St.), 202-429-2200

■ Diplomats and internationals in-the-know are utterly at home in this "beautiful" Downtown Iberian, as is anyone who delights in "refined" yet gutsy Spanish food, "lots of privacy" and "artful" service; a branch of one of Madrid's "world-class" restaurants, it lends a "sense of occasion" to a "wonderful" business meal or evening event.

TACHIBANA S | 25 | 19 | 22 | $27 |
6715 Lowell Ave. (Emerson Ave.), McLean, VA, 703-847-1771

■ McLean sushi lovers "still can't believe" their good fortune in having this highly rated Nipponese settle into facilities near a major shopping hub; they happily note, while crowding into its "relaxing setting", that "the Japanese go there" for "huge, fresh portions" of "phenomenal" fish, delicate dumplings and "intriguing" dishes.

Tahoga [S] | 23 | 21 | 21 | $40

2815 M St., NW (bet. 28th & 29th Sts.), 202-338-5380

■ "Great beginnings" made its "minimalist" Georgetown digs a stage set for the stylish, yet this New American "keeps working on getting it right"; despite a chef change, its "generally good" food is becoming "even better", and its sometimes "overconfident staff" is settling down; one of the "best new restaurants" in the area, it has a "hidden courtyard" that's the most romantic place in town.

Taipei/Tokyo Cafe [S]⊄ | 21 | 6 | 13 | $12

Metro Ctr. Plaza, 11510-A Rockville Pike (Nicholson Ln.), Rockville, MD, 301-881-8388

■ "What a value, what a crowd" – what do you expect from a Rockville Chinese-Japanese providing "decent", "made-to-order" sushi "without the usual fuss"; while fans say this two-sided Sino-sushi stop is "dirt cheap", they "pay with decor and service", since they get very little of each.

Tako Grill [S] | 23 | 17 | 19 | $22

7758 Wisconsin Ave. (Cheltenham Rd.), Bethesda, MD, 301-652-7030

■ With "top-tier sushi", "great" "grilled anything" and the "nicest waiters", this Bethesda Japanese "appeals to all the senses" – that is, if you like its recently renovated "Isaac Mizrahi on acid" decor; a "best bet" for a sensible meal, there's "a long wait, but you will empty your plate."

Tara Thai [S] | 24 | 22 | 20 | $22

4828 Bethesda Ave. (bet. Arlington Rd. & Wisconsin Ave.), Bethesda, MD, 301-657-0488

7501-E Leesburg Pike (Pimmit Dr.), Falls Church, VA, 703-506-9788

226 Maple Ave. (bet. Lawyer's Rd. & Nutley St.), Vienna, VA, 703-255-2467

■ "Dining under the sea" at these "upbeat" suburban Thais may be more "aquatic" than "authentic", but few Asians provide such a "well-priced" and winning mix of "consistently good", "fresh flavors" and a "high-energy environment", generating "clamor", crowds and "raves"; "attractive decor, people and food – make a reservation."

TASTE OF SAIGON [S] | 25 | 20 | 22 | $22

410 Hungerford Dr. (Beall Ave.), Rockville, MD, 301-424-7222

8201 Greensboro Dr. (International Dr.), Tysons Corner, VA, 703-790-0700

■ "Unspoiled by success" (or expansion), this *Survey's* top Vietnamese keep getting everything right; their "stylish" black lacquer, marble and glass settings work for business, the kids or couples, as does the "wonderful variety and quality" of their "delicious" Indochine cuisine ("don't miss the black pepper shrimp"); best of all, their family treats you and yours "like you want to be treated" – "if all suburban restaurants matched up to these, we'd never go Downtown."

Taverna Cretekou [S] 21 | 21 | 20 | $29

818 King St. (bet. Alfred & Columbus Sts.), Alexandria, VA, 703-548-8688

◪ Forget the 'net, for virtual transport "to the Greek Isles", try this Old Town taverna's "arbored courtyard" on a "hot summer night" or when the waiters start singing, dancing and "busting plates" in its whitewashed dining rooms on weekends; even if the "good Greek food" "sometimes misses", the exuberant *'opa'* ambiance won't.

Teaism [S] 20 | 20 | 16 | $13

2009 R St., NW (Connecticut Ave.), 202-667-3827

◪ This handsome, "restorative" teahouse serving snacks and "light meals" wasn't "undiscovered long enough" to suit its Dupont Circle devotees; a "fascinating selection of teas", "interesting" Pan-Asian fare, "good bento boxes" and homey all-American sweets are sold in a "purist" space that's sometimes "too crowded for a true Zen experience."

Tel Aviv Cafe ◐ [S] 17 | 16 | 15 | $21

4869 Cordell Ave. (Norfolk Ave.), Bethesda, MD, 301-718-9068

◪ Maybe you "don't go to Israel for the food", but that doesn't keep Bethesda's extended families and "chic youngsters on cell phones" from mobbing this "noisy" Israeli cafe; apparently, its "rudeness", "subway station" intimacy and only "ok" Middle Eastern cooking are overlooked for "nice noshes" (falafel, *meze*, breads) and sidewalk schmoozing.

Tempo [S] 21 | 17 | 19 | $31

4231 Duke St. (N. Gordon St.), Alexandria, VA, 703-370-7900

◪ The talented kitchen at this "cosmopolitan ex–gas station" in Alexandria isn't afraid to "try new things", turning out a "fine mix" of Italian, French and Californian dishes that keep the customers happy; service and food "inconsistencies" make some slow to sing Tempo's praises, but the majority is quick to point out that "when it's good, it's very good."

Terrazza ▽ 21 | 18 | 20 | $38

2 Wisconsin Circle (bet. Western & Wisconsin Aves.), Chevy Chase, MD, 301-951-9292

◪ A "promising" Chevy Chase newcomer and "toned-down replacement" for Duca di Milano that gets the nod for its Northern Italian pastas, fish and veal and "attentive" servers; it "may pull it off in this location", but "noise" has dogged every restaurant that's preceded it.

T.H.A.I. [S] 22 | 23 | 20 | $21

Village at Shirlington, 4029 S. 28th St. (Randolph St.), Arlington, VA, 703-931-3203

■ Jazzed-up ethnic dining is hot, as evidenced by the popularity of this "stylish" Shirlington Thai and others of its ilk (Tara Thai, Busara); here, the "bright", "beautiful" dining room and "imaginative" presentations almost overshadow the "agreeable" eating – "add hot sauce" for more "heat."

Washington, D.C.

	F	D	S	C

Thai Chef S
▽ | 15 | 11 | 15 | $18

1712 Connecticut Ave., NW (bet. R & S Sts.), 202-234-5698
■ With wildly popular City Lights of China across the street, which shares Dupont Circle "tourist" traffic, some wonder why this Thai hasn't done better; perhaps because reports of "good food" are mixed with shrugs of "not very impressive."

Thai Kingdom S
21 | 19 | 19 | $21

2021 K St., NW (bet. 20th & 21st Sts.), 202-835-1700
■ This "reliable" lion still roars on K Street, with food "so authentic" and an atmosphere so "friendly" that no one hesitates to "take Thai clients" here; it looks a bit "tacky", but if "you want spicy, you got spicy" at this spot.

That's Amore S
17 | 16 | 18 | $23

5225 Wisconsin Ave., NW (Jennifer St.), 202-237-7800
15201 Shady Grove Rd. (Research Blvd.), Rockville, MD, 301-670-9666
Potomac Run Shopping Ctr., 46300 Potomac Run Plaza (Cascades Pkwy. & Leesburg Pike), Sterling, VA, 703-406-4900
Danor Plaza, 150 Branch Rd. (Rte. 123), Vienna, VA, 703-281-7777
■ If 'more is never enough' for your "garlic-loving" clan (and they're always ready "to cart food home"), head for these "hectic", "reasonably priced" Italian banquet halls; but naysayers shudder at the "parody" of Neapolitan family dining – "not great, but big."

Thyme Square S
20 | 20 | 19 | $24

4735 Bethesda Ave. (Woodmont Ave.), Bethesda, MD, 301-657-9077
■ "Joy" abounds at this Crayola-bright Bethesda celebration of "fresh", veggie-oriented eating that's supplemented by an "imaginative" Eclectic mix of fish and pasta, along with "sumptuous" desserts; while supporters say it "breaks all the stereotypes about health food", the less-enthused gripe the fare "tastes bland" and some "combos are ill-conceived."

Tia Queta S
– | – | – | M

4839 Del Ray Ave. (Norfolk Ave.), Bethesda, MD, 301-654-4443
Seafood that seems to come "straight from a Mexican grandma's kitchen" is "back" in Bethesda at this "lively" cantina's new locale; while the artifact-filled rooms and roof garden are an "improvement" over its old digs, you'll recognize its "interesting" menu and kid-friendly grins.

Tivoli
22 | 21 | 21 | $33

1700 N. Moore St. (19th St.), Rosslyn, VA, 703-524-8900
■ "Downtown class" (with on-site parking), a "spectacular DC view" and "excellent Continental" food are the draws at this Rosslyn old reliable; it's a "little dated", but its conservative image helps "impress clients", and the bean counters and contingency planners that have made this a "Pentagon hangout" know how to spot a "pre-theater value", as well as leave room for "irresistible desserts."

Washington, D.C.　　　　　　　F | D | S | C

Tomato Tango S　　　　　▽ 15 | 14 | 18 | $16
Olney Towne Ctr., 18115 Towne Ctr. Dr. (bet. Rte. 108 & Spartan Rd.), Olney, MD, 301-570-5247

Judging by reports of "tons of garlic" and "too many spices dumped on" dishes, the "new ownership" doesn't seem to have gotten a grip on this Olney Cal-Ital; yet, despite rumors that its major asset, "portion size", had shrunk to merely "massive", this "pleasant" spot remains overrun with "too many kids" and their kin.

Tomokazu S　　　　　　▽ 21 | 17 | 22 | $21
2322 W. University Blvd. (Elkins Ave.), Silver Spring, MD, 301-962-9062

"An excellent, new place", this spacious, "gracious" Wheaton Japanese offers a "vast menu" of "authentic dishes" – whether steamed, griddled, grilled or fried – as well as a "variety" of "fresh sushi"; "late" hours and "reasonable prices" are additional pluses.

Tom Tom S　　　　　　　14 | 16 | 12 | $20
2333 18th St., NW (bet. Belmont St. & Kalorama Rd.), 202-588-1300

Although tapas are back on the Mediterranean menu and the "rooftop in summer is prime real estate", the in-"crowds have moved on" and this "arty hangout" is no longer the Adams Morgan hot spot, prompting ex-acolytes to ask "what happened" here?

Tony & Joe's Seafood Place S　15 | 19 | 15 | $29
Washington Harbour, 3000 K St., NW (30th St.), 202-944-4545

A "delightful location" with "beautiful" Potomac river views, a blockbuster bar and "unparalleled" people-watching are the point at this Washington Harbour fish house; its seafood and service are not as "good" and are not the "reason to go."

Tony Cheng's Mongolian S　　20 | 14 | 18 | $20
619 H St., NW (bet. 6th & 7th Sts.), 202-842-8669
Tony Cheng's Seafood S
619 H St., NW (bet. 6th & 7th Sts.), 202-371-8669

At this "all-you-can-eat" Mongolian BBQ that's "great for dress-down Friday lunches" diners choose ingredients for cooking in tabletop hot pots, producing an experience that's sometimes more fun to "watch" than "to eat"; upstairs, there's "delicious" dim sum and seafood daily.

Tragara S　　　　　　　22 | 21 | 20 | $40
4935 Cordell Ave. (bet. Norfolk Ave. & Old Georgetown Rd.), Bethesda, MD, 301-951-4935

Chef Michel Laudier's "classic approach" to Northern Italian cuisine is evident in his "delicious pastas" and "splendid" fish; however, while pros praise the "impressive surroundings", cons counter the "jackets preferred but not required" dictum seems "stuffy" for Bethesda.

Trattoria da Franco [S] ▽ 15 14 15 $27
305 S. Washington St. (Duke St.), Alexandria, VA, 703-548-9338
◪ Soaking up Old Town "local color" on this "family" Italian's patio or in its "very cozy" dining room is generally of more interest than its food, which surveyors say is "basic" and "could improve"; but monthly opera nights are applauded – ebullient owner Franco Abbruzetti joins the singers and $35 gets you a buffet and a bottle of wine.

Tsukiji – – – I
Ritchie Shopping Ctr., 785-K Rockville Pike (Ritchie Hwy.), Rockville, MD, 301-294-9160
"A little beat-up looking", this "family-style Japanese" could be on an Asian side street instead of on Rockville Pike; its "basic sushi", simple salads and grills won't win awards, but are inexpensive, "authentic and tasty."

Tunnicliff's Tavern [S] 14 14 14 $18
222 Seventh St., SE (bet. 2nd & 3rd Sts.), 202-546-3663
◪ "Tucked behind the Capitol", this ancient American watering hole serves the neighborhood "bearable burgers", bloodies and bonhomie, supplemented by "good" gumbo; however, "the real excitement is at the bar" on live jazz nights or sitting "outside on Saturdays" across from Eastern Market.

Tuscana West 18 19 17 $29
1350 I St., NW (bet. 13th & 14th Sts.), 202-289-7300
◪ In this "slick" Italian environment, Downtown lawyers get one good "lunch deal" while making another; although there's "nothing exceptional" about its food ("dated recipes") and service is "slow", the place has a bit of "European flair", a lively happy hour and "nifty opera nights on Thursday"; however, with the debut of DC Coast nearby, it finally has some "competition."

219 [S] 20 23 19 $31
219 King St. (Fairfax St.), Alexandria, VA, 703-549-1141
◪ Reactions to this beckoning bit of Victorian "New Orleans" in Old Town are as varied as its diverse dining spaces: while loyalists like the "downstairs bar at lunch" for its good buys on Creole cooking and the "cozy", "romantic" dining room, critics contend the latter is "off-puttingly formal, as is the food"; what there's no debate about though is the "super upstairs jazz", "terrific brunch" and heated porch.

Two Quail [S] 22 24 23 $31
320 Massachusetts Ave., NE (bet. 3rd & 4th Sts.), 202-543-8030
◪ Hundreds of loyalists laud this endearingly "eclectic" Capitol Hill Victorian's "mismatched", "overstuffed", knickknacked "nooks and crannies", "interesting" American concoctions and "polite" help; but critics counter it's "billed as 'romantic'" but it looks like "Grandma's attic", with its "unkempt clutter"; still, "if you're not a member of Congress", don't go without a reservation.

Washington, D.C. | F | D | S | C |

Udupi Palace S | 22 | 13 | 17 | $17 |
1325 University Blvd. (New Hampshire Ave.), Langley Park, MD, 301-434-1431
■ "Crummy on the outside, yummy inside": the "full house" of "ethnic" families and wallet-watchers "says it all" about this Langley Park South Indian; its "extremely flavorful" food, prepared without meat, fish or eggs, adds exotic words like "*dosas*" (crisp, filled pancakes) to local vegans' vocabulary.

Umberto's S | 20 | 12 | 18 | $22 |
7745 Tuckerman Ln. (Seven Locks Rd.), Potomac, MD, 301-983-5566
◪ The "only cheap Italian within miles" satisfies Potomac pizza and pasta cravings and is "quick" for carryout; while it's "good, tasty, convenient and exactly as a neighborhood restaurant should be", it's a "standard" "spaghetti and meatballs place" where "nothing stands out."

Uncle Jed's Roadhouse S | 14 | 12 | 15 | $16 |
7525 Old Georgetown Rd. (Wisconsin Ave.), Bethesda, MD, 301-913-0026
◪ A roadhouse where a "chatty" staff serves "large quantities" of Southern "home cooking" under "glaring" lights or out on a "busy street"-side patio; most find the food and mood "unremarkable", or as Bethesda's country boys bluntly put it: "this dog don't hunt."

Union Street Public House S | 17 | 18 | 17 | $21 |
121 S. Union St. (bet. King & Prince Sts.), Alexandria, VA, 703-548-1785
■ This "popular Old Town brewhouse" has "historic" connections (to George Washington's tobacco warehouse) and multigenerational appeal; singles party and "pub grub" it in the "crowded" bar downstairs, but "thirtysomethings"-plus find it "worth going up a flight" for smoke-free seating, Dixie-influenced "honest meal deals" and great beers.

U-topia S | 19 | 20 | 19 | $22 |
1418 U St., NW (bet. 14th & 15th Sts.), 202-483-7669
■ In "no man's land" in the New U, this "hip" collage of "live music" and Eclectic dining suits a neighborhood willing to "forgive lapses", like "spacey" staffers, for the sake of its burgers and some of the "best martinis" around; if it acts "too excited about itself" that's one thing that ain't "cool."

Vegetable Garden S | 18 | 14 | 18 | $16 |
11618 Rockville Pike (bet. Nicholson Ln. & Old Georgetown Rd.), Rockville, MD, 301-468-9301
◪ Those with a Sinophilic vegetarian in their dining circle will appreciate the "pages of meatless dishes" on this Rockville Chinese's menu and ability to "make tofu edible" in "mock" meat and fowl preparations; however, skeptics scoff that there's "no atmosphere", not much service and the "real thing is usually better."

Vegetaria [S] ▽ 20 | 14 | 20 | $15

2465-J Centerville Rd. (Fox Mill Rd.), Herndon, VA, 703-713-0442

◪ The healthy eating craze brought this Pan-Asian veggie "adventure" to Herndon where its faux meat (soy protein and wheat gluten) and fresh produce make it a "great place to take vegetarian and kosher" friends; the "menu with photos" helps you preview the colorful food but, noting that staff is in short supply, some surveyors recommend its "tasty" buffet (lunch $6.25; dinner weekends only $8.95).

Velocity Grill [S] – | – | – | M

MCI Ctr., 601 F St., NW (6th St.), 202-347-7780

Revving up for prime time, this multilevel, multimedia, multicolor MCI Center American-Eclectic eatery and exercise in sensory overload offers 88 TVs and hockey practice, not to mention gussied-up bar snacks and meal-sized salads; respondents remark it's not yet up-to-speed, but add it has the "best Key lime pie – what else do you need?"

Veneziano [S] 22 | 18 | 21 | $31

2305 18th St., NW (Kalorama Rd.), 202-483-9300

■ "You're in good hands" at this "welcoming", rather "pretty" Adams Morgan Northern Italian, since its Venetian seafood, game and risotto are nearly as impressive as its "great" selection of more than "300 grappas"; it would probably be more popular were it not for "the parking problem and no Metro" nearby.

VIDALIA [S] 26 | 23 | 24 | $43

1990 M St., NW (bet. 19th & 20th Sts.), 202-659-1990

■ It's not just the "namesake onions" that chef-owner Jeffrey Buben transforms into "downright glamorous" fare; his "imaginative" renditions of Southern classics have made his "sunny basement dining room" ("looks like Van Gogh by way of Valdosta") a "premier" M Street site for "expense-account comfort food"; be sure to ask about his "fine wines."

Vienna Inn [S] 16 | 11 | 13 | $11

120 E. Maple Ave. (bet. Center & Park Sts.), Vienna, VA, 703-938-9548

■ Although many Vienna residents won't admit to knowing this "landmark" "dive of all dives" even exists, its parking lot is jammed from breakfast on; fans frequent it for "cheap" American eats and the "best damn [chile] dogs and fake cheese on fries in town"; P.S. at lunchtime, "abusive service is the point" and the "pride" of the place.

Villa d'Este [S] ▽ 22 | 19 | 21 | $33

818 St. Asaph St. (Montgomery St.), Alexandria, VA, 703-549-9477

■ Tucked away from Old Town's crowded shopping streets, this old-fashioned, white-tablecloth Italian is "treasured" for its "understated" atmosphere and "solid, reliable" recipes; specials can be "memorable", but its "attentively" served meals have been known to take awhile.

Washington, D.C. F | D | S | C

Villa Franco S — | — | — | E
601 Pennsylvania Ave., NW (Indiana Ave.), 202-638-2423
Within sight of the Capitol and in the heart of happening Downtown, this smashing sun-washed evocation of an Italian villa is becoming a major dining destination; the light pastas and seafood grills are revelations to Americans accustomed to the red-sauced stuff that passes for Neapolitan cooking; the production is orchestrated by seasoned pro Franco Nuschese (Cafe Milano).

Village Bistro S 23 | 16 | 20 | $27
Colonial Village, 1723 Wilson Blvd. (Quinn St.), Arlington, VA, 703-522-0284
■ A "modest place", with immoderately "good" Continental-French seafood and a "crème brûlée like no other", this "small", "bustling" bistro brings "good value", "unfailing quality" dining to Arlington; publicity has brought yupsters to its "unassuming strip mall" location.

Vintage ▽ 22 | 17 | 18 | $42
2809 M St., NW (bet. 28th & 29th Sts.), 202-625-0077
◪ Appreciators applaud Gerard Pangaud's (Gerard's Place) "elegant" Georgetown bistro-cum-cigar-and-wine bar for its "marvelous fish soup and good peasant plus French food"; however, while the more critical concede this relative newcomer is "up-and-coming", they say it needs "time", as most vintages do.

Virginia Beverage Co. ●S 16 | 18 | 16 | $21
607 King St. (bet. St. Asaph & S. Washington Sts.), Alexandria, VA, 703-684-5397
◪ "High hops" are frequently dashed by the "disappointing food and service" at this "ambitious" King Street brewpub where the American "menu is interesting but the execution is unpredictable"; however, "lots of good beer and lots of atmosphere" satisfy foam fans.

Vox Artis 18 | 20 | 18 | $31
839 17th St., NW (I St.), 202-974-4260
◪ "In warm weather", an open front welcomes "high-powered" and "political types" to picture-postcard Paris on Lafayette Square; most find the "intime" ambiance of this French brasserie "authentic", "less so" the "uneven", "pricey" food and the "doting" waiters' "false Euro accents"; however, "lunch is worth watching."

Vox Populi 20 | 17 | 17 | $20
800 Connecticut Ave., NW (H St.), 202-835-2233
◪ The "high-quality", "cafeteria-style French" fare can't be faulted and it's "pretty successful at transplanting" a European feel to this prime people-watching prospect "across from the White House"; still, that doesn't altogether justify its "soup and salad, that'll be $20" pricing; open weekdays 9:30 AM–2 PM.

Washington, D.C. | F | D | S | C |

Warehouse Bar & Grill S | 22 | 19 | 21 | $29 |
214 King St. (bet. Fairfax & Lee Sts.), Alexandria, VA, 703-683-6868

▲ "Lots of tourists" join prominent Alexandria "locals" (match their faces to their caricatures on the walls) for Cajun-Creole steaks, fish and "fun" at this younger, bigger, more "institutional" relation of Arlandria's R.T.'s; however, plaudits for some of "Old Town's best seafood" are mixed with reports of "spicy hot but tasteless" dishes; perhaps its acquisition of The Wharf restaurant across the street stretched it thin.

West End Cafe ●S | 19 | 19 | 19 | $30 |
1 Washington Circle (New Hampshire Ave.), 202-293-5390

■ A "courteous", "comfortable shoe" for West Enders and Kennedy Center theatergoers with a "convenient" Ken-Cen shuttle, this supper club features a "civilized" lunch buffet ($9.95) and a "dependable" New American prix fixe menu; late nights aren't quite the same without Burnett Thompson at the piano, but "fabulous" hostess Gerlinda Burr is still "serving Goldwasser" to her pets.

West End Grill S | 19 | 16 | 18 | $28 |
7904 Woodmont Ave. (bet. Fairmont & St. Elmo Aves.), Bethesda, MD, 301-951-9696

▲ Pros praise this "welcome Bethesda addition" for its "good" contemporary Continental food at "modest prices", "friendly" staff and weekend "upstairs jazz dinner"; however, foes feel there are "some wrinkles", such as "uneven" food, "hectic and erratic" service and the fact that "no reservations [downstairs] means you must go early."

White Tiger S | 22 | 19 | 19 | $21 |
301 Massachusetts Ave., NE (3rd St.), 202-546-5900

■ Mouthwatering "aromas" herald the "best tasting Indian lunch buffet" on Capitol Hill; besides "great food", this "worthy" subcontinental commands a "lovely, large patio", with "loads of [upscale] atmosphere" inside, and such "nice" waiters that each could single-handedly improve his native country's congressional relations.

WILLARD ROOM | 24 | 28 | 25 | $52 |
Willard Hotel, 1401 Pennsylvania Ave., NW (14th St.), 202-637-7440

■ "One of the most elegant", "impressive" and "stately" dining rooms in DC, this Edwardian treasure Downtown simply "drips money", power and "first-rate service"; the arrival of "rising star" chef Gerard Mandani may not be fully reflected in the above food rating, but his "wonderful" Contemporary American–French cuisine is eliminating comments like "if only you could eat the room."

Washington, D.C. F | D | S | C

Willow Grove Inn S ▽ | 24 | 23 | 23 | $40
Willow Grove Inn, 14079 Plantation Way (Rte. 15, 1 mi. north of Orange), Orange, VA, 540-672-5982
■ A "delicious, friendly" and "romantic" place "to eat and stay" when you're visiting Monticello and Charlottesville; there's something about this engaging post–Civil War mansion's "real country" setting, Regional American food and "beautiful dining room" that makes it "really special", even on those occasional days when the cooking is "just ok."

Woo Lae Oak S 23 | 17 | 18 | $25
River House, 1500 S. Joyce St. (15th St.), Arlington, VA, 703-521-3706
■ Westerners can satisfy "Seoul food cravings" with "flavorful", grill-your-own BBQ, dumplings and other staples at this "kitschy Korean" with a largely Asian clientele in Arlington; since the staff is "not [always] helpful" to novices, it takes going with a guide "who knows how to order" in Korean to get the "real thing."

Woomi Garden S ▽ | 15 | 24 | 17 | $23
2423 Hickerson Dr. (Georgia Ave.), Silver Spring, MD, 301-933-0100
■ Real money was apparently spent on the decor here, yet the rest of this Korean-Japanese production in Silver Spring seems rather ragged; reports of "delicious dumplings and good beef" are contradicted by complaints about "average", "overpriced and underseasoned" food and being "rushed" by help that "doesn't speak much English."

Wrap Works S 17 | 14 | 14 | $10
1601 Connecticut Ave., NW (Q St.), 202-265-4200
1079 Wisconsin Ave. (bet. K & M Sts.), 202-333-0220
Reston Town Ctr., 1820 Discovery St. (Reston Pkwy.), Reston, VA, 703-318-5200
■ If the "wrap rage" (trendy combos of internationally flavored fillings in colorful tortillas) is "already a cliché", why do hundreds of surveyors brave "long lines" for these "high-pressured" cafes?; 'cause they're "fast", "cheap", "healthy" and the help is "cute"; those who would rather give them a bad rap simply sniff "more hype than taste" – "mush in a tube."

Wurzburg-Haus S 19 | 16 | 18 | $22
Red Mill Shopping Ctr., 7236 Mancaster Mill Rd. (Shady Grove Rd.), Rockville, MD, 301-330-0402
■ There's still a "beer hall atmosphere" at this Rockville Bavarian with accordion music, costumed servers and "heavy-duty" German food; however, new owners have made some changes, adding some lighter eating options to the "great bratwurst, spaetzle and potato pancakes" that dominated the menu, which could explain why some diehards declare that the place is "not what it used to be."

Washington, D.C. | F | D | S | C |

Xando ◐ S | 16 | 22 | 13 | $14 |
1350 Connecticut Ave. (Dupont Circle), 202-296-9341
1647 20th St., NW (R St.), 202-332-6364
■ Gen Xers "lose Saturday mornings" (and late nights) hanging out at this "coffee drink joint", martini bar and "do-your-own-s'mores" (marshmallows, graham crackers and chocolate cooked on a hibachi) spot off Dupont Circle; utter "chaos" characterizes the scramble for seats and sight lines, "slow" describes the service; no matter, "so cool, it's hot – wear black"; N.B. the branch above Dupont Circle, near R street, is new and unrated.

Yokohama S | ▽ 23 | 15 | 20 | $23 |
11300 Georgia Ave. (University Blvd.), Wheaton, MD, 301-949-7403
■ Masao Kim "holds court at the sushi bar" of this "undistinguished"-looking Wheaton storefront, where his "successful blend of Japanese and Korean" cooking, "friendly" demeanor and "generous" values (like $1 apiece sushi at lunch) earn kudos; no wonder reviewers beg "don't tell everyone how good the food is", we "don't want to start waiting in line."

Yosaku S | 21 | 15 | 19 | $25 |
4712 Wisconsin Ave., NW (Davenport St.), 202-363-4453
■ A Friendship Heights movie and shopping "standby" where the sushi is "dependable", the yosenabe winter-warming and the "shabu-shabu not [too] shabby"; sure, it's a bit "slapdash" and could be "spiffed up", but steady customers (including food-savvy "shrinks" and some faces) can always "get in."

Zed's S | 21 | 11 | 18 | $18 |
3318 M St., NW (bet. 33rd & 34th Sts.), 202-333-4710
◪ This nondescript Georgetown Ethiopian may lack the charged "atmosphere of its Adams Morgan" brethren, but "adventurous" vegetarians and diplomats attest to its "high-quality", "interesting" cuisine; however, eating "gooey", "spicy" stews with one's fingers, while "popular" for some "first dates", is probably "not for your mother" unless she was a Peace Corps volunteer.

Zuki Moon S | 21 | 19 | 19 | $24 |
824 New Hampshire Ave., NW (bet. I & K Sts.), 202-333-3312
■ At her "perfect for Kennedy Center" location, Mary Richter previews the "future of Asian cuisine" with "wonderful noodle soups", "delicious" seared tuna 'sushi' and "superb" ice creams; her "refreshing" take on Japanese and Indochinese classics "thrills" her many fans (it's "too healthy" for a few phobes), but even they say the "dollhouse miniature chairs" need replacing and the service should be brought up to speed.

Indexes to Washington, D.C. Restaurants

Special Features and Appeals

TYPES OF CUISINE

Afghan
Faryab
Kabul Caravan
Panjshir
Paradise

American (New)
Addie's
American Grill
Aquarelle
Ardeo
Ashby Inn
BET on Jazz
Bistro
Bistro Bistro
Bleu Rock Inn
Blue Plate
Cafe Bethesda
Cafe on M
Carlyle Grand
Cashion's
Chardonnay
Coeur De Lion
DC Coast
Dean & DeLuca
Elysium
Evening Star Cafe
Fedora Cafe
Felix
4 & 20 Blackbirds
Greenwood's
Indigo
Inn/Little Washington
Jasmine Cafe
Jefferson Rest.
Kinkead's
Lafayette
M & S Grill
Mark
Market St. B&G
Melrose
Mendocino Grille
Metro Center Grille
Morrison-Clark Inn
Mrs. Simpson's
New Heights
Nora
Occidental Grill
Old Angler's Inn
Oval Room
Persimmon
Pesce
Rhodeside Grill
Ritz-Carlton, Grill
Riverside Grille
Roof Terrace
Rupperts
Seasons
701
Silverado
Soper's on M
Starland Cafe
Stella's
Stone Manor
Sweetwater Tavern
Tabard Inn
Tahoga
Two Quail
Vidalia
West End Cafe

American (Regional)
Addie's
Blue & Gold
Cafe Marianna
Crisfield
Crisfield/Lee Plaza
DC Coast
Georgia Brown's
Inn/Little Washington
Morrison-Clark Inn
Old Angler's Inn
Red Sage
1789
Shelly's Woodroast
Soper's on M
Stone Manor
Vidalia
Willow Grove Inn

American (Traditional)
America
Amphora's Diner
Artie's
Belmont Kitchen
Bilbo Baggins
Blue & Gold
Bob & Edith's
Cafe Deluxe
Calvert Grille
Capital Grille
Capitol City Brewing
Carlyle Grand

Washington, D.C. Indexes

Cedar Knoll Inn
C.F. Folks
Charley's Place
Cheesecake Factory
Chicken Out
Chris'
Clyde's
Daily Grill
Dave & Busters
District ChopHse.
Evans Farm Inn
Gadsby's Tavern
Hard Rock Cafe
Hard Times Cafe
Hogate's
Houston's
Hunter's Inn
Inn at Glen Echo
Jerry Seafood
John Harvard's
J. Paul's
King St. Blues
Kramerbooks
Legal Sea Food
Luna Grill
Martin's Tavern
Max's of Washington
McCormick & Schmick's
Meadowlark Inn
Metro 29
Mike Baker's 10th St.
Mike's American
Monocle
Montgomery's Grille
Morrison-Clark Inn
Morton's of Chicago
Occidental Grill
Old Ebbitt Grill
Olde Towne Tavern
Old Glory BBQ
Old Hickory Grill
Olney Ale House
Original Pancake Hse.
Phillips Seafood Grill
Planet Hollywood
Polly's Cafe
Potowmack Landing
Ramparts
Red Hot & Blue
Rock Bottom Brewery
Royal Rest.
Sequoia
Shelly's Woodroast
Silver Diner
Sweetwater Tavern
Tunnicliff's Tavern
Union St. Public Hse.
Velocity Grill
Vienna Inn
Virginia Bev. Co.
Warehouse B&G

Asian
Asia Garden
Asia Nora
Bangkok St. Grill
Burma
Cafe Asia
Germaine's
Oodles Noodles
Raku
Saigon Crystal
Spices
Stardust
Straits of Malaya
Teaism
Vegetaria
Zuki Moon

Bakeries
Bread Line
Cafe Marianna
Carlyle Grand
Firehook Bakery
La Madeleine
Maggiano's
Patisserie Cafe Didier
Samadi Sweets

Bar-B-Q
George Starke's
Houston's
King St. Blues
Memphis Bar-B-Q
Old Glory BBQ
Old Hickory Grill
Red Hot & Blue
Rockland's

Brazilian
Coco Loco
Greenfield Churrascaria
Grill from Ipanema
Malibu Grill

Cajun/Creole
Blue & Gold
Cafe Marianna
Cajun Bangkok

115

Washington, D.C. Indexes

Louisiana Express
R.T.'s
R.T.'s Seafood
Sea Catch
219
Warehouse B&G

Californian

California Pizza Kit.
California Tortilla
Cheesecake Factory
Citronelle
Fedora Cafe
Paolo's
Tempo

Caribbean

Banana Cafe
BET on Jazz
Hibiscus Cafe
Mango Mike's
Rainforest Cafe

Chinese

A&J Rest.
Asia Garden
BD's Mongolian
Canton Cafe
Charlie Chiang's
China Canteen
City Lights of China
Dynasty
Eat First
Foong Lin
Fortune
Four Rivers
Full Kee
Full Key
Golden Palace
Good Fortune
Hollywood East
Hunan Chinatown
Hunan Lion
Hunan Lion II
Hunan Number One
Hunan Palace
Majestic
Mongolian Grill
Mr. K's
Mr. Yung's
Oriental Star
Paul Kee
Peking Gourmet Inn
P.F. Chang's

Seven Seas
Sunny Garden
Taipei/Tokyo Cafe
Tony Cheng's
Vegetable Garden

Coffeehouses/Desserts

Dean & DeLuca
Firehook Bakery
Kramerbooks
Le Bon Cafe
Patisserie Cafe Didier
Savory
Xando

Coffee Shops/Diners

Amphora's Diner
Blue Plate
Bob & Edith's
C.F. Folks
Florida Ave. Grill
Luna Grill
Metro 29
Silver Diner

Continental

Bilbo Baggins
Cafe Renaissance
Cafe Royal
Jockey Club
Lafayette
Normandie Farm
Ritz-Carlton, Rest.
Serbian Crown
Tivoli
Two Quail
Village Bistro
West End Grill

Cuban

Banana Cafe
Havana Cafe

Delis

Cafe Mozart
Krupin's
Lucia's
Parkway Deli

Dim Sum

A&J Rest.
Charlie Chiang's
Fortune
Four Rivers
Good Fortune

116

Washington, D.C. Indexes

Hunan Number One
Mr. Yung's
Seven Seas
Tony Cheng's

Eclectic/International
Bread Line
Capital Wrapps
C.F. Folks
Cities
Felix
Levante's
Lewie's
Little Fountain Cafe
Mark
Mezza 9
Perry's
Rainforest Cafe
Rhodeside Grill
Savory
Stardust
Thyme Square
Two Quail
U-topia
Velocity Grill
West End Grill
Wrap Works

Ethiopian
Meskerem
Red Sea
Zed's

French
Bistro Francais
Bistro 123
Bistrot Lepic
Cafe de Paris
Cafe Renaissance
Cafe Royal
Gerard's Place
Jean-Michel
La Bergerie
La Chaumiere
La Colline
La Cote d'Or Cafe
La Ferme
La Fourchette
La Miche
La Provence
L'Auberge Chez Francois
L'Auberge Provencale
Lavandou
Le Gaulois

Le Paradis
Le Refuge
Le Rivage
Les Halles
Lespinasse
Le Vieux Logis
Prince Michel
Vintage
Vox Artis
Willard Room

French Bistro
Au Pied du Cochon
Bistro Francais
Bistro 123
Bistrot Lepic
Cafe de Paris
Cafe Parisien
Cafe Royal
La Brasserie
La Chaumiere
La Colline
La Cote d'Or Cafe
La Fourchette
La Madeleine
La Miche
La Provence
Lavandou
Le Bon Cafe
Le Gaulois
Le Petit Mistral
Le Refuge
Les Halles
Patisserie Cafe Didier
Village Bistro
Vintage
Vox Artis
Vox Populi

French (New)
Citronelle
Gerard's Place
La Colline
Lespinasse
Vintage
Willard Room

German
Cafe Berlin
Cafe Mozart
Old Europe
Wurzburg-Haus

Greek
Aegean Taverna
Amphora's Diner

Washington, D.C. Indexes

Levante's
Mykonos
Taverna Cretekou

Hamburgers
Addie's
Artie's
Carlyle Grand
Clyde's
Hard Rock Cafe
Houston's
Hunter's Inn
J. Paul's
Martin's Tavern
Mike Baker's 10th St.
Mike's American
Montgomery's Grille
Occidental Grill
Old Brogue Irish
Old Ebbitt Grill
Planet Hollywood
Polly's Cafe
Rock Bottom Brewery
Union St. Public Hse.
Virginia Bev. Co.

Indian
Aangan
Aaranthi
Aditi
Aroma
Bombay Bistro
Bombay Club
Bombay Curry Co.
Bombay Palace
Cafe New Delhi
Cafe Taj
Connaught Place
Delhi Dhaba
Food Factory
Haandi
Mehak
Udupi Palace
White Tiger

Indonesian
Ivy's Place
Sabang
Straits of Malaya

Irish
Fadó Irish Pub
Ireland's 4 Courts
Old Brogue Irish

Italian
(N=Northern; S=Southern;
N&S=Includes both)
Al Tiramisu (N&S)
Arucola (N&S)
A.V. Rist. Italiano (S)
Barolo (N)
Bertolini's (N&S)
Bertucci's (N&S)
Buon Giorno (N&S)
Cafe Milano (N)
Cafe Mileto (N&S)
Cafe Oggi (N&S)
California Pizza Kit. (N)
Cesco (N)
"Ciao baby" Cucina (N&S)
Coppi's (N&S)
Coppi's Vignorelli (N)
Da Domenico (N&S)
Dante (N)
Dolcetto (N)
Donatello (N&S)
Ecco Cafe (N&S)
Faccia Luna (N&S)
Fedora Cafe (N&S)
Fellini (N&S)
Filomena (N&S)
Fiorentino's (N&S)
Galileo (N)
Generous George's (N&S)
Geppetto (N&S)
Geranio (N&S)
Goldoni (N)
Il Borgo (N&S)
Il Cigno (N)
Il Pizzico (N&S)
Il Radicchio (N&S)
Il Ritrovo (S)
I Matti (N&S)
I Ricchi (N)
La Dolce Vita (N&S)
Landini Bros. (N)
La Panetteria (N&S)
La Tomate (N&S)
Listrani's (N&S)
Lucia's (N&S)
Luigino (N&S)
Maggiano's (S)
Mare e Monti (N&S)
Monroe's (N&S)
Obelisk (N)
Paolo's (N&S)
Pariolo (N&S)
Pasta Plus (N&S)

Washington, D.C. Indexes

Petitto's (N&S)
Pines of Rome (N&S)
Positano (N&S)
Primi Piatti (N&S)
Provence (N&S)
Red Tomato Cafe (N&S)
Renato (N&S)
Ricciuti's (N&S)
Sesto Senso (N)
Sostanza (N&S)
Tempo (N&S)
Terrazza (N)
That's Amore (N&S)
Tivoli (N&S)
Tomato Tango (N&S)
Tragara (N)
Trattoria da Franco (N&S)
Tuscana West (N&S)
Umberto's (N&S)
Veneziano (N)
Villa d'Este (N&S)
Villa Franco (N)

Japanese
Akasaka
Appetizer Plus
Asia Garden
Atami
Blue Ocean
Hinode
Hisago
Ichiban
Jin-Ga
Kawasaki
Makoto
Matuba
Miyagi
Nulbom
Sakana
Sam Woo
Sushi Chalet
Sushi-Ko
Sushi Sushi
Sushi Taro
Tachibana
Taipei/Tokyo Cafe
Tako Grill
Tomokazu
Tsukiji
Woomi Garden
Yokohama
Yosaku
Zuki Moon

Jewish
Felix
Tel Aviv Cafe

Korean
Hee Been
Ichiban
Jin-Ga
Nulbom
Sam Woo
Sushi Chalet
Woo Lae Oak
Woomi Garden
Yokohama

Latin American
Cafe Atlantico
Chicken Place
Coco Loco
Crisp & Juicy
El Gavilan
Gabriel
Hibiscus Cafe
Las Placitas

Malaysian
Asia Garden
Straits of Malaya

Mediterranean
Bacchus
BeDuCi
Cafe Promenade
Cedar Knoll Inn
Fellini
Il Ritrovo
Isabella
Lebanese Taverna
Levante's
Mediterranee
Mezza 9
Provence
Samadi Sweets
Skewers/Cafe Luna
Tom Tom

Mexican/Tex-Mex
Alamo
Austin Grill
Burrito Bros.
Burro
Cactus Cantina
La Lomita
Las Placitas
Lauriol Plaza

119

Washington, D.C. Indexes

Mi Rancho
On the Border
Rio Grande Cafe
South Austin Grill
Tia Queta

Middle Eastern
Bacchus
Faryab
Lebanese Taverna
Moby Dick
Paradise
Pasha Cafe
Samadi Sweets
Skewers/Cafe Luna
Tel Aviv Cafe

Persian
Caravan Grill
Hautam Kebobs
Moby Dick
Paradise
Shamshiry

Peruvian
Chicken Place
Crisp & Juicy
🌶 Pollo Rico

Pizza
A.V. Rist. Italiano
Bertolini's
Bertucci's
Cafe Mileto
California Pizza Kit.
Coppi's
Coppi's Vignorelli
Ecco Cafe
Faccia Luna
Generous George's
Geppetto
Il Radicchio
I Matti
La Dolce Vita
Listrani's
Mare e Monti
Monroe's
Paolo's
Pasta Plus
Pines of Rome
Pizza de Resistance
Pizzeria Paradiso
Primi Piatti
Red Tomato Cafe
Ricciuti's

Thyme Square
Tomato Tango
Tuscana West
Umberto's

Russian
Serbian Crown

Salvadoran
El Catalan
El Tamarindo
La Lomita
Los Chorros
Mi Rancho

Seafood
Ardeo
Blue Point Grill
Chart House
Crisfield
Crisfield/Lee Plaza
DC Coast
Georgetown Seafood
Grillfish
Hogate's
Jerry Seafood
Kinkead's
Legal Sea Food
Le Rivage
M & S Grill
McCormick & Schmick's
Palm
Pesce
Phillips Seafood Grill
Ritz-Carlton, Rest.
R.T.'s
R.T.'s Seafood
Sea Catch
Seven Seas
Sostanza
Stardust
Tony & Joe's
Village Bistro
Warehouse B&G

Southern/Soul
B. Smith's
Florida Ave. Grill
Georgia Brown's
Gulf Coast Kitchen
King St. Blues
Morrison-Clark Inn
Music City Roadhse.
Southside 815
Uncle Jed's
Vidalia

Washington, D.C. Indexes

Southwestern
Adobe Grill
Austin Grill
Cottonwood Ranch
Gabriel
Red Sage
Rio Grande Cafe
Santa Fe East
Silverado
South Austin Grill
Sweetwater Tavern

Spanish
Andalucia
Barcelona
El Catalan
Gabriel
Jaleo
La Costa/Las Tapas
Lauriol Plaza
Taberna del Alabardero

Steakhouses
Bugaboo Creek
Capital Grille
Chart House
Chris'
District ChopHse.
Fran O'Brien's
Les Halles
M & S Grill
Max's of Washington
Morton's of Chicago
Outback Steakhouse
Palm
Prime Rib
Ruth's Chris
Sam & Harry's
Sostanza

Tapas
Barcelona
El Catalan
Gabriel
Jaleo
La Costa/Las Tapas
Mezza 9
Taberna del Alabardero
Tom Tom

Tearooms
Teaism

Thai
Asia Garden
Bangkok Bistro
Bangkok Garden
Bangkok St. Grill
Benjarong
Bua
Busara
Cajun Bangkok
Crystal Thai
Duangrat's
Dusit
Haad Thai
Ivy's Place
Oriental Star
Pilin Thai
Po Siam
Rabieng
Sala Thai
Stardust
Star of Siam
Tara Thai
T.H.A.I.
Thai Chef
Thai Kingdom

Turkish
Kazan
Levante's
Nizam's

Vegetarian
(* Vegetarian-friendly)
Ardeo*
Blue Plate*
Bombay Club*
Burro*
California Tortilla*
Faryab*
Greenwood's*
Inn/Little Washington*
Levante's*
Morrison-Clark Inn*
New Heights*
Raku*
Tako Grill*
Taste of Saigon
Tel Aviv Cafe*
Thyme Square
Udupi Palace
Vegetable Garden
Vegetaria

Vietnamese
Asia Garden
Cafe Dalat
Cafe Saigon

Washington, D.C. Indexes

- Del Ray Garden
- Galaxy
- Little Viet Garden
- Majestic
- Miss Saigon
- Nam's
- Nam Viet
- Pho Cali
- Pho 95
- Pho 75
- Queen Bee
- Saigon Crystal
- Saigon Gourmet
- Saigon Inn
- Saigonnais
- Song Ho/Pho Tay Ho
- Taste of Saigon

Washington, D.C. Indexes

NEIGHBORHOOD LOCATIONS

WASHINGTON, D.C.

Capitol Hill
America
Banana Cafe
Barolo
B. Smith's
Burrito Bros.
Cafe Berlin
Capitol City Brewing
Il Radicchio
La Brasserie
La Colline
La Lomita
Las Placitas
Le Bon Cafe
Monocle
Tunnicliff's Tavern
Two Quail
White Tiger

Chinatown/Convention Center/Penn Quarter
Austin Grill
A.V. Rist. Italiano
Bertolini's
Bertucci's
BET on Jazz
Burma
Cafe Atlantico
Capital Grille
Capitol City Brewing
Charlie Chiang's
Coco Loco
Coeur De Lion
Dean & DeLuca
District ChopHse.
Eat First
El Catalan
Fadó Irish Pub
Full Kee
Golden Palace
Haad Thai
Hunan Chinatown
Jaleo
John Harvard's
Les Halles
Luigino
M & S Grill
Mark
Metro Center Grille
Mike Baker's 10th St.
Morrison-Clark Inn
Mr. Yung's
Occidental Grill
Old Ebbitt Grill
Planet Hollywood
Rupperts
701
Tony Cheng's
Velocity Grill
Villa Franco
Willard Room

Downtown/Dupont Circle South
Bombay Club
Burrito Bros.
Burro
Cafe Mozart
Cafe Promenade
Chardonnay
"Ciao baby" Cucina
Daily Grill
DC Coast
Fellini
Firehook Bakery
Fran O'Brien's
Galileo
Georgetown Seafood
Georgia Brown's
Gerard's Place
Goldoni
Grillfish
Hard Rock Cafe
I Ricchi
Isabella
Jefferson Rest.
Kawasaki
Lafayette
Lespinasse
Max's of Washington
McCormick & Schmick's
Morton's of Chicago
Oodles Noodles
Palm
Red Sage
Red Tomato Cafe
Sam & Harry's
Soper's on M

123

Washington, D.C. Indexes

Star of Siam
Tuscana West
Vidalia
Vox Artis
Vox Populi
Xando

Dupont Circle
Al Tiramisu
Bacchus
BeDuCi
Blue Plate
Burrito Bros.
Burro
Cafe Asia
California Pizza Kit.
C.F. Folks
City Lights of China
Firehook Bakery
Gabriel
Jockey Club
Kramerbooks
La Tomate
Luna Grill
Nora
Obelisk
Pesce
Pizzeria Paradiso
Raku
Ruth's Chris
Sakana
Sala Thai
Sesto Senso
Sostanza
Tabard Inn
Teaism
Thai Chef
Wrap Works
Xando

Dupont Circle East/Adams Morgan
Belmont Kitchen
Bua
Burrito Bros.
Caravan Grill
Cashion's
Cities
El Tamarindo
Felix
Florida Ave. Grill
Grill from Ipanema
Il Radicchio
I Matti

La Fourchette
Las Placitas
Lauriol Plaza
Little Fountain Cafe
Meskerem
Perry's
Red Sea
Saigonnais
Skewers/Cafe Luna
Star of Siam
Straits of Malaya
Sushi Taro
Tom Tom
Veneziano

Foggy Bottom/K Street
Aquarelle
Aroma
Asia Nora
Bertucci's
Bombay Palace
Bread Line
Burro
Dean & DeLuca
Donatello
Kinkead's
Legal Sea Food
Mr. K's
Mykonos
Oval Room
Prime Rib
Primi Piatti
Roof Terrace
Taberna del Alabardero
Thai Kingdom
Zuki Moon

Georgetown
Aditi
Adobe Grill
Au Pied du Cochon
Austin Grill
Bangkok Bistro
Bistro Francais
Burrito Bros.
Cafe Milano
Citronelle
Clyde's
Dean & DeLuca
Filomena
Firehook Bakery
Hibiscus Cafe
Hisago
Houston's

124

Washington, D.C. Indexes

Il Radicchio
J. Paul's
La Chaumiere
La Madeleine
Martin's Tavern
Mendocino Grille
Miss Saigon
Moby Dick
Morton's of Chicago
Music City Roadhse.
Old Glory BBQ
Paolo's
Patisserie Cafe Didier
Riverside Grille
Saigon Inn
Sea Catch
Seasons
Sequoia
1789
Tahoga
Tony & Joe's
Vintage
Wrap Works
Zed's

Maine Avenue/SW Waterfront
American Grill
Hogate's
Le Rivage
Phillips Seafood Grill

New "U"
Coppi's
Polly's Cafe
U-topia

Upper NW
Ardeo
Arucola

Bistrot Lepic
Busara
Cactus Cantina
Cafe Deluxe
California Pizza Kit.
Cheesecake Factory
Chicken Out
Coppi's Vignorelli
Dolcetto
El Tamarindo
Germaine's
Greenwood's
Ivy's Place
Krupin's
Lavandou
Lebanese Taverna
Listrani's
Makoto
Mrs. Simpson's
Nam Viet
New Heights
Old Europe
Petitto's
Rockland's
Saigon Gourmet
Saigon Inn
Spices
Starland Cafe
Sushi-Ko
That's Amore
Yosaku

West End
Bistro
Cafe on M
Jin-Ga
Melrose
Provence
West End Cafe

NEARBY MARYLAND

Bethesda/Chevy Chase
Aangan
Andalucia
Bacchus
Bangkok Garden
BD's Mongolian
Bertolini's
Buon Giorno
Cafe Bethesda
California Pizza Kit.

California Tortilla
Capital Wrapps
Capitol City Brewing
Cesco
Chicken Out
Clyde's
Cottonwood Ranch
Delhi Dhaba
Del Ray Garden
Faccia Luna
Faryab
Foong Lin

125

Washington, D.C. Indexes

Geppetto
Gulf Coast Kitchen
Haandi
Hinode
Houston's
Il Ritrovo
Ivy's Place
Jean-Michel
La Ferme
La Madeleine
La Miche
La Panetteria
Levante's
Le Vieux Logis
Lewie's
Louisiana Express
Matuba
Moby Dick
Mongolian Grill
Montgomery's Grille
Nam's
Oodles Noodles
Original Pancake Hse.
Outback Steakhouse
Paradise
Pariolo
Persimmon
Pines of Rome
Positano
Raku
Red Tomato Cafe
Rio Grande Cafe
Rock Bottom Brewery
Ruth's Chris
South Austin Grill
Sushi Chalet
Sushi Sushi
Tako Grill
Tara Thai
Tel Aviv Cafe
Terrazza
Thyme Square
Tia Queta
Tragara
Uncle Jed's
West End Grill

Gaithersburg/ Shady Grove/Olney

Bugaboo Creek
Cafe Mileto
Chicken Out
Chris'
Cottonwood Ranch
Fiorentino's
Hunan Palace
Hunter's Inn
Ichiban
Le Paradis
Los Chorros
Meadowlark Inn
Mi Rancho
Olde Towne Tavern
Olney Ale House
Outback Steakhouse
Red Hot & Blue
Ricciuti's
Stone Manor
Sushi Chalet
Tomato Tango

Potomac/Glen Echo

Cafe Royal
Chicken Out
Hunter's Inn
Inn at Glen Echo
Normandie Farm
Old Angler's Inn
Renato
Umberto's

Rockville/ White Flint/ Garrett Park

A&J Rest.
Addie's
Andalucia
Asia Garden
Benjarong
Bombay Bistro
Canton Cafe
Cheesecake Factory
Chicken Out
China Canteen
Crisp & Juicy
Dave & Busters
Four Rivers
George Starke's
Greenfield Churrascaria
Hard Times Cafe
Hautam Kebobs
Hinode
Houston's
Il Pizzico
La Madeleine
Nulbom
On the Border
Original Pancake Hse.

Washington, D.C. Indexes

Pho 95
Pho 75
Sam Woo
Seven Seas
Shelly's Woodroast
Silver Diner
Sunny Garden
Taipei/Tokyo Cafe
Taste of Saigon
That's Amore
Tsukiji
Vegetable Garden
Wurzburg-Haus

Silver Spring/Wheaton/ Langley Park/Laurel/ Landover

Cafe de Paris
Chicken Place
Crisfield
Crisfield/Lee Plaza
Crisp & Juicy
Dusit
Dynasty
El Gavilan
El Pollo Rico
Food Factory
Full Key
Good Fortune
Hollywood East
Jerry Seafood
Los Chorros
Lucia's
Mare e Monti
Mi Rancho
Nam's
Old Hickory Grill
Outback Steakhouse
Parkway Deli
Pasta Plus
Paul Kee
Pho 75
Red Hot & Blue
Sabang
Savory
Silver Diner
Tomokazu
Udupi Palace
Woomi Garden
Yokohama

NEARBY VIRGINIA

Alexandria

Akasaka
Alamo
Austin Grill
Barcelona
Bilbo Baggins
Blue Point Grill
Bombay Curry Co.
Cafe Marianna
Cajun Bangkok
California Pizza Kit.
Calvert Grille
Cedar Knoll Inn
Chart House
Clyde's
Ecco Cafe
Elysium
Evening Star Cafe
Firehook Bakery
Gadsby's Tavern
Generous George's
Geranio
Hard Times Cafe
King St. Blues
La Bergerie
La Costa/Las Tapas
La Madeleine
Landini Bros.
Le Gaulois
Le Refuge
Mango Mike's
Monroe's
Oriental Star
Outback Steakhouse
Po Siam
Potowmack Landing
Ramparts
Royal Rest.
R.T.'s
Santa Fe East
Southside 815
Stardust
Stella's
Taverna Cretekou
Tempo
Trattoria da Franco
219
Union St. Public Hse.
Villa d'Este
Virginia Bev. Co.
Warehouse B&G

127

Washington, D.C. Indexes

Arlington
Aegean Taverna
Atami
Bistro Bistro
Blue & Gold
Bob & Edith's
Cafe Dalat
Cafe New Delhi
Cafe Parisien
Cafe Saigon
California Pizza Kit.
Crisp & Juicy
Crystal Thai
Delhi Dhaba
El Pollo Rico
Faccia Luna
Food Factory
Hard Times Cafe
Havana Cafe
Hunan Number One
Il Radicchio
Kabul Caravan
La Cote d'Or Cafe
Landini Bros.
Lebanese Taverna
Little Viet Garden
Luna Grill
Matuba
Mediterranee
Memphis Bar-B-Q
Metro 29
Moby Dick
Nam Viet
Outback Steakhouse
Pasha Cafe
Pho Cali
Pho 75
Queen Bee
Red Hot & Blue
Rio Grande Cafe
Ritz-Carlton, Grill
Rockland's
R.T.'s Seafood
Ruth's Chris
Saigon Crystal
Silver Diner
Village Bistro
Woo Lae Oak

Falls Church/Baileys Crossroads/Shirlington
Bangkok St. Grill
Capitol City Brewing
Carlyle Grand
Duangrat's
Fortune
Galaxy
Haandi
La Madeleine
Malibu Grill
Mehak
Panjshir
Peking Gourmet Inn
Pho 75
Pilin Thai
Rabieng
Samadi Sweets
Song Ho/Pho Tay Ho
Tara Thai
T.H.A.I.

Great Falls
Dante
Indigo
L'Auberge Chez Francois
Old Brogue Irish
Serbian Crown

McLean
Busara
Cafe Oggi
Cafe Taj
Charley's Place
Chicken Out
Evans Farm Inn
Il Borgo
Kazan
Le Petit Mistral
Miyagi
Tachibana

Reston/Herndon/Chantilly
Amphora's Diner
Bertucci's
Bistro Bistro
Burrito Bros.
Chicken Out
Clyde's
Food Factory
Fortune
Hard Times Cafe
Il Cigno
Jasmine Cafe
La Madeleine
Market St. B&G
McCormick & Schmick's
Memphis Bar-B-Q

Washington, D.C. Indexes

On the Border
Outback Steakhouse
Paolo's
Red Hot & Blue
Rio Grande Cafe
Silver Diner
Vegetaria
Wrap Works

Rosslyn/Courthouse

Appetizer Plus
Ireland's 4 Courts
Mezza 9
Pizza de Resistance
Red Hot & Blue
Rhodeside Grill
Tivoli

Springfield/Fairfax/Annandale/Centreville

Artie's
Austin Grill
Bertucci's
Blue Ocean
Bombay Bistro
Bugaboo Creek
Chicken Out
Connaught Place
El Pollo Rico
Generous George's
Hee Been
La Dolce Vita
Majestic
Memphis Bar-B-Q
Mike's American
Outback Steakhouse
Red Hot & Blue
Silverado
Silver Diner
Sweetwater Tavern
That's Amore

Tysons Corner/Vienna

Aaranthi
America
Bertucci's
Bistro 123
Cafe Renaissance
California Pizza Kit.
Da Domenico
Fedora Cafe
Hunan Lion
Hunan Lion II
La Madeleine
La Provence
Legal Sea Food
Maggiano's
Moby Dick
Morton's of Chicago
Nizam's
On the Border
Outback Steakhouse
Panjshir
P.F. Chang's
Phillips Seafood Grill
Primi Piatti
Rainforest Cafe
Ritz-Carlton, Rest.
Sam & Harry's
Shamshiry
Silver Diner
Sweetwater Tavern
Tara Thai
Taste of Saigon
That's Amore
Vienna Inn

Washington, VA/Flint Hill/White Post/Orange

Ashby Inn
Bleu Rock Inn
4 & 20 Blackbirds
Inn/Little Washington
L'Auberge Provencale
Prince Michel
Willow Grove Inn

Washington, D.C. Indexes

SPECIAL FEATURES AND APPEALS

Breakfast
(All hotels and the following standouts)
Bob & Edith's
Bread Line
Cafe Promenade
Galileo
La Brasserie
La Colline
La Madeleine
Martin's Tavern
Old Ebbitt Grill
Original Pancake Hse.
Patisserie Cafe Didier
Teaism
Vienna Inn

Brunch
(Best of many)
Aquarelle
BET on Jazz
Bilbo Baggins
Bleu Rock Inn
B. Smith's
Cashion's
Clyde's
4 & 20 Blackbirds
Gabriel
Jaleo
Kinkead's
Malibu Grill
Melrose
Morrison-Clark Inn
Music City Roadhse.
New Heights
Old Brogue Irish
Old Ebbitt Grill
Olde Towne Tavern
Perry's
Rhodeside Grill
Ritz-Carlton, Grill
Ritz-Carlton, Rest.
Roof Terrace
Seasons
Tabard Inn

Buffet Served
(Check prices, days and times)
Aroma
BD's Mongolian
Bombay Bistro
Bombay Palace
Cafe New Delhi
Cafe Promenade
Canton Cafe
Caravan Grill
Charlie Chiang's
El Tamarindo
Evans Farm Inn
Filomena
Gabriel
Generous George's
Greenfield Churrascaria
Haandi
Hautam Kebobs
Hee Been
Hinode
Hogate's
Ichiban
Lewie's
Malibu Grill
Metro Center Grille
Mongolian Grill
Paradise
Pho Cali
Ritz-Carlton, Grill
Ritz-Carlton, Rest.
Royal Rest.
Sam Woo
Seasons
Sushi Chalet
Tomokazu
Tony Cheng's
Velocity Grill
West End Cafe
West End Grill
White Tiger
Yokohama

Business Dining
Addie's
Artie's
Bombay Club
Cafe Promenade
Cesco
Daily Grill
DC Coast
El Catalan
Galileo
Gerard's Place
Hunan Lion
Hunan Lion II

Washington, D.C. Indexes

Kinkead's
Lespinasse
M & S Grill
Mark
Market St. B&G
Max's of Washington
McCormick & Schmick's
Melrose
Mezza 9
Monocle
Montgomery's Grille
Morrison-Clark Inn
Morton's of Chicago
Mr. K's
Occidental Grill
Old Ebbitt Grill
Oval Room
Palm
Pesce
P.F. Chang's
Prime Rib
Primi Piatti
Provence
Red Sage
Ritz-Carlton, Grill
Ritz-Carlton, Rest.
Sam & Harry's
Seasons
701
1789
Sostanza
Taberna del Alabardero
Tahoga
Taste of Saigon
Terrazza
T.H.A.I.
Thyme Square
Tivoli
Tragara
Vidalia
Villa Franco
Vintage
Warehouse B&G
West End Cafe
Willard Room
Zuki Moon

Caters

(Best of many)
Addie's
Aditi
Al Tiramisu
Amphora's Diner
Bacchus
Bombay Club
Bread Line
B. Smith's
Burrito Bros.
Burro
Cafe Bethesda
Cafe Marianna
C.F. Folks
Chicken Out
Citronelle
Dean & DeLuca
George Starke's
Germaine's
Hibiscus Cafe
Il Radicchio
Jasmine Cafe
Krupin's
La Madeleine
Lebanese Taverna
Le Bon Cafe
Listrani's
Louisiana Express
Mango Mike's
Mare e Monti
Old Glory BBQ
Parkway Deli
Pasha Cafe
Patisserie Cafe Didier
Peking Gourmet Inn
Primi Piatti
Raku
Red Hot & Blue
Ritz-Carlton, Grill
Rockland's
Sam Woo
Sea Catch
701
Silver Diner
Sushi-Ko
Tako Grill
Tara Thai
Taste of Saigon
Taverna Cretekou
Tel Aviv Cafe
Vidalia
Vox Populi
Willow Grove Inn
Xando
Zed's
Zuki Moon

Cigar Friendly

Barolo
Clyde's

131

Washington, D.C. Indexes

Fadó Irish Pub
Fellini
Les Halles
Martin's Tavern
McCormick & Schmick's
Morton's of Chicago
Palm
Prime Rib
Ruth's Chris
Sam & Harry's
Sesto Senso
Shelly's Woodroast
Taberna del Alabardero
Vintage

Dancing/Entertainment
(Check days, times and performers for entertainment; D=dancing; best of many)
Alamo (bands)
Andalucia (guitar/Spanish)
BET on Jazz (jazz)
Bistro Bistro (jazz)
Blue & Gold (blues/jazz)
Bombay Club (piano)
B. Smith's (jazz)
Clyde's (guitar/jazz)
Duangrat's (Thai dance)
Elysium (piano)
Evans Farm Inn (piano)
Evening Star Cafe (bands)
Fadó Irish Pub (Celtic)
Felix (D/DJ)
Fellini (D)
Fran O'Brien's (piano)
Gadsby's Tavern (D)
Galaxy (D)
Georgia Brown's (blues)
Ireland's 4 Courts (Irish)
Jefferson Rest. (D/jazz/piano)
King St. Blues (blues/jazz)
Kinkead's (piano)
Melrose (D)
Music City Roadhse. (blues/gospel)
Old Brogue Irish (varies)
Olde Towne Tavern (varies)
Old Europe (piano)
Old Glory BBQ (varies)
Paolo's (varies)
Perry's (varies)
Petitto's (opera)
Rhodeside Grill (varies)
Starland Cafe (varies)

Taberna del Alabardero (Spanish)
Tony & Joe's (varies)
Trattoria da Franco (piano)
Tuscana West (opera)
219 (jazz)
U-topia (jazz)
West End Cafe (piano)
Willard Room (piano)

Delivers*/Takeout
(Nearly all Asians, coffee shops, delis, diners and pasta/pizzerias deliver or do takeout; here are some interesting possibilities; D=delivery, T=takeout; *call to check range and charges, if any)
Addie's (T)
Andalucia (T)
Arucola (D,T)
Asia Nora (T)
Austin Grill (T)
Bacchus (T)
Bangkok Bistro (T)
Benjarong (D,T)
Bistro Bistro (D,T)
Bombay Bistro (D,T)
Bombay Club (T)
Bombay Palace (T)
Cafe Marianna (T)
Cafe Mileto (D,T)
Cafe Mozart (T)
Cafe Oggi (T)
Cafe Parisien (T)
California Tortilla (T)
Calvert Grille (T)
Capital Grille (T)
Capital Wrapps (D,T)
C.F. Folks (T)
Chicken Out (D,T)
Chicken Place (T)
"Ciao baby" Cucina (T)
City Lights of China (T)
Clyde's (T)
Cottonwood Ranch (T)
Crisfield (T)
Crisfield/Lee Plaza (T)
Crisp & Juicy (T)
Da Domenico (T)
Daily Grill (T)
Dean & DeLuca (D,T)
Duangrat's (T)

132

Washington, D.C. Indexes

Faryab (T)
Felix (T)
Fellini (T)
Filomena (T)
Firehook Bakery (T)
Gabriel (T)
Galileo (T)
George Starke's (T)
Georgetown Seafood (T)
Georgia Brown's (T)
Germaine's (T)
Goldoni (T)
Hard Times Cafe (T)
Hinode (T)
Hunter's Inn (T)
Il Pizzico (T)
Il Radicchio (T)
Il Ritrovo (T)
Jaleo (T)
Jerry Seafood (T)
La Brasserie (T)
La Chaumiere (T)
La Dolce Vita (T)
La Ferme (T)
Lebanese Taverna (T)
Legal Sea Food (T)
Le Gaulois (T)
Levante's (T)
Louisiana Express (D,T)
Luigino (T)
Mark (T)
Market St. B&G (T)
Martin's Tavern (T)
McCormick & Schmick's (T)
Memphis Bar-B-Q (D,T)
Metro Center Grille (T)
Old Brogue Irish (T)
Old Ebbitt Grill (T)
Old Europe (D,T)
Old Hickory Grill (T)
Oodles Noodles (T)
Pariolo (T)
Pasha Cafe (T)
Pasta Plus (T)
Patisserie Cafe Didier (T)
Perry's (T)
Pesce (T)
Phillips Seafood Grill (T)
Pizzeria Paradiso (T)
Red Hot & Blue (T)
Ricciuti's (T)
Rockland's (T)
R.T.'s (T)

R.T.'s Seafood (T)
Sushi-Ko (T)
Tako Grill (T)
Taste of Saigon (T)
Teaism (D,T)
Tomokazu (T)
Tony & Joe's (T)
219 (T)
Umberto's (T)
Vegetaria (T)
Vidalia (T)
Villa Franco (T)
Warehouse B&G (T)
West End Grill (T)
Wrap Works (T)
Xando (T)
Yosaku (T)
Zed's (T)

Dessert/Ice Cream
Addie's
Cheesecake Factory
Dean & DeLuca
Firehook Bakery
4 & 20 Blackbirds
Inn/Little Washington
Kinkead's
Melrose
Morrison-Clark Inn
Obelisk
Old Ebbitt Grill
Patisserie Cafe Didier
Samadi Sweets
Seasons
1789
Thyme Square
Tivoli
Tragara
Vidalia

Dining Alone
(Other than hotels, coffee shops, sushi bars and places with counter service)
Blue Plate
Bread Line
Carlyle Grand
C.F. Folks
Clyde's
Daily Grill
Dean & DeLuca
Jaleo
Kinkead's
Morrison-Clark Inn

Washington, D.C. Indexes

Old Ebbitt Grill
Pizzeria Paradiso
Raku
Red Sage
701
Teaism
Vidalia
Vienna Inn
Vintage
Vox Populi
Wrap Works

Family Style
Arucola
Evans Farm Inn
Maggiano's
Music City Roadhse.
That's Amore

Fireplaces
Al Tiramisu
Bilbo Baggins
Bleu Rock Inn
Chart House
4 & 20 Blackbirds
Indigo
Inn/Little Washington
Jefferson Rest.
La Chaumiere
La Ferme
La Madeleine
L'Auberge Chez Francois
L'Auberge Provencale
Le Gaulois
Mike Baker's 10th St.
Monocle
Morrison-Clark Inn
Normandie Farm
Old Angler's Inn
Olney Ale House
Polly's Cafe
Potowmack Landing
Red Sage
Ritz-Carlton, Grill
Ruth's Chris
Sea Catch
1789
Stone Manor
Tabard Inn
Trattoria da Franco
219
Willow Grove Inn

Health/Spa Menus
(Most places cook to order to meet any dietary request; call in advance to check; almost all Chinese, Indian and other ethnics have health-conscious meals, as do the following)
Andalucia
Burro
Cafe Atlantico
California Tortilla
Clyde's
La Ferme
Le Vieux Logis
Melrose
Morrison-Clark Inn
Seasons
Tako Grill
Thyme Square
Tragara
Vegetable Garden
Vegetaria

Historic Interest
(Year opened; *building)
1750 Alamo*
1753 L'Auberge Provencale
1778 Willow Grove Inn
1792 Gadsby's Tavern*
1800 Bilbo Baggins
1800 Santa Fe East
1856 Music City Roadhse.
1860 Old Angler's Inn
1860 1789*
1865 Morrison-Clark Inn*
1867 Martin's Tavern*
1887 Tabard Inn
1890 Rupperts
1904 Two Quail
1906 Olde Towne Tavern*
1908 B. Smith's*
1910 4 & 20 Blackbirds
1920 Olney Ale House

Hotel Dining
ANA Hotel
  Bistro
Ashby Inn
  Ashby Inn
Bleu Rock Inn
  Bleu Rock Inn
Capitol Hilton Hotel
  Fran O'Brien's

Washington, D.C. Indexes

Doubletree Park Terrace
  Chardonnay
Four Seasons Hotel
  Seasons
Hay-Adams Hotel
  Lafayette
Henley Park Hotel
  Coeur De Lion
Hilton Hotel
  Landini Bros.
Hyatt Arlington
  Mezza 9
Hyatt Hotel
  Market St. B&G
Inn at Little Washington
  Inn/Little Washington
Jefferson Hotel
  Jefferson Rest.
Latham Hotel
  Citronelle
L'Auberge Provencale
  L'Auberge Provencale
Loews L'Enfant Plaza
  American Grill
Marriott at Metro Center
  Metro Center Grille
Mayflower Hotel
  Cafe Promenade
Morrison-Clark Inn
  Morrison-Clark Inn
Morrison House Hotel
  Elysium
Park Hyatt Hotel
  Melrose
Radisson-Barcelo
  Gabriel
Ritz-Carlton/Pentagon City
  Ritz-Carlton, Grill
Ritz-Carlton/Tysons II
  Ritz-Carlton, Rest.
Sheraton Carlton Hotel
  Lespinasse
Tabard Inn
  Tabard Inn
Watergate Hotel
  Aquarelle
Westin Fairfax
  Jockey Club
Westin Hotel
  Cafe on M
Willard Hotel
  Willard Room
Willow Grove Inn
  Willow Grove Inn

"In" Places

Cafe Milano
Cafe Promenade
Capital Grille
Cashion's
Galileo
Germaine's
McCormick & Schmick's
Morton's of Chicago
New Heights
Nora
Obelisk
Old Brogue Irish
Olde Towne Tavern
Oval Room
Pesce
Pizzeria Paradiso
Provence
Rhodeside Grill
Ritz-Carlton, Rest.
R.T.'s
R.T.'s Seafood
Ruppers
Seasons
Sesto Senso
701
Tabard Inn
Tahoga
Tel Aviv Cafe
Vienna Inn
Villa Franco
Vintage

Late Late – After 12:30

(All hours are AM)
Au Pied du Cochon (24 hrs.)
Bistro Francais (3)
Bob & Edith's (24 hrs.)
Canton Cafe (1)
Carlyle Grand (1)
Coppi's (1)
Dave & Busters (1)
Dynasty (1:30)
El Tamarindo (2)
Fadó Irish Pub (2)
Full Kee (1)
Full Key (1:30)
Good Fortune (1)
Hard Rock Cafe (1)
Hollywood East (1)
Hunan Number One (1:45)
Kramerbooks (1)
Metro 29 (1)
Nulbom (1)

135

Washington, D.C. Indexes

Old Ebbitt Grill (1)
Olde Towne Tavern (1)
Paul Kee (1)
Polly's Cafe (1)
Seven Seas (1)
Silver Diner (2)
Tel Aviv Cafe (1)
Xando (1)

Meet for a Drink
(Most top hotels and the following standouts)
America
Artie's
BET on Jazz
Bistro Bistro
Cafe Atlantico
Cafe Milano
Capitol City Brewing
"Ciao baby" Cucina
Clyde's
Coco Loco
DC Coast
Fadó Irish Pub
Gabriel
McCormick & Schmick's
Melrose
Mendocino Grille
Mike's American
Montgomery's Grille
Old Brogue Irish
Old Ebbitt Grill
Olde Towne Tavern
Oval Room
Seasons
Sequoia
701
Shelly's Woodroast
Tabard Inn
Tahoga
Teaism
That's Amore
Vienna Inn
Vintage
West End Cafe
Xando

Noteworthy Newcomers (39)
Ardeo
Barolo
BET on Jazz
Bistro 123
Bread Line
Cesco
Charlie Chiang's
DC Coast
Dolcetto
El Catalan
Fadó Irish Pub
Fellini
Greenwood's
Hollywood East
Indigo
Le Petit Mistral
Levante's
Lewie's
Malibu Grill
M & S Grill
Mark
Max's of Washington
McCormick & Schmick's
Mezza 9
Mike Baker's 10th St.
On the Border
Persimmon
P.F. Chang's
Saigon Crystal
Soper's on M
Sostanza
Stardust
Tahoga
Tomokazu
Velocity Grill
Villa Franco
Vintage
Xando
Zuki Moon

Offbeat
Asia Nora
Bob & Edith's
Florida Ave. Grill
Germaine's
Hibiscus Cafe
Olney Ale House
Ruppert's
Tabard Inn
Teaism
U-topia
Vienna Inn

Outdoor Dining
(G=garden; P=patio; S=sidewalk; T=terrace; W=waterside)
Aangan (P)
Addie's (P)

136

Washington, D.C. Indexes

Aegean Taverna (S)
America (S)
Aroma (S)
Arucola (S)
Ashby Inn (P)
Bacchus (P)
Banana Cafe (S)
Bangkok Bistro (P)
BD's Mongolian (P)
BeDuCi (S)
Belmont Kitchen (S)
Bertolini's (S)
Bistro (P)
Bistro Bistro (S)
Bleu Rock Inn (T)
Bombay Club (S)
Bread Line (S)
Bua (P)
Busara (P)
Cactus Cantina (S)
Cafe Atlantico (S)
Cafe Berlin (P,S)
Cafe Bethesda (S)
Cafe Dalat (S)
Cafe Deluxe (S)
Cafe de Paris (S)
Cafe Marianna (G,S)
Cafe Milano (P,S)
Cafe Mileto (P,S)
Cafe Mozart (S)
Cafe New Delhi (P)
Cafe Roval (P)
Cafe Taj (P)
California Tortilla (P)
Carlyle Grand (P)
Cashion's (S)
Cesco (S)
C.F. Folks (P)
Chardonnay (G)
Chart House (P,W)
Clyde's (T)
Coco Loco (P)
Cottonwood Ranch (P)
Crystal Thai (T)
Dean & DeLuca (P)
District ChopHse. (S)
Dolcetto (P)
Donatello (T)
Duangrat's (S)
El Tamarindo (S)
Evans Farm Inn (G)
Faccia Luna (P)
Fedora Cafe (S)
Firehook Bakery (P)

Gabriel (P,S)
Gadsby's Tavern (P)
Galileo (P)
Georgetown Seafood (P)
Geppetto (P)
Gerard's Place (S)
Greenwood's (S)
Grill from Ipanema (T)
Gulf Coast Kitchen (T)
Hibiscus Cafe (P)
Hisago (P)
Hogate's (P,W)
Hunter's Inn (P)
Il Cigno (P)
Il Ritrovo (S)
Indigo (P)
Inn at Glen Echo (T)
Inn/Little Washington (P)
Ireland's 4 Courts (S)
Isabella (S)
Jasmine Cafe (T)
Kabul Caravan (T)
Kinkead's (S)
Kramerbooks (S)
La Brasserie (S)
La Colline (S,T)
La Cote d'Or Cafe (P)
La Ferme (G)
La Fourchette (S)
La Madeleine (P)
La Tomate (P)
L'Auberge Chez Francois (G)
L'Auberge Provencale (T)
Lauriol Plaza (S)
Le Bon Cafe (S)
Le Rivage (T)
Les Halles (P,S)
Levante's (P)
Le Vieux Logis (P)
Little Viet Garden (P)
Luigino (P)
Luna Grill (P)
Malibu Grill (P)
Mango Mike's (P)
Market St. B&G (P)
Melrose (G)
Mi Rancho (P)
Monroe's (P)
Montgomery's Grille (P)
Morton's of Chicago (T)
Mrs. Simpson's (P)
Music City Roadhse. (T)
Nam Viet (P)

137

Washington, D.C. Indexes

New Heights (S)
Old Angler's Inn (T)
Old Brogue Irish (P)
Olde Towne Tavern (T)
Olney Ale House (G)
On the Border (P)
Oodles Noodles (S)
Oval Room (S)
Paolo's (S)
Pariolo (T)
Perry's (T)
Phillips Seafood Grill (S,W)
Pho Cali (P)
Pizza de Resistance (P)
Polly's Cafe (S)
Primi Piatti (S)
Prince Michel (P)
Raku (S)
Red Sea (S)
Red Tomato Cafe (S)
Rhodeside Grill (S)
Rio Grande Cafe (P,S)
Riverside Grille (T,W)
Rock Bottom Brewery (S)
Ruth's Chris (S)
Saigon Crystal (P)
Saigon Gourmet (S)
Saigon Inn (S)
Saigonnais (P)
Santa Fe East (P)
Savory (P)
Sea Catch (P,W)
Sequoia (W)
701 (P)
Skewers/Cafe Luna (T)
Soper's on M (P)
Sostanza (S)
Southside 815 (S)
Starland Cafe (P)
Star of Siam (S,T)
Stella's (P)
Stone Manor (P)
Straits of Malaya (T)
Sweetwater Tavern (P)
Tabard Inn (G)
Taberna del Alabardero (P,S)
Tahoga (G)
Taste of Saigon (P)
Taverna Cretekou (G)
Tel Aviv Cafe (S)
Tempo (P)
Terrazza (T)
T.H.A.I. (S)
That's Amore (P,S)

Tia Queta (T)
Tivoli (P)
Tom Tom (S,T)
Tony & Joe's (T,W)
Trattoria da Franco (P,S)
Tunnicliff's Tavern (P,S)
Tuscana West (S)
219 (T)
Uncle Jed's (S)
Villa Franco (S)
Vox Populi (S)
Willow Grove Inn (T)
Xando (S)
Zuki Moon (P)

Outstanding Views

Bleu Rock Inn
Chart House
Il Cigno
L'Auberge Chez Francois
Le Rivage
New Heights
Perry's
Potowmack Landing
Roof Terrace
Ruth's Chris
Seasons
Sequoia
Tony & Joe's

Parking

(L=parking lot;
V=valet parking;
*=validated parking)
Aangan (L)
Aaranthi (L)
Addie's (L)
Aegean Taverna (L)
Akasaka (L,V)
Al Tiramisu (V)
America*
American Grill (V)
Amphora's Diner (L)
Andalucia (L)
Aquarelle (V)
Ardeo (V)
Artie's (L)
Asia Garden (L)
Asia Nora (L)
Atami (L)
Austin Grill (L)
A.V. Rist. Italiano (L)
Bacchus (V)
Bangkok Bistro (V)

Washington, D.C. Indexes

Bangkok St. Grill (L)
Barcelona (V)
BD's Mongolian (L)
BeDuCi (V)*
Benjarong
Bertolini's (L,V)
BET on Jazz (V)
Bistro (L)
Bistro Bistro (L)*
Bistro Francais (V)
Bistro 123 (L)
Bleu Rock Inn (V)
Blue & Gold*
Blue Ocean (L)
Bob & Edith's (L)
Bombay Bistro (L)
Bombay Club (V)
Bombay Palace*
B. Smith's*
Bugaboo Creek (L)
Buon Giorno*
Busara (V)
Cafe Atlantico (V)
Cafe Bethesda (V)
Cafe Deluxe (V)
Cafe de Paris (L)
Cafe Milano (V)*
Cafe Mileto (L)
Cafe Mozart*
Cafe New Delhi (V)
Cafe Oggi (L)
Cafe on M (L)
Cafe Parisien (L)
Cafe Promenade (V)*
Cafe Renaissance (L)
Cafe Roval (L)
Cafe Saigon (L)
Cafe Taj (L)
California Pizza Kit. (L)
Calvert Grille (L)*
Capital Grille (V)*
Carlyle Grand (L)
Cashion's (V)
Cedar Knoll Inn (L)
Cesco (V)
Chardonnay (L,V)*
Charley's Place (L)
Chicken Out (L)*
Chicken Place (L)
China Canteen (L)
Chris' (L)
Cities (V)
Citronelle (V)
Clyde's (L,V)*

Coco Loco (V)
Coeur De Lion (L)
Connaught Place (L)
Cottonwood Ranch (V)
Crisfield (L)
Crisfield/Lee Plaza (L)
Crisp & Juicy (L)
Crystal Thai (L)
Da Domenico (L)
Dante (L)
Dave & Busters (L)
DC Coast (V)
Dean & DeLuca (L)
Delhi Dhaba (L)
Del Ray Garden (V)
District ChopHse. (V)
Dolcetto (L)*
Donatello*
Duangrat's (L)
Dusit (L)
Ecco Cafe (L)*
El Catalan (V)
El Gavilan (L)
El Pollo Rico (L)
Elysium (V)
Evans Farm Inn (L)
Faccia Luna (L)
Fadó Irish Pub (V)
Fedora Cafe (L)
Felix (L)
Fellini*
Food Factory (L)
Foong Lin (L)*
Fortune (L)
4 & 20 Blackbirds (L)
Four Rivers (L)
Full Key (L)
Gabriel (L,V)*
Galaxy (L)
Galileo (V)
Generous George's (L)
Georgetown Seafood (V)
Georgia Brown's (V)
Geppetto (L)
Gerard's Place (V)
Germaine's (V)
Goldoni (L,V)
Greenfield Churrascaria (L)
Greenwood's (L)
Haandi (L)
Hard Times Cafe (L)
Hee Been (L)
Hinode (L)
Hisago (L)

139

Washington, D.C. Indexes

Hogate's*
Hollywood East (L)
Houston's (L,V)
Hunan Lion (L)
Hunan Number One (L)
Hunan Palace (L)
Hunter's Inn (L)
Ichiban (L)
Il Borgo (L)
Il Cigno (L)
Il Pizzico (L)
Il Ritrovo (L)
I Matti (V)
Indigo (L)
Inn at Glen Echo (L)
Isabella (V)
Jaleo*
Jasmine Cafe (L)
Jean-Michel (L)
Jefferson Rest.*
Jerry Seafood (L)
Jockey Club (V)
Kabul Caravan (L)
Kawasaki (L)*
Kazan (L)
Kinkead's (V)
La Bergerie*
La Brasserie (V)
La Chaumiere*
La Colline*
La Costa/Las Tapas (V)
La Cote d'Or Cafe (L)
La Dolce Vita (L)
Lafayette (V)
La Ferme (L)
La Madeleine (L)
La Miche (L)
Landini Bros.*
La Provence (L)
La Tomate (L)
L'Auberge Chez Francois (L)
Lauriol Plaza*
Lavandou*
Lebanese Taverna (L)
Legal Sea Food (V)
Le Gaulois (L)
Le Paradis (L)
Le Petit Mistral (L)
Le Rivage (V)
Les Halles (V)
Lespinasse (V)
Levante's (L)
Le Vieux Logis (V)
Lewie's (L)

Little Viet Garden (L)
Los Chorros (L)
Luna Grill (L)
Malibu Grill (L)
M & S Grill (V)
Mark*
Market St. B&G (L)
Martin's Tavern*
Matuba (L)
Max's of Washington (V)
McCormick & Schmick's (L,V)
Meadowlark Inn (L)
Mediterranee (L)
Melrose (L,V)
Memphis Bar-B-Q (L)
Mendocino Grille (V)
Metro Center Grille (L)*
Metro 29 (L)
Mezza 9 (V)
Mike's American (L)
Mi Rancho (L)
Miyagi (L)
Moby Dick (L)
Mongolian Grill (L)
Monroe's (L)
Montgomery's Grille (L)*
Morrison-Clark Inn (V)
Morton's of Chicago (L,V)*
Mr. K's (V)
Music City Roadhse.*
Mykonos (V)
Nam's (L,V)
Nam Viet (L)
New Heights (V)
Nizam's (L)
Nora (V)
Nulbom (L)
Occidental Grill*
Old Angler's Inn (L)
Old Brogue Irish (L)
Old Ebbitt Grill (V)*
Olde Towne Tavern (L)
Old Hickory Grill (L)
Olney Ale House (L)
Oriental Star (L)
Outback Steakhouse (L)
Oval Room (V)
Palm (V)
Panjshir (L)
Paolo's (L,V)
Paradise (L)
Pariolo (V)
Parkway Deli (L)
Pasha Cafe (L)

140

Washington, D.C. Indexes

Pasta Plus (L)
Paul Kee (L)
Peking Gourmet Inn (L)
Pesce (V)*
Phillips Seafood Grill (L)
Pho Cali (L)
Pho 95 (L)
Pho 75 (L)
Pilin Thai (L)
Pizza de Resistance (L)
Po Siam (L)
Potowmack Landing (L)
Prime Rib (V)
Primi Piatti (L,V)
Prince Michel (L)
Provence (V)
Rabieng (L)
Red Hot & Blue (L)
Red Sage*
Renato (L)
Rhodeside Grill (L)
Rio Grande Cafe (L)
Ritz-Carlton, Grill (V)
Ritz-Carlton, Rest. (V)
Rockland's (L)
Roof Terrace (L)
Royal Rest. (L)
R.T.'s Seafood (L)
Rupperts (L,V)
Ruth's Chris (V)
Sabang (L)
Saigon Gourmet (L)
Sam & Harry's (L,V)
Sam Woo (L)
Santa Fe East*
Savory (L)
Sea Catch (L)*
Seasons (L,V)
Sequoia (L)
Serbian Crown (L)
Sesto Senso (V)
701 (V)
Seven Seas (L)
1789 (V)
Shamshiry (L)
Shelly's Woodroast (L)
Silverado (L)
Silver Diner (L)
Sostanza (V)
Southside 815 (L)
Spices (L)
Star of Siam (L)
Stella's (L)*
Stone Manor (L)

Sunny Garden (L)
Sushi Chalet (L)
Sushi-Ko (V)
Sweetwater Tavern (L)
Taberna del Alabardero (L,V)
Tachibana (L)
Tahoga (V)
Taipei/Tokyo Cafe (L)
Tako Grill (L)
Tara Thai (L)
Taste of Saigon (L)
Tel Aviv Cafe (V)
Tempo (L)
Terrazza*
T.H.A.I.*
Thai Kingdom (L)
That's Amore (L)*
Thyme Square (L)
Tivoli (L)
Tomato Tango (L)
Tomokazu (L)
Tragara (V)
Trattoria da Franco*
Tsukiji (L)
Tuscana West (V)
Umberto's (L)
U-topia (L)
Vegetable Garden (L)
Vegetaria (L)
Veneziano (L)
Vidalia (V)
Vienna Inn (L)
Villa Franco (V)
Village Bistro (L)
Vox Populi (L)
Warehouse B&G (L)*
West End Cafe*
Willard Room (L,V)
Willow Grove Inn (L)
Woo Lae Oak (L)
Woomi Garden (L)
Wrap Works (L)
Wurzburg-Haus (L)
Zuki Moon (V)

Parties & Private Rooms
(Any nightclub or restaurant charges less at off-times; * indicates private rooms available; most top hotels and the following standouts)
Addie's
Alamo*
America*

Washington, D.C. Indexes

Bilbo Baggins*
Bleu Rock Inn*
B. Smith's*
Busara*
Cafe Milano*
Capital Grille*
Cities*
Clyde's*
Coco Loco*
Dolcetto*
Duangrat's*
Ecco Cafe*
Evans Farm Inn*
Felix*
Fortune*
Gabriel*
Gadsby's Tavern
Galileo*
Generous George's*
Germaine's*
I Matti
Indigo*
King St. Blues*
Kinkead's*
L'Auberge Chez Francois*
Les Halles*
Le Vieux Logis*
Luigino*
Nora*
Old Ebbitt Grill*
Oval Room*
Palm*
Peking Gourmet Inn*
Prime Rib
Primi Piatti*
Red Hot & Blue
Rhodeside Grill*
Ruppers*
Ruth's Chris*
Sam & Harry's*
Santa Fe East*
Sea Catch*
701*
1789*
Sostanza*
Stone Manor*
Taberna del Alabardero*
Tahoga*
That's Amore*
Tivoli*
Tragara*
219*
Two Quail*
Vidalia*
Xando*

People-Watching
America
Au Pied du Cochon
Austin Grill
Bob & Edith's
B. Smith's
Cafe Milano
Cashion's
Dean & DeLuca
Galileo
Georgia Brown's
Kinkead's
Mark
McCormick & Schmick's
Monocle
Morton's of Chicago
Nora
Old Ebbitt Grill
Olde Towne Tavern
Old Glory BBQ
Oval Room
Palm
Perry's
Red Sage
Red Tomato Cafe
Ruppers
Sam & Harry's
Seasons
Sequoia
701
Tahoga
T.H.A.I.
Tom Tom
Vintage

Power Scenes
Ardeo
Barolo
Bombay Club
B. Smith's
Capital Grille
Cesco
Citronelle
Daily Grill
DC Coast
El Catalan
Elysium
Galileo
Georgia Brown's
Germaine's
Inn/Little Washington
I Ricchi
Jefferson Rest.
Kinkead's

Washington, D.C. Indexes

La Brasserie
La Colline
M & S Grill
Max's of Washington
McCormick & Schmick's
Monocle
Morrison-Clark Inn
Morton's of Chicago
Nora
Old Ebbitt Grill
Oval Room
Palm
Prime Rib
Red Sage
Ritz-Carlton, Grill
Ritz-Carlton, Rest.
Rupperts
Ruth's Chris
Sam & Harry's
Seasons
701
1789
Taberna del Alabardero
Taste of Saigon
Vidalia
Villa Franco
Vintage
Willard Room

Pre-/Post-Theater Dining
(Call to check prices, days and times; best of many)
Aquarelle
Bistro Bistro
Bistro Francais
Bombay Club
Clyde's
Donatello
Le Rivage
McCormick & Schmick's
Old Ebbitt Grill
Tivoli
West End Cafe

Prix Fixe Menus
(Call to check prices, days and times; best of many)
Bacchus
BET on Jazz
Citronelle
Felix
Fiorentino's
Indigo
Jin-Ga
L'Auberge Chez Francois
Le Petit Mistral
Le Rivage
Morrison-Clark Inn
Obelisk
Oval Room
Prince Michel
701
1789
Stone Manor
Taberna del Alabardero
Tivoli
Willard Room

Pubs/Bars/Microbreweries
Blue & Gold
Clyde's
District ChopHse.
Fadó Irish Pub
Houston's
Inn at Glen Echo
John Harvard's
J. Paul's
King St. Blues
Martin's Tavern
Old Brogue Irish
Old Ebbitt Grill
Olde Towne Tavern
Olney Ale House
Polly's Cafe
Ramparts
Rock Bottom Brewery
R.T.'s
Southside 815
Sweetwater Tavern
Union St. Public Hse.
Vienna Inn
Virginia Bev. Co.

Quiet Conversation
Asia Nora
Bombay Club
Chardonnay
DC Coast
Dolcetto
Elysium
Melrose
Morrison-Clark Inn
New Heights
Obelisk
Patisserie Cafe Didier
Seasons
701

143

Washington, D.C. Indexes

Sostanza
Teaism
Terrazza
Zuki Moon

Raw Bars
Blue Point Grill
Clyde's
Georgetown Seafood
Hogate's
J. Paul's
Kinkead's
Legal Sea Food
Old Ebbitt Grill
Sea Catch

Reservations Essential
Bacchus
Bleu Rock Inn
Citronelle
Elysium
Germaine's
Inn/Little Washington
L'Auberge Chez Francois
L'Auberge Provencale
Nora
Obelisk
Palm
Prince Michel
Ritz-Carlton, Grill
Rupperts
Stone Manor
Taberna del Alabardero

Romantic Spots
Bombay Club
Citronelle
Coeur De Lion
Inn/Little Washington
L'Auberge Chez Francois
Le Refuge
Mrs. Simpson's
New Heights
Old Angler's Inn
1789
Straits of Malaya
Tahoga
Two Quail

Saturday Lunch – Best Bets
Aangan
Addie's
Aquarelle
Ardeo
Arucola

Austin Grill
Barcelona
Barolo
Belmont Kitchen
Bistro
Bistro Bistro
Bistrot Lepic
Blue Plate
Blue Point Grill
Bombay Palace
B. Smith's
Cactus Cantina
Cafe Deluxe
Cafe Marianna
Cafe Milano
Cafe Mileto
Cafe on M
Cafe Promenade
Cafe Taj
Calvert Grille
Capital Grille
Caravan Grill
Carlyle Grand
Cedar Knoll Inn
Chardonnay
Charley's Place
Charlie Chiang's
Cheesecake Factory
Citronelle
Clyde's
Daily Grill
Duangrat's
El Catalan
Elysium
Evans Farm Inn
Fadó Irish Pub
Filomena
Florida Ave. Grill
Gabriel
Gadsby's Tavern
George Starke's
Greenfield Churrascaria
Grill from Ipanema
Hard Times Cafe
Havana Cafe
Hunter's Inn
Il Radicchio
I Matti
Inn at Glen Echo
Jaleo
Jefferson Rest.
Jockey Club
J. Paul's
King St. Blues

144

Washington, D.C. Indexes

Kinkead's
Krupin's
La Bergerie
La Colline
La Costa/Las Tapas
La Cote d'Or Cafe
La Dolce Vita
Lafayette
Landini Bros.
La Provence
La Tomate
Lauriol Plaza
Legal Sea Food
Le Gaulois
Le Paradis
Les Halles
Lewie's
Listrani's
Luigino
Makoto
M & S Grill
Mango Mike's
Mark
Martin's Tavern
McCormick & Schmick's
Meadowlark Inn
Melrose
Mendocino Grille
Mike Baker's 10th St.
Mike's American
Mrs. Simpson's
Occidental Grill
Old Angler's Inn
Old Brogue Irish
Old Ebbitt Grill
Olde Towne Tavern
Old Hickory Grill
Olney Ale House
Paolo's
Paradise
Pasha Cafe
Patisserie Cafe Didier
Pesce
P.F. Chang's
Phillips Seafood Grill
Pizzeria Paradiso
Potowmack Landing
Rainforest Cafe
Red Hot & Blue
Red Sage
Red Tomato Cafe
Ricciuti's
Ritz-Carlton, Grill
Ritz-Carlton, Rest.

Rockland's
R.T.'s
Santa Fe East
Sea Catch
South Austin Grill
Tabard Inn
Tachibana
Tara Thai
Taste of Saigon
Taverna Cretekou
Teaism
T.H.A.I.
Thyme Square
Tomato Tango
Tony & Joe's
219
Union St. Public Hse.
Vienna Inn
Warehouse B&G

Sunday Dining – Best Bets
(B=brunch; L=lunch;
D=dinner; plus all hotels
and most Asians)
America (B,L)
Ardeo (B,D)
Artie's (B,L,D)
Austin Grill (B,L,D)
Belmont Kitchen (B,L,D)
Bilbo Baggins (B,D)
Bistro Bistro (B,D,L)
Bistrot Lepic (L,D)
Bleu Rock Inn (B,D)
Blue Plate (B,L,D)
Blue Point Grill (B,L,D)
Bombay Club (B,D)
B. Smith's (B,D)
Cafe Atlantico (D)
Cafe Deluxe (B,L,D)
Cafe Promenade (B,L,D)
Capital Grille (L,D)
Caravan Grill (L,D)
Carlyle Grand (B,L,D)
Cashion's (B,D)
Cheesecake Factory (B,L,D)
Clyde's (B,L,D)
Crisfield (L,D)
Crisfield/Lee Plaza (L,D)
Daily Grill (L,D)
Dave & Busters (L,D)
Duangrat's (L,D)
Ecco Cafe (B,L,D)
Evans Farm Inn (B,D)
Evening Star Cafe (B,D)

145

Washington, D.C. Indexes

Fadó Irish Pub (L,D)
Felix (B,D)
Filomena (L,D)
Georgia Brown's (B,D)
Greenfield Churrascaria (L,D)
Greenwood's (D)
Il Radicchio (L)
Indigo (B,D)
Inn at Glen Echo (B,D)
Jaleo (L,D)
Kinkead's (B,L,D)
Kramerbooks (B,D)
La Brasserie (B,L,D)
La Cote d'Or Cafe (B,L,D)
La Dolce Vita (L,D)
Lauriol Plaza (L,D)
Les Halles (L,D)
Levante's (L,D)
Luigino (L,D)
M & S Grill (D)
Mark (B,D)
McCormick & Schmick's (B,L,D)
Meadowlark Inn (L,D)
Mediterranee (B)
Mike's American (L,D)
Music City Roadhse. (B,D)
New Heights (B,D)
Occidental Grill (L,D)
Old Angler's Inn (B,L,D)
Old Brogue Irish (B,L,D)
Old Ebbitt Grill (B,L,D)
Olde Towne Tavern (B,L,D)
Old Glory BBQ (B,L,D)
Old Hickory Grill (L,D)
Olney Ale House (L,D)
Paolo's (B,L,D)
Perry's (B,D)
Pesce (D)
P.F. Chang's (L,D)
Phillips Seafood Grill (B,D,L)
Pizzeria Paradiso (L,D)
Polly's Cafe (B,D)
Potowmack Landing (B,L,D)
Rainforest Cafe (L,D)
Ramparts (L,D)
Red Hot & Blue (L,D)
Rhodeside Grill (B,D)
Rio Grande Cafe (B,D)
Roof Terrace (B,D)
Sam & Harry's (L,D)
Sequoia (B,D)
South Austin Grill (B,L,D)
Stardust (B,D)
Starland Cafe (B,D)

Tachibana (L,D)
Tara Thai (B,L,D)
Taste of Saigon (B,L,D)
Taverna Cretekou (B,L,D)
Thyme Square (L,D)
Tony & Joe's (B,L,D)
219 (B,L,D)
Union St. Public Hse. (B,L,D)
Villa Franco (D)
Warehouse B&G (B,L,D)
Willow Grove Inn (B,D)

Singles Scenes
Artie's
Austin Grill
Cafe Atlantico
Cafe Deluxe
Cafe Milano
"Ciao baby" Cucina
Coco Loco
Fedora Cafe
Fellini
J. Paul's
Mango Mike's
Mike's American
Montgomery's Grille
Olde Towne Tavern
Old Glory BBQ
Perry's
Red Tomato Cafe
Rhodeside Grill
Sequoia
Sesto Senso
Sweetwater Tavern
Tom Tom
Tony & Joe's
Tuscana West
Union St. Public Hse.
U-topia
Xando

Sleepers
(Good to excellent food, but little known)
Bistro 123
Cafe de Paris
Cafe Marianna
Cafe Mileto
Cafe New Delhi
Cafe Taj
Del Ray Garden
Elysium
Galaxy
Hautam Kebobs

Washington, D.C. Indexes

Hollywood East
Jerry Seafood
Jin-Ga
Kabul Caravan
Kawasaki
Majestic
Mare e Monti
Miyagi
Old Hickory Grill
Paradise
Pho Cali
Ricciuti's
Sakana
Sushi Sushi
Tomokazu
Willow Grove Inn
Yokohama

Teflons
(Get lots of business, despite so-so food, i.e. they have other attractions that prevent criticism from sticking)
America
Amphora's Diner
Au Pied du Cochon
Blue & Gold
Bugaboo Creek
Capitol City Brewing
Dave & Busters
Evans Farm Inn
Hard Rock Cafe
Hogate's
Montgomery's Grille
Planet Hollywood
Rainforest Cafe
Rock Bottom Brewery
Shelly's Woodroast
Silver Diner

Smoking Prohibited
(May be permissible at bar or outdoors)
Aangan
Addie's
BD's Mongolian
Bread Line
Cafe Bethesda
Cafe de Paris
Cafe Marianna
Cesco
Dolcetto
Gadsby's Tavern
Generous George's
Good Fortune
Greenfield Churrascaria
Haandi
Hinode
Jean-Michel
Levante's
Le Vieux Logis
Mi Rancho
Miyagi
Mongolian Grill
Montgomery's Grille
Obelisk
Olney Ale House
Original Pancake Hse.
Pizzeria Paradiso
Queen Bee
Rainforest Cafe
Raku
Ricciuti's
Rupperts
Stone Manor
Tako Grill
Teaism
Terrazza
Thyme Square
Tragara
Vegetable Garden
Vegetaria

Teas
Aquarelle
Coeur De Lion
Elysium
Jefferson Rest.
Lafayette
Lespinasse
Melrose
Morrison-Clark Inn
Patisserie Cafe Didier
Seasons
Teaism

Transporting Experiences
Bistrot Lepic
Dave & Busters
El Catalan
Hard Rock Cafe
Inn/Little Washington
Makoto
Planet Hollywood
Rainforest Cafe
Stone Manor
Tara Thai
Taverna Cretekou

Washington, D.C. Indexes

Visitors on Expense Accounts
Ardeo
Capital Grille
DC Coast
El Catalan
Elysium
Galileo
Lespinasse
M & S Grill
Max's of Washington
Melrose
Morton's of Chicago
Mr. K's
Old Angler's Inn
Palm
Prime Rib
Provence
Red Sage
Ritz-Carlton, Grill
Ritz-Carlton, Rest.
Rupperts
Ruth's Chris
Sam & Harry's
Seasons
Serbian Crown
701
1789
Soper's on M
Sostanza
Stone Manor
Taberna del Alabardero
Vidalia
Villa Franco
Vintage
Willard Room

Wheelchair Access
(Most places now have wheelchair access; call in advance to check)

Winning Wine Lists
Ashby Inn
Bistro Francais
Cashion's
Chardonnay
Citronelle
Galileo
Gerard's Place
Inn/Little Washington
Kinkead's
La Ferme
L'Auberge Chez Francois
Lespinasse
Melrose
Mendocino Grille
Morrison-Clark Inn
Morton's of Chicago
Obelisk
Palm
Prime Rib
Prince Michel
Rhodeside Grill
Rupperts
Ruth's Chris
Sam & Harry's
Seasons
Sostanza
Taberna del Alabardero
Tivoli
Vidalia
Vintage

Worth a Trip
MARYLAND
Glen Echo
   Inn at Glen Echo
Middletown
   Stone Manor
Potomac
   Old Angler's Inn
VIRGINIA
Flint Hill
   4 & 20 Blackbirds
Great Falls
   L'Auberge Chez Francois
Leon
   Prince Michel
Orange
   Willow Grove Inn
Paris
   Ashby Inn
Washington
   Bleu Rock Inn
   Inn/Little Washington
White Post
   L'Auberge Provencale

Young Children
(Besides the normal fast-food places; * indicates children's menu available)
Arucola
Austin Grill
Bertucci's*
Cactus Cantina
Calvert Grille

148

Washington, D.C. Indexes

Chart House*
Clyde's*
Dave & Busters
Evans Farm Inn
Generous George's
Hard Rock Cafe
Hard Times Cafe
Lebanese Taverna
Listrani's
Matuba

Olney Ale House
Original Pancake Hse.
Planet Hollywood
Rainforest Cafe
Red Hot & Blue
Rio Grande Cafe
Silver Diner
Tara Thai
T.H.A.I.
Union St. Public Hse.

Baltimore

Baltimore's Favorites

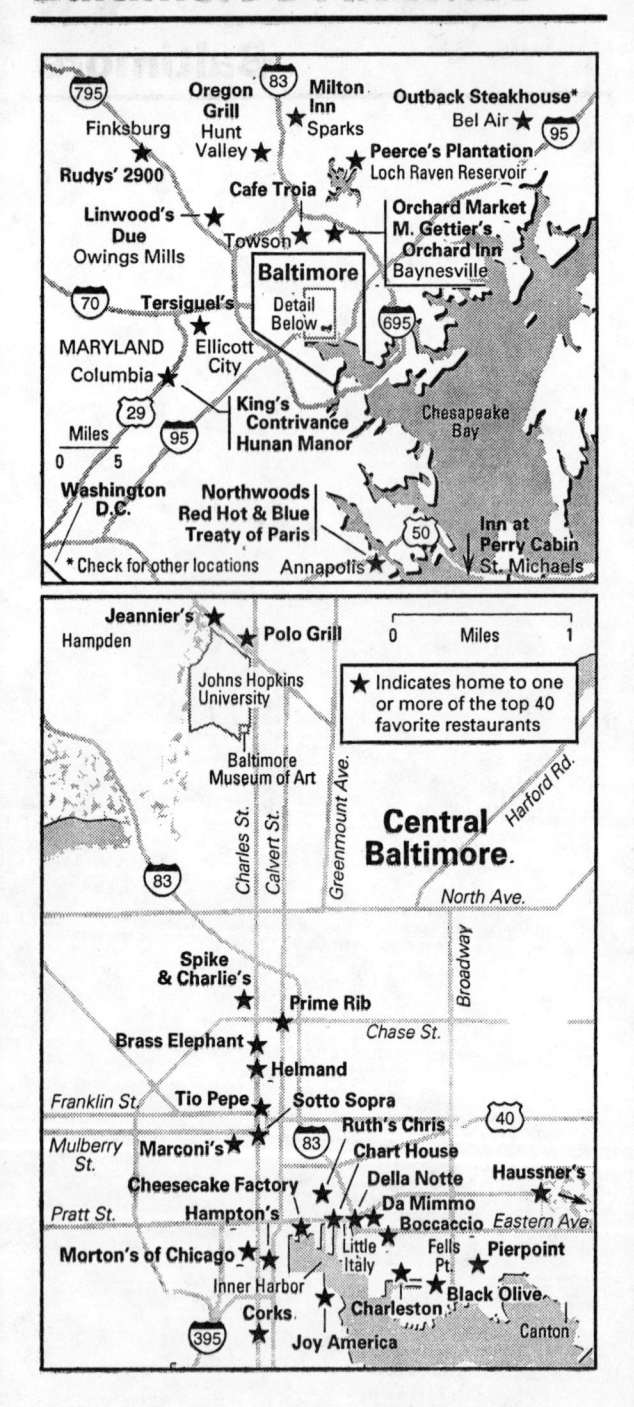

Baltimore (Detail Below)

- Oregon Grill — Hunt Valley
- Milton Inn — Sparks
- Outback Steakhouse* — Bel Air
- Finksburg (795)
- (83)
- Peerce's Plantation — Loch Raven Reservoir
- (95)
- Rudys' 2900
- Cafe Troia
- Linwood's Due — Owings Mills
- Towson
- Orchard Market, M. Gettier's, Orchard Inn — Baynesville
- (70)
- Tersiguel's
- (695)
- MARYLAND
- Columbia
- Ellicott City
- Chesapeake Bay
- (29)
- (95)
- King's Contrivance
- Hunan Manor
- Miles 0 — 5
- Washington D.C.
- Northwoods, Red Hot & Blue, Treaty of Paris
- (50)
- Inn at Perry Cabin — St. Michaels
- Annapolis

*Check for other locations

Central Baltimore

- Jeannier's — Hampden
- Polo Grill
- Johns Hopkins University
- Baltimore Museum of Art
- Charles St.
- Calvert St.
- Greenmount Ave.
- Harford Rd.
- (83)
- North Ave.
- Spike & Charlie's
- Prime Rib
- Brass Elephant
- Chase St.
- Helmand
- Broadway
- Franklin St.
- Tio Pepe
- Sotto Sopra
- Ruth's Chris
- Chart House
- (40)
- Mulberry St.
- Marconi's
- (83)
- Della Notte
- Haussner's
- Cheesecake Factory
- Da Mimmo
- Pratt St.
- Hampton's
- Boccaccio
- Eastern Ave.
- Morton's of Chicago
- Little Italy
- Fells Pt.
- Pierpoint
- Inner Harbor
- Corks
- Charleston
- Black Olive
- Canton
- (395)
- Joy America

0 — Miles — 1

★ Indicates home to one or more of the top 40 favorite restaurants

152

Baltimore's Favorite Restaurants

Each of our reviewers has been asked to name his or her five favorite restaurants. The 40 spots most frequently named, in order of their popularity, are:

1. Tio Pepe
2. Prime Rib
3. Linwood's
4. Ruth's Chris
5. Cheesecake Factory
6. Polo Grill
7. Hampton's
8. Morton's of Chicago
9. Brass Elephant
10. Boccaccio
11. Helmand
12. Outback Steakhouse
13. Haussner's
14. Charleston
15. Joy America
16. Jeannier's
17. Della Notte
18. Oregon Grill*
19. Tersiguel's*
20. M. Gettier's Orchard Inn
21. Rudys' 2900*
22. Red Hot & Blue/A
23. Spike & Charlie's
24. Pierpoint
25. Inn at Perry Cabin/A
26. Due
27. Sotto Sopra
28. Cafe Troia
29. Marconi's
30. Corks
31. Peerce's Plantation
32. Northwoods/A
33. Da Mimmo
34. Orchard Market*
35. Milton Inn
36. King's Contrivance/C
37. Treaty of Paris/A*
38. Black Olive
39. Chart House*
40. Hunan Manor/C*

It's obvious that most of the restaurants on the above list are among the most expensive, but Baltimore diners love a bargain. Were popularity calibrated to price, we suspect that a number of other restaurants would join the above ranks. Thus, we have listed over 130 "Best Buys" on pages 158 and 159.

A = Annapolis/Eastern Shore, C = Columbia.
* Tied in score with the restaurant listed directly above it.

153

Top Ratings*

Top 40 Food Ranking

28 Prime Rib
27 Hampton's
Linwood's
208 Talbot/A
Charleston
Inn at Perry Cabin/A
26 Milton Inn
Lenny's Chop House
Lewnes' Steakhouse/A
Boccaccio
Rudys' 2900
Black Olive
Polo Grill
Morton's of Chicago
25 Helmand
Tersiguel's
Pierpoint
La Piccola Roma/A
Hamilton's
Matsuri

Tio Pepe
Northwoods/A
Brass Elephant
24 Peter's Inn
Antrim 1844
Da Mimmo
Ruth's Chris
Oregon Grill
Hunan Manor/C
Joy America
Orchard Market
Corks
Thai
Jeannier's
Narrows/A
Brighton's
Michael Rork's/A
23 Banjara
Harry Browne's/A
Due

Top Spots by Cuisine

Top American
26 Milton Inn
24 Oregon Grill
Narrows/A
Brighton's
23 Marconi's

Top American (New)
27 Hampton's
Linwood's
208 Talbot/A
Charleston
26 Polo Grill

Top Asian/Pan-Asian
23 Purple Orchid
22 Cafe Zen
21 Hoang's
Thai Orient
20 Orient

Top Breakfast**
23 Morning Edition
20 Blue Moon Cafe
Woman's Ind. Exch.
19 One World Cafe
16 Cafe Hon

Top Brunch
27 Hampton's
26 Polo Grill
25 Pierpoint
24 Joy America
23 Morning Edition

Top Business Lunch
27 Linwood's
26 Boccaccio
Polo Grill
25 Helmand
La Piccola Roma/A

---

* Excluding restaurants with low voting.
** Other than hotels.
A = Annapolis/Eastern Shore, C = Columbia.

Top Chinese
- *24* Hunan Manor/C
- *22* Szechuan Best
  Cafe Zen
  Jumbo Seafood
- *21* Tony Cheng's

Top Continental
- *27* Inn at Perry Cabin/A
- *26* Rudys' 2900
- *25* Tio Pepe
  Northwoods/A
  Brass Elephant

Top Crab Houses
- *22* Cantler's Riverside/A
- *21* Crab Claw/A
  Obrycki's
- *20* Bo Brooks Crab Hse.
- *19* Harris Crab Hse./A

Top Family Dining
- *22* Cantler's Riverside/A
- *21* Cheesecake Factory
- *20* Friendly Farms
- *19* Tomato Palace/C
- *16* Baugher's

Top French
- *25* Tersiguel's
- *24* Jeannier's
- *23* Purple Orchid
- *21* Martick's
- *20* Cafe Normandie/A

Top Hotel Dining
- *27* Hampton's/
  Harbor Court Hotel
  Inn at Perry Cabin/
  Inn at Perry Cabin/A
- *26* Polo Grill/
  Inn at the Colonnade
- *24* Brighton's/
  Harbor Court Hotel
- *23* Corinthian/
  Loews Annapolis/A

Top Indian
- *23* Banjara
  Bombay Grill
- *22* Mughal Garden
- *21* Ambassador Din. Rm.
- *20* Akbar

Top Italian
- *26* Boccaccio
- *25* La Piccola Roma/A
- *24* Da Mimmo
- *23* Due
  Cafe Troia

Top Japanese
- *25* Matsuri
- *21* Hoang's
  Kawasaki*
  Nichi Bei Kai
- *20* Sushi-Ya

Top Newcomers/Rated
- *27* Charleston
- *26* Lenny's Chop House
  Black Olive
- *25* Hamilton's
- *24* Oregon Grill

Top Newcomers/Unrated
- Cafe Madrid
- ESPN Zone
- McCormick & Schmick's
- Shula's Steak House
- SoBo Cafe

Top Seafood
- *26* Black Olive
- *25* Pierpoint
- *24* Narrows/A
  Michael Rork's/A
- *22* Cantler's Riverside/A

Top Steakhouses
- *28* Prime Rib
- *26* Lenny's Chop House
  Lewnes' Steakhouse/A
  Morton's of Chicago
- *24* Ruth's Chris

Top Vegetarian
- *23* Margaret's Cafe
- *21* Wild Mushroom
- *20* Liquid Earth**
  Puffins/Sin Carne
- *19* One World Cafe

Top Worth a Trip
- *27* 208 Talbot/
  St. Michaels, MD
  Inn at Perry Cabin/
  St. Michaels, MD
- *24* Antrim 1844/
  Taneytown, MD
  Michael Rork's/
  St. Michaels, MD
- *22* Tilghman Island Inn**/
  Tilghman Island, MD

---

* Tied in score with the restaurant listed directly above it.
** Low votes.

Top 40 Decor Ranking

28 Hampton's
Inn at Perry Cabin/A
Antrim 1844
27 Lenny's Chop House
Oregon Grill
26 Brighton's
Brass Elephant
Milton Inn
Linwood's
25 Charleston
Prime Rib
Elkridge Furnace Inn
Polo Grill
24 Joy America
Haussner's
Brewer's Art
Sotto Sopra
23 208 Talbot/A
Boccaccio
King's Contrivance

Hamilton's
Corinthian/A
Windows*
Treaty of Paris/A
Tersiguel's
Robert Morris Inn/A
22 Due
Owl Bar
Peerce's Plantation
Ruth's Chris
Della Notte
Carrol's Creek Cafe/A
Northwoods/A
Troia at The Walters
Ruby Lounge
Ambassador Din. Rm.
Morton's of Chicago
Rudys' 2900
Narrows/A
Tio Pepe

Top Outdoor

Ambassador Din. Rm.
Cantler's Riverside/A
Carrol's Creek Cafe/A
Chart House/A
Cheesecake Factory
Inn at Perry Cabin/A
J. Leonard's Waterside
Joy America
McGarvey's/A

Middleton Tavern/A
Oregon Grill
Paolo's
Peerce's Plantation
Piccolo's
River Watch
Rusty Scupper
Sanders' Corner
Windows on the Bay

Top Rooms

Antrim 1884
Brass Elephant
Hampton's
Haussner's
Inn at Perry Cabin/A

McCormick & Schmick's
Polo Grill
Prime Rib
Sotto Sopra
Troia at the Walters

Top Views

Baldwins Station
Bay Cafe
Carrol's Creek Cafe/A
Chart House/A
Hampton's
Inn at Perry Cabin/A
Joy America
McCormick & Schmick's

Michael Rork's/A
Narrows/A
Peerce's Plantation
Piccolo's
Pisces
Rusty Scupper
Tilghman Island Inn/A
Windows

---

* Tied in score with the restaurant listed directly above it.

Top 40 Service Ranking

- **27** Hampton's
- **26** Inn at Perry Cabin/A
  Charleston
- **25** Prime Rib
  Antrim 1844
  Linwood's
  Milton Inn
- **24** Marconi's
  Polo Grill
  Brass Elephant
  208 Talbot/A
  Boccaccio
  Tersiguel's
  Brighton's
  Rudys' 2900
- **23** Morton's of Chicago
  Northwoods/A
  Lenny's Chop House
  La Piccola Roma/A
  Harry Browne's/A

Ruth's Chris
Helmand
Banjara
Corinthian/A
- **22** Due
  Tio Pepe
  Helen's Garden
  Ambassador Din. Rm.
  Purple Orchid
  Michael Rork's/A
  Oregon Grill
  Jeannier's
  Joy America
  Peerce's Plantation
  Corks
  Da Mimmo
  Haussner's
  Elkridge Furnace Inn
  Hamilton's
  Margaret's Cafe

157

Best Buys

Top 100 Bangs For The Buck

This list reflects the best dining values in our *Survey*. It is produced by dividing the cost of a meal into the combined ratings for food, decor and service.

1. One World Cafe
2. Attman's Deli
3. Woman's Ind. Exch.
4. Margaret's Cafe
5. Rallo's
6. Holy Frijoles
7. Adrian's Book Cafe
8. Jimmy's
9. Helen's Garden
10. Canopy
11. Ze Mean Bean Café
12. Baugher's
13. Chick & Ruth's/A
14. Duda's Tavern
15. PaperMoon Diner
16. Cafe Zen
17. City Cafe
18. Desert Cafe
19. Café Pangea
20. Peter's Inn
21. Nick's Inner Harbor
22. Double T Diner
23. Morning Edition
24. Nacho Mama's
25. Blue Moon Cafe
26. New Towne Diner
27. Hunan Manor/C
28. Al Pacino Cafe
29. Faidley's
30. Sanders' Corner
31. Cafe Hon
32. Banjara
33. Thai Orient
34. Szechuan Best
35. Mr. Chan's
36. Thai
37. Hull St. Blues
38. Silver Diner
39. Bill Bateman's
40. Claddagh Pub
41. Donna's
42. Bandaloops
43. Helmand
44. Tomato Palace/C
45. Ban Thai
46. Jumbo Seafood
47. Louie's Bookstore
48. Mama Lucia
49. Bertucci's
50. Romano's Macaroni
51. Orient
52. Thai Landing
53. No Way Jose
54. Akbar
55. Orchard Market
56. John Steven, Ltd.
57. Bangkok Place
58. Sushi-Ya
59. Mughal Garden
60. Ambassador Din. Rm.
61. Friendly Farms
62. California Pizza Kit.
63. Loco Hombre
64. New No Da Ji
65. Zorba's B&G
66. Red Hot & Blue/A
67. Alonso's
68. Bombay Grill
69. Perring Place
70. Ram's Head Tavern/A
71. Tenosix
72. Amicci's
73. Ransome's Harbor Hill
74. Buddy's Crabs & Ribs/A
75. Bahama Mamas
76. Griffin's/A
77. River Watch
78. Matsuri
79. Cheesecake Factory
80. Cantler's Riverside/A
81. Regi's
82. Casa Mia's
83. Bertha's
84. McCabe's
85. Della Notte
86. Hard Rock Cafe
87. Ralphie's Diner
88. Henninger's Tavern
89. Bare Bones
90. Haussner's
91. Bamboo Hse.
92. Owl Bar
93. Sisson's
94. Ellicott Mills
95. Vito's Cafe
96. McGarvey's/A
97. Capitol City Brewing
98. Wild Mushroom
99. Ikaros
100. Tony Cheng's

A = Annapolis/Eastern Shore, C = Columbia.

Additional Good Values
(A bit more expensive, but worth every penny)

Acropolis
Angler/A
Anne Arundel Seafood
Braznell's
Cafe Bretton
Calvert House
Ciao/A
Fazzini's
G & M
Giolitti Deli/A
Golden Gate Noodle Hse.
Golden West Cafe
Grand Palace
Holly's/A
Kelly's
Kelsey's
Liquid Earth
Mamie's
Mangia Mangia
Nam Kang
Olive Grove
Purim Oak
Rotisseria
Saigon Palace/A
Samos
San Sushi
Silk Road
SoBo Cafe
Surfin' Bull
Suzie's Soba
Vera's Bakery/A
Wolford's Bakery

Alphabetical Directory of Baltimore, Annapolis and the Eastern Shore Restaurants

Baltimore

F	D	S	C

Acropolis — | — | — | M
4714-4718 Eastern Ave. (Oldham St.), 410-675-3384
An "excellent value in the heart of Greektown", this Hellenic offers overwhelming servings of grilled fish and lamb that are matched by generous hospitality from a family that is "really pleased to serve you"; "recently remodeled", its crisp blue-and-white decor is an added draw.

Adam's Ribs S 19 | 11 | 18 | $21
589 Baltimore-Annapolis Blvd. (McKinsey Rd.), Severna Park, 410-647-5757
See review in Annapolis and Eastern Shore Directory.

Adrian's Book Cafe S 16 | 17 | 15 | $11
714 S. Broadway (bet. Aliceanna & Lancaster Sts.), 410-732-1048
◪ "Flirting" is one way to "get better service" and relieve the boredom of the "same old" "sprouty fare" at this Fells Point bookstore/cafe; other diversions include desserts, "local musicians" and a "funky, '50s revisited" "living room atmosphere" that is most appealing to those too young to have experienced the real thing.

Akbar S 20 | 15 | 19 | $18
823 N. Charles St. (bet. Madison & Read Sts.), 410-539-0944
Columbia Mktpl., 9400 Snowden River Pkwy. (Rte. 175), Columbia, 410-381-3600
3541 Brenbrook Dr. (Liberty Rd.), Randallstown, 410-655-1600
■ "Indian food is 'in' now", due, in part, to this "reasonable", "reliable" Mt. Vernon subcontinental (and its suburban offshoot); for years, this forerunner has provided a "cozy environment" for private discussions; N.B. the Randallstown branch is now independently owned.

Alonso's S 15 | 7 | 13 | $13
415 W. Cold Spring Ln. (Keswick Rd.), 410-235-3433
■ This "Roland Park landmark" is being absorbed into Loco Hombre next door; although its name will stay on the door, the "world-class bar food" menu will be Mediterranean-ized; reports are that the one-pound-plus "deathburger" will be spared, but the fate of its "great garlic pizza" is up for grabs.

Al Pacino Cafe S 18 | 12 | 16 | $13
Lake Forest Village, 6084 Falls Rd. (Lake Ave.), 410-377-3132 (carryout/delivery only)
Al Pacino Cafe/Cafe Isis S
900 Cathedral St. (Read St.), 410-962-8859
12240 W. Padonia Rd. (York Rd.), Cockeysville, 410-666-4888

Baltimore | F | D | S | C |

Al Pacino Cafe/Cafe Isis (Cont.)
Festival at Woodholme, 1809 Reisterstown Rd. (Hooks Ln.), Pikesville, 410-653-6868
Egyptian Pizza S
Belvedere Sq., 542 E. Belvedere Ave. (York Rd.), 410-323-7060
Nile Cafe S
811 S. Broadway (bet. Lancaster & Thomas Sts.), 410-327-0005
■ Besides giving pizza a Mediterranean "twist", these Egyptian sibs serve some of Baltimore's best Middle Eastern food, including "fantastic vegetarian platters" and kebabs; while a number have some of the area's most "cramped", dispiriting settings ("sit near the window"), Cockeysville actually has some ambiance, but here, as at some of its other offshoots, servers can "bond with you" or act "indifferent."

Ambassador Dining Room S | 21 | 22 | 22 | $23 |
3811 Canterbury Rd. (University Pkwy.), 410-366-1484
■ Unexpectedly, this grande dame dining room "has come alive" as the perfect "British Empire" setting for some very good, "refined" Anglo-Indian food; one of the most "beautiful" gardens anywhere, "gracious" hosts and a value-laden lunch buffet bring words like "worthy" and "superior" to mind.

Amicci's S | 19 | 13 | 18 | $18 |
231 S. High St. (bet. Fawn & Stiles Sts.), 410-528-1096
◪ Trading on its "hole-in-the-wall" Little Italy location, "cute" props and "Sinatra crooning in the background", this trendy Italian keeps the "party" going with "cheap", "heavy on the garlic and tomato" sauce staples; however, the less enthused counter "its casual atmosphere results in food that is casually prepared."

Angelina's S | 19 | 11 | 17 | $22 |
7135 Harford Rd. (Rosalie Ave.), 410-444-5545
■ It sounds like heresy to ignore this Northeast Baltimore Irish-Italian saloon's main claim to culinary fame, but if you "look past" its legendary crab cakes ("the biggest and maybe the best in the world"), you'll find some really "good bar food served by real hons"; insiders advise you to treat its "blue-collar atmosphere" as "an attraction in its own right."

Anne Arundel Seafood S | ▽ 20 | 7 | 15 | $14 |
230 Mountain Rd. (Solley Rd.), Pasadena, 410-255-3344
■ Chesapeake Bay–bound boaters, "neighborhood" families and biz lunchers "share picnic tables" on this Pasadena seafood outlet's vast enclosed porch for the sake of "wonderful all-lump crab cakes", raw bar fare and choose-your-own, fried-to-order fish; its self-serve, "eat and get out'" ethic is counterbalanced by the fact that you get "plenty of seafood" "fast" and cheap.

Baltimore | F | D | S | C |

ANTRIM 1844 COUNTRY INN S | 24 | 28 | 25 | $53 |
Antrim 1844 Country Inn, 30 Trevanion Rd. (Rte. 140), Taneytown, 410-756-6812
■ Butlers serving "hors d'oeuvres while you wander" through magnificent rooms with "antiques, flowers and fireplaces", as well as the "lovely gardens" of this "gorgeous" restoration near Gettysburg, set the tone for a prix fixe New American meal; a few wallet-watchers warn that unless you "go with someone special", the evening may not be "worth the price and the drive."

A-1 Crab Haven | 16 | 10 | 17 | $21 |
1600 Old Eastern Ave. (Back River Neck Rd.), 410-687-6000
◪ "Stick with the steamed crabs" and "great Greek salad" at this old-line Essex seafooder; crabby types carp the rest of the fare is only "so-so" and the "decor is dated."

Ashley M's ☾S | – | – | – | M |
911 N. Charles St. (bet. Eager & Read Sts.), 410-837-2424
In his fledgling second-story boîte on North Charles Street, Ed Rogers, chef-owner of La Tesso Tana, serves his trademark amalgam of Italian and rich tasting American classics, with an emphasis on wild game; named after his young daughter, the place has charming vibes.

Attman's Delicatessen S | 22 | 8 | 16 | $9 |
1019 E. Lombard St. (bet. Central Ave. & Fallsway), 410-563-2666
◪ "Appropriately tacky", this Lombard Street relic still "smells [and acts] like a deli" – "who else serves a kosher dog with fried baloney", stacks its "amazing" corned beef "high" and respects chutzpah (its own and its customers')? but the neighborhood is "lousy", so devotees declare "don't linger"; delivery is the other option.

Austin Grill S | 18 | 17 | 18 | $18 |
American Can Co., 2400 Boston St. (Hudson St.), 410-534-0606
See review in Washington, DC Directory.

Azeb's Ethiopian S | ▽ 20 | 14 | 21 | $16 |
322 N. Charles St. (bet. Mulberry & W. Saratoga Sts.), 410-625-9787
■ Adventuresome Charles Street diners find it "fun to eat with fingers Ethiopian-style", scooping up spicy stews with spongy bread; this "exotic" fare is served in an airy space that's suitable for business dining but, upstairs, "traditional" low stools make for a more casual mood.

Bahama Mamas S | 17 | 11 | 16 | $16 |
601 Wise Ave. (bet. Merritt Blvd. & North Point Rd.), 410-477-1261
■ "Fantastic crabs, great steamed shrimp and beautiful ribs" are dished up in a "funky", "noisy" atmosphere dominated by live bands and a tropical bar frequented by "tank-top" types; you can dock your boat or bike at this "redneck" warren in Dundalk, but best leave the BMW at home.

Baldwins Station [S] ▽ 16 19 17 $29

7618 Main St. (railroad tracks), Sykesville, 410-795-1041

◪ It would be hard to imagine a more picturesque "small town" setting than this beautifully "restored train station" in Sykesville where the locomotives still whistle by; don't miss the Wednesday night dinner concerts when live music helps tune-up "well-prepared" New American food.

Bamboo House 20 20 20 $23

Yorktowne Plaza Shopping Ctr., 26 Cranbrook St. (York Rd.), Cockeysville, 410-666-9550

Joey Chiu's Greenspring Inn [S]

10801 Falls Rd. (Greenspring Valley Rd.), Brooklandville, 410-823-1125

◪ The "Far East distilled for the blue hair set" means that this duo's "comfortable and pretty" surroundings put the Valley's old guard at ease; the fact that the Chinese food and sushi are "as 'American' as it gets" doesn't mean that they aren't "tasty", "pricey" and pleasantly served.

Bandaloops 18 19 18 $17

1024 S. Charles St. (bet. Cross & Hamburg Sts.), 410-727-1355

■ An "eclectic mix of people, food" and artwork gives this SoBo American "raw-brick-and-fern" bar "character", while its "casual" manners and "glorified bar food" keep it full; it's a "short walk from the harbor for lunch" (go for "good specials"), while at night "serious drinkers" find it "up to date" (in more ways than one).

Bangkok Place [S] 21 11 18 $17

5230 York Rd. (bet. Cold Spring Ln. & Woodbourne Ave.), 410-433-0040

■ "For years", this North Baltimore Asian's "light and fragrant" curries have been converting people who "don't usually eat Thai food", while its "low" prices have kept them fast friends; the decor may be "pedestrian", but its "offbeat location" boasts a free parking lot.

Banjara [S] 23 19 23 $19

1017 S. Charles St. (bet. Cross & Hamburg Sts.), 410-962-1554

■ When some of the top "hot and spicy" Indian food in town is served by "doting" waiters who want to "refill your water after every sip", a "dark" South Baltimore "hole-in-the-wall" becomes a "delight"; surveyors are equally enthused about getting its "good value" in the form of "deliveries at home."

Ban Thai [S] 21 14 19 $17

340 N. Charles St. (Mulberry St.), 410-727-7971

◪ It may be a little too pink, "overlit" and occasionally "slow", but this "reliable" Downtown Thai is appealing enough to rate "take a date" or a colleague status; it offers "something for everyone" as long as one likes highly flavored Siamese food – "they really use lemon grass" and don't stint on spice.

Baltimore F | D | S | C

Bare Bones S 18 | 15 | 18 | $19
St. John's Plaza, 9150 Baltimore Nat'l Pike (west of Rte. 29), Ellicott City, 410-461-0770
Head for this "typical strip mall joint" in Ellicott City for a "great deal on all-you-can-eat ribs", as well as microbrews and good rings; but critics have a bone to pick, calling the 'cue here "unexciting" and only "ok."

Baugher's S 16 | 11 | 17 | $11
289 W. Main St. Ext. (Rtes. 31 & 32), Westminster, 410-848-7413
Time-travelers by the busload "step back into the '50s" at this Carroll County "country" restaurant/farmstand where the "old-fashioned", mostly "fried" family food is unbelievably "cheap"; while the period-piece waitresses and setting are almost "too homey", they won't keep most from appreciating its "outstanding" fruit pies, produce and ice cream.

Bay Cafe S 14 | 17 | 14 | $17
2809 Boston St. (Linwood Ave.), 410-522-3377
"Youthful energy" – "it's great if you're drunk and 23 years old" – is so pervasive at this "tropical paradise" that many grown-ups lament the "waste" of one of Baltimore's "finest waterside settings"; the American food is "generic", so stick to the "legendary shrimp salad sandwich", sit by the water and try to keep the "lousy service" at bay.

Bertha's S 17 | 16 | 16 | $18
734 S. Broadway (Lancaster St.), 410-327-5795
The dark "English pub with real beer" that "gentrified Fells Point" with music and a "delightful afternoon tea" (by reservation) is still flexing its mussels; although seafood is its "strength", you might find better bivalves elsewhere, but there is nothing like its electric "atmosphere", which is "very Bawlmer" and "always fun."

Bertucci's S 17 | 15 | 16 | $16
12 Bel Air S. Pkwy. (Rte. 24), Bel Air, 410-569-4600
Snowden Sq., 9081 Snowden River Pkwy. (Robert Fulton Dr.), Columbia, 410-312-4800
Owings Mills Mall, Owings Mills Blvd. (I-795), Owings Mills, 410-356-5515
1818 York Rd. (Ridgely Rd.), Timonium, 410-561-7000
8130 Corporate Dr. (bet. Honeygo & Perry Hall Blvds.), White Marsh, 410-931-0900
See review in Washington, DC Directory.

Bill Bateman's Bistro ●S 16 | 13 | 15 | $14
7800 York Rd. (Cross Campus Dr.), Towson, 410-296-2737
"Good basic grunge food" and the "best grease" in town are turned out by the "college-oriented kitchen" of this "noisy" sports bar near Towson U; it's cheap, chock full of TV screens and other distractions – i.e. if you're "over 30", you'll feel "forgotten by the waiter" but will "love the decor of 20-year-old ladies" and "cute guys."

Baltimore   F | D | S | C

Birds of a Feather   22 | 15 | 19 | $25
1712 Aliceanna St. (Broadway), 410-675-8466

■ "Hidden behind" this smoky Fells Point bar, which is stocked with more than "100 single-malt scotches", is a "pretty, little" dining room featuring "creative" Contemporary American food and an "eclectic wine list", where a "warm and friendly" family "takes itself [and its customers] seriously"; while this results in a few snipes about "attitude", they're tempered with high praise for a "delicious meal."

BLACK OLIVE S   26 | 18 | 21 | $38
814 S. Bond St. (Shakespeare St.), 410-276-7141

■ "Great everything" – no wonder this young Greek scored high food ratings on its first try, proving that in Fells Point, as on the Aegean, classically "simple" preparations and hands-on "hospitality" impress; its white brick and wood decor "is like being in a Greek fishing village", yet a few feel entitled to more "for the price."

Blue Moon Cafe S   20 | 16 | 18 | $15
1621 Aliceanna St. (bet. Bond St. & Broadway), 410-522-3940

◪ Breakfast lovers mellow out just thinking of this Gen X comfort station's "totally homemade" cinnamon buns and biscuits and the "relaxing", country cottage atmosphere in which they're served; but weekend Fells Point crowds mean "major bummer sidewalk waits" for "low-priced" breakfasts, lunches and desserts; N.B. open 7 AM–3 PM six days a week and all-night Friday and Saturday.

Blue Nile S   ▽ 18 | 11 | 17 | $15
2101 N. Charles St. (bet. 20th & 21st Sts.), 410-783-0982

◪ It's "plain" and in an Uptown area that's "uncomfortable" at night, yet this BYO Ethiopian has a "cozy" "third world feel", which enhances the "eating-with-fingers" appeal of its cuisine; if you're up for a "novel" experience requiring a high tolerance for fiery food, you'll find it here.

Bo Brooks Crab House S   20 | 10 | 17 | $23
5415 Belair Rd. (Frankford Ave.), 410-488-8144

■ For the "quintessential" steamed crab encounter – "just you, a pile of crabs, a mallet and a beer" – this Northeast "bunker" has few, if any, city peers; maybe the crabs aren't always "from Maryland", but they're big, fresh and "cooked the Baltimore way" (coated with peppery spice) and everything from the "appropriate" lack of decor and service to the "crab fluffs" is typically "home town."

BOCCACCIO S   26 | 23 | 24 | $41
925 Eastern Ave. (bet. Exeter & High Sts.), 410-234-1322

■ The "chef receives in the kitchen" of this "high-end", "celebrity-filled", "real [Northern] Italian" where he shows Baltimore that there is more to Little Italy than "red sauce" pastas; perhaps "reservations are not always on time", but the "wonderful" veal chop is.

Bombay Grill [S] 23 | 19 | 21 | $22
2 E. Madison St. (N. Charles St.), 410-837-2973
Bombay Peacock Grill
10005 Old Columbia Rd. (Eden Brook Dr.), Columbia, 410-381-7111
■ "A tag team of top-notch tandoori, thali and tasty temptations" score points for these high-ranking Indians; check out their talents at the "great variety" lunch buffets or opt for a "leisurely" (verging on "slow") dinner served by a "courteous" staff in attractive surroundings.

Boomerang Pub [S] 15 | 21 | 18 | $22
1110 S. Charles St. (Cross St.), 410-727-2333
◪ "Truly Aussie" accents like "wonderful" down under murals lend a matey mood to this "brash" Federal Hill watering hole housed in a converted "old bank building"; its kitchen dishes out seafood and steak, along with "unusual" items "for the brave", like kangaroo stew and emu.

BRASS ELEPHANT [S] 25 | 26 | 24 | $38
924 N. Charles St. (bet. Eager & Read Sts.), 410-547-8480
■ "Impressive but not snooty", this Edwardian dining room in a "beautiful townhouse" is a "client"-pleaser, while its upstairs marble bar offers "elegant" "deals"; the "terrific" Italian-Continental cooking mostly "matches" its "wear a cloche and drink martinis" mood; "safe parking" is yet another reason why it's a "lovely place to go."

Braznell's Carribean Kitchen [S] ▽ 18 | 16 | 15 | $21
1623 E. Baltimore St. (Broadway), 410-327-2445
◪ Regulars "call ahead" when they "want spice", because Alfred and Esme Braznell, who run this Butcher's Hill Caribbean, aren't always there; but when they're cooking they're cookin' "authentic" island food; the operation's a bit "unpolished", but that's why folks "love her" and dig him.

Brewer's Art [S] 18 | 24 | 17 | $24
1106 N. Charles St. (bet. Biddle & Chase Sts.), 410-547-6925
◪ "Beaucoup bohemian" Mt. Vernon "scene place" where most people "love" the "charming" vintage parlor decor, "outstanding" beer and scotch selections and "house-brewed Belgian-style ales", but feel the Eclectic cuisine and the service "need improvement"; most conclude that it "works better" as a "hip" "bar with food than a restaurant."

Brighton's [S] 24 | 26 | 24 | $38
Harbor Court Hotel, 550 Light St. (bet. Conway & Lee Sts.), 410-347-9750
■ It's a pleasure to take clients to this "bright and cheery", more "affordable", "relaxed version of Hampton's" (the hotel's luxury restaurant), with its "great view", "interesting" New American cooking and "hard working staff"; while it's technically a "coffee shop, the food's better than most hotels'" top dining rooms; P.S. it's a "must for afternoon tea."

Baltimore   F | D | S | C

Cacao Lane 🆂   18 | 20 | 17 | $22
8066 Main St. (Tiber Alley), Ellicott City, 410-461-1378
◪ "Stone walls, an amazing crab dip", weekend music and a "nice outside deck" are the draws at this Ellicott City fixture; since the service and '70s Continental menu have "needed work" for years, and "winter heat" would help, the "quaint" atmosphere must be what carries this place, though even that's "not like it used to be."

Caesar's Den 🆂   22 | 16 | 21 | $33
223 S. High St. (Stiles St.), 410-547-0820
◪ With its "old-fashioned, fine Italian food", far from ordinary (albeit "pricey") wines and standout service, you can tell the owner "cares"; if sometimes its "cooks do the tourist stuff", the restaurant remains a "good value" and a "Little Italy standard bearer."

Cafe Bombay 🆂   ▽ 19 | 16 | 18 | $20
114 E. Lombard St. (Calvert St.), 410-539-2233
◪ The "variety and value" of this Downtown Indian's lunch buffet, which features *dosas* (platter-sized filled pancakes) and unusual breads, make this step-down cafe a good place to explore Southern India's interesting cuisine; the "helpful" staff is another plus.

Cafe Bretton   ▽ 24 | 21 | 19 | $34
849 Baltimore-Annapolis Blvd. (McKinsey Rd.), Severna Park, 410-647-8222
◼ Transplanting a "little bit of France" to Severna Park isn't as easy as this French-Continental makes it seem; of course, its "French country house exterior" gives it a running start, but making use of the fresh produce from its "herb and veggie garden" in the mostly "well-prepared" Gallic food is the result of "try hard" determination.

Cafe Hon 🆂   16 | 15 | 15 | $13
1002 W. 36th St. (bet. Falls Rd. & Roland Ave.), 410-243-1230
◪ Perhaps it was inevitable that this wildly popular, "kitschy" Hampden American would lose a little of its luster; after all, when you crave "homey, plain" "comfort" food — BLT's, fries, bread pudding — you want a surrogate "mom" in the kitchen, not a "hectic" "cultural icon"; still, most maintain it's a "great place to meet a friend for lunch."

Cafe Madrid 🆂   – | – | – | M
505 S. Broadway (Eastern Ave.), 410-276-7700
The intimate, candlelit Fells Point townhouse that once housed M. Gettier is equally suited to this charming young Spaniard; go for tapas and sherry or properly prepared and served Iberian-Continental specialties like paella and lamb.

Baltimore

| F | D | S | C |

Café Pangea ⓢ 19 | 19 | 18 | $15
4007 Falls Rd. (bet. 40th & 41st Sts.), 410-662-0500
You "can web surf while you wait" at this Hampden cybercafe, but you really should click on the "fresh, made-to-order" sandwiches, salads and "imaginative" snacks; while the "delightful" outdoor porch setting attracts "everyone from yuppies and hippies" to media faces (headquartered nearby), a few critics complain that the experience is "too cyberspacey" (i.e. "not consistent", with "service that's too casual").

Cafe Tattoo ⓢ ▽ 13 | 10 | 15 | $13
4825 Belair Rd. (Moravia Rd.), 410-325-7427
For 'cue and "chile mixed with cigar smoke, loud blues and friendly people", regulars hit this no-frills, "character"-full Northeast bar; but the surveyor who would "never eat there, but did get my tattoo, upstairs" ain't atypical either.

Cafe Troia ⓢ 23 | 20 | 22 | $32
28 W. Allegheny Ave. (Washington Ave.), Towson, 410-337-0133
Locals imagine they're eating "in Italy" in this prettified Towson office building (the "room to the left is very romantic"); but while pros praise "premium quality" classics like "superb spaghetti Bolognese" and osso buco that are complemented by "great" wines, cons counter that "success has spoiled" some of its "classy", casual appeal – it's become "pricey" and the waiters are "arrogant at times."

Cafe Zen ⓢ 22 | 15 | 19 | $14
438 E. Belvedere Ave. (York Rd.), 410-532-0022
"Spa Chinese" served in "bright, airy" but "spartan" surroundings that's often double-billed with the nearby Senator movie theater – so "get there early because the place gets packed" and service slows; affordable (BYO) and "child-friendly", its "interesting Oriental-American" cuisine is cooked with lots of veggies and a "healthy" hand.

California Pizza Kitchen ⓢ 17 | 13 | 16 | $16
Harborplace, 201 E. Pratt St. (Light St.), 410-783-9339
See review in Washington, DC Directory.

Calvert House – | – | – | M
347 N. Calvert St. (Saratoga St.), 410-539-3627
The straightforward charm of this old-time business district establishment is the not-so-well-kept secret of nearby worker bees looking for an upscale lunch; its dark, quiet, comfortable dining room, pleasant manners and classic Maryland seafood/steak and Italian menu provide a gastronomic glimpse of a vanishing way of life.

170

Baltimore | F | D | S | C |

Candle Light Inn S | 18 | 20 | 20 | $26 |
1835 Frederick Rd. (Rolling Rd.), Catonsville, 410-788-6076
■ It "feels like a country inn, without the drive", so if you yearn for the "old family tradition of Sunday dinner, white tablecloths and gentle manners", this Catonsville Continental is your kind of place; it's adept at "accommodating large groups" at holidays, and if it's a tad "old-fashioned", so is its "steady" clientele.

Canopy, The S | 16 | 6 | 12 | $8 |
Peddler Sq. Shopping Ctr., 2030 Liberty Rd. (Monroe Ave.), Eldersburg, 410-549-2880
9319 Baltimore Nat'l Pike (Chatham Rd.), Ellicott City, 410-465-5718
5 Vernon Ave., NW (Ritchie Hwy.), Glen Burnie, 410-768-1719
Roberts Field Shopping Ctr., 721 Hanover Pike (N. Woods Trail), Hampstead, 410-239-4089
Festival, 8125-P Ritchie Hwy. (Jumpers Hole Rd.), Pasadena, 410-647-7722
607 E. Main St. (Chartley Dr.), Reisterstown, 410-526-4229
140 Village Shopping Ctr., Westminster, 410-848-7443
5820 Johnnycake Rd. (Ingleside Ave.), Woodlawn, 410-744-2188
■ "Nice pit beef sandwiches and fries" are Baltimore's native "fast foods" – hence, the persistence of these "grubby", self-serve, kid-friendly pit stops; their "honest meat and potatoes" fare is "sloppy, tasty and exactly what you pay for", but if you aren't from these environs, you sure wouldn't call it 'cue.

Capitol City Brewing Co. S | 14 | 16 | 16 | $18 |
Harborplace, 301 Light St. Pavilion (Pratt St.), 410-539-7468
See review in Washington, DC Directory.

Captain Harvey's S | 17 | 14 | 16 | $24 |
11510 Reisterstown Rd. (Nicodemus Rd.), Reisterstown, 410-356-7550
■ Its hundred-year-old steamed crab formula is only one of the "surprises" at this "big boat" of a Reisterstown restaurant; "outstanding fresh seafood", bar food and steaks are served in a "conservative", "bland atmosphere" that strikes outsiders as "very snobby."

Casa Mia's ◐ | 15 | 10 | 14 | $15 |
40 York Rd. (Burke Ave.), Towson, 410-321-8707
■ There's "a little of this and a little of that" at this Towson Greek-Italian, which is "trying to please students and seniors simultaneously"; the former advise "stick to pizza and subs and they will stick to you"; others carp that crab cakes and such can "take forever" to arrive.

Baltimore | F | D | S | C |

Chameleon S   ▽ | 23 | 18 | 19 | $24 |
32 W. Main St. (bet. John St. & Railroad Ave.),
Westminster, 410-751-2422
■ Bringing "refreshing" "charm to a land of boring food" is the change this chameleon's "creative" American menu has wrought in Westminster; plus it's a "great"-looking place with a patio, cozy bar and "funky wall murals."

CHARLESTON S | 27 | 25 | 26 | $40 |
1000 Lancaster St. (bet. Central & Exeter Sts.),
410-332-7373
■ Even though it only opened shortly before our *Baltimore Survey* was conducted, this "stunning" Southern American vaulted to No. 5 for Food, 3 for Service and 10 for Decor; chef-owner Cindy Wolf and her husband Tony Forman's stellar performance at the defunct Savannah continues here with "unique, delicious" takes on "Low Country delicacies" and one of the "best wine cellars in town"; even the harbor-view office building location is "smashing", if "totally un-Baltimore."

Chart House S | 19 | 21 | 19 | $30 |
Pier 4, 601 E. Pratt St. (Market Pl.), 410-539-6616
See review in Washington, DC Directory.

CHEESECAKE FACTORY ☾ S | 21 | 18 | 18 | $21 |
Harborplace, Pratt St. Pavilion (Calvert St.), 410-234-3990
See review in Washington, DC Directory.

Chiapparelli's S | 18 | 15 | 18 | $23 |
237 S. High St. (Fawn St.), 410-837-0309
◪ Little Italy "staple", with "mainstream" "red spaghetti sauce" fare, "12,000 calorie house salad" and "Chip family" hospitality; while supporters say it's still a local "favorite", foes who recall "long waits", "tired decor" and the "same" old food ask "why?"

Ciao Bella   ▽ | 19 | 18 | 20 | $27 |
236 S. High St. (bet. Fawn & Stiles Sts.), 410-685-7733
◪ An "intimate" Italian whose enthusiasts cite some of the "best calamari", plus a "particularly excellent marinara"; however, those who are less than enamored insist there are "better choices in Little Italy."

City Cafe S | 18 | 19 | 16 | $14 |
1001 Cathedral St. (Eager St.), 410-539-4252
■ This chic Downtown "drop in" coffeehouse/restaurant has "filled a neighborhood void nicely" with upscale snacks, desserts and an eclectic menu; here, "space is the place", with oversized windows, "great Southern exposure", art-filled walls and an impressive copper-fronted bar; while service can be "abrupt", that doesn't stop it from being a "safe hangout" for "diverse" urbanites.

Claddagh Pub [S] 19 | 15 | 17 | $16

Canton Sq., 2918 O'Donnell St. (Curley St.), 410-522-4220

■ Raucous good times rule at this "solid Irish pub" in Canton, where almost everything is "great" – the "beef", "burgers", "wings and beer specials", the "bartenders", "happy hour" and the noise level.

Clyde's ◐ [S] 18 | 21 | 19 | $23

10221 Wincopin Circle (Little Patuxent Pkwy.), Columbia, 410-730-2829

See review in Washington, DC Directory.

Corks [S] 24 | 20 | 22 | $34

1026 S. Charles St. (bet. Cross & Hamburg Sts.), 410-752-3810

■ "Dynamic" and "engaging", this "innovative" New American's "kitchen is well complemented by a varied", "friendly" and "incredibly priced wine list" and a "well-informed" staff; the Federal Hill townhouse setting and "nonstuffy atmosphere" put novices and experts at ease, although it strikes some as a "bit overpriced."

Corner Stable [S] 17 | 9 | 14 | $18

9942 York Rd. (Church Ln.), Cockeysville, 410-666-8722

■ It's "easy to get sloppy" at this Cockeysville bar, a "Baltimore tradition" for some of the "best" baby back ribs ("heartburn on the hog") and garlic-salted fries, which is why no one seems to mind the "dark, smoky", "don't look down at the floor" premises or the "sluggish service"; N.B. this is the original "CS", others with the same name are separately owned.

Costas Inn ◐ [S] ▽ 20 | 10 | 17 | $23

4100 North Point Blvd. (New Battle Grove Rd.), Dundalk, 410-477-1975

■ A steady supply of some of the "best steamed crabs in crab city" is the "reason to go" to this blue-collar venue in Dundalk; it manages to fill a "football field–sized, functional room" with "family warmth" and doesn't do a bad job with other things on its "varied" steak and seafood menu.

Crease, The [S] 11 | 12 | 12 | $19

523 York Rd. (bet. Allegheny & Pennsylvania Aves.), Towson, 410-823-0395

◪ Not so affectionately known as the "Grease", this lacrosse-obsessed sports bar is a place for "tired jocks" and collegians to "get sloshed"; its pub fare "doesn't enter into the equation" and neither does the so-called help.

Dalesio's of Little Italy [S] 21 | 19 | 20 | $30

829 Eastern Ave. (Albemarle St.), 410-539-1965

◪ On Little Italy's "main drag", this softly lit townhouse is best known for its Italian "spa cuisine", "tasty seafood dishes", "great Italian wines" and "after-theater" desserts; while a few find the experience "dull", for most it personifies the proverbial "little joint at its best."

Da Mimmo [S] 24 | 20 | 22 | $43

217 S. High St. (Stiles St.), 410-727-6876

◩ "Ridiculously expensive and worth it"? – that depends on your point of view on this tiny, "dimly lit", "celebrity" stronghold in Little Italy; boosters call it a bastion of "wonderful, traditional Italian" cooking where you get treated "like an underworld kingpin" in a '50s atmosphere"; but some say that they "push specials for mega bucks", "insult" you and "don't honor reservations."

DELLA NOTTE [S] 20 | 22 | 20 | $23

801 Eastern Ave. (President St.), 410-837-5500

■ Misgivings about "cheesy" Little Italy "tourist locations" quickly turn to praise for "on-site parking" and "fast, easy", "modern day Italian" dining in an "airy, spacious" room; this "on the way up" youngster is "still finding its way", but offers enough good choices – brick-oven pizza, "fantastic salads", "homemade pastas" and "even-better desserts" – to ensure that most "people leave with a smile."

Desert Cafe ⊄ 19 | 14 | 15 | $13

1605-07 Sulgrave Ave. (Newbury St.), 410-367-5808

◩ This "small, funky" Mt. Washington spot has a "nice Mideast menu" full of "vegetarian" options and many "good" desserts; with just a few tables and comfy chairs, it's "like being in someone's home", making it just right for a "rainy day cup of tea and a chat."

Donna's at Bibelot [S] 19 | 18 | 17 | $17

American Can Co., 2400 Boston St. (Hudson St.), 410-276-9212

Festival at Woodholme, 1819 Reisterstown Rd. (2 blocks north of I-695), Pikesville, 410-653-6939

Timonium Crossing Shopping Ctr., 2080 York Rd. (Timonium Rd.), Timonium, 410-308-2041

Donna's at the Gallery [S]

Harborplace, 200 W. Pratt St. (bet. Lombard & South Sts.), 410-752-9040

Donna's at University Hospital

22 S. Green St. (Baltimore St.), 410-328-1962 (Mon.-Fri.)

Donna's Charles Village [S]

3101 St. Paul St. (31st St.), 410-889-3410

Donna's Coffee Bar [S]

2 W. Madison St. (N. Charles St.), Mt. Vernon, 410-385-0180

◩ Quips about "McDonna's", 'the coffee shop that swallowed Baltimore' aside, these "clean" California-inspired eateries are a "phenomenon" precisely because they meet people's needs for "great sandwiches", salads and sweets; sure they do the "whole trendy foccacia and arugula bit", they've "gotten predictable" and their "service is erratic", but where would we be without them?; N.B. the new megastore in Harborplace does everything the others do and more.

Baltimore F | D | S | C

Dooby's Bar & Grill ●S ▽ 22 | 19 | 18 | $16
3123 Elliott St. (Robinson St.), 410-534-0556

◨ Judging by this "noisy" Canton "hideaway", "lava lamps and glass beads" are making a comeback, while "gourmet pizza", "good bar food" and an Eclectic menu never go out of style; while they haven't quite nailed down the "basics", everyone is "trying hard" here and the "seafood specials" are "usually very good."

Double T Diner ●S 15 | 14 | 16 | $12
6300 Baltimore Nat'l Pike (Rolling Rd.), Catonsville, 410-744-4151
1 Mountain Rd. (Ritchie Hwy.), Glen Burnie, 410-766-9669
10741 Pulaski Hwy. (Ebenezer Rd.), White Marsh, 410-344-1020

◨ One "eats", not dines, at the "best diner in Charm City", a "cheap, noisy, greasy", sprawling Catonsville fixture where you can get a "square meal" (and then some) and incomparable people-watching "24 hours a day"; P.S. some surveyors say that the "new Double T's [on Ritchie Highway and Route 40E] are better run and more pleasant", but somehow they don't suit to the original T.

DuClaw Brewing Company S – | – | – | M
16-A Bel Air S. Pkwy. (Rte. 24), Bel Air, 410-515-3222

Bringing a glass-walled, Seattle-style brewpub to this burgeoning 'burb was a no-brainer, and almost instantly, there were lines out the door; early reports cite the "great menu" of snacks, American classics and "unique steak sauces" that complement the cooling brews; N.B. it gets loud and beery at night.

Duda's Tavern ● 21 | 15 | 19 | $14
1600 Thames St. (Bond St.), 410-276-9719

■ There's no shortage of atmospheric "neighborhood taverns" in the area, yet this slot-sized, "burger and beer joint that predates Fells Point's gentrification" is consistently "the best" of the bunch; it's nothing more (or less) than a "good bar with satisfying food" – "great blue plate specials", crab cakes, "fresh" sweet potato fries – and "friendly folks."

Due S 23 | 22 | 22 | $31
McDonough Crossroads, 25 Crossroads Dr. (McDonough & Reisterstown Rds.), Owings Mills, 410-356-4147

■ "Joined at the hip to Linwood's", this "upscale" Italian has the same "informal but classy" and "innovative" approach to '90s dining as its next door Owings Mills sib; the Tuscan-inspired menu includes some "excellent" dishes – "pastas galore", "wonderful osso buco", house-made breads and desserts – but the price of popularity is paid with some "misses" and "loud" weekend crowds.

Edo Sushi [S] — | — | — | M
53 E. Padonia Rd. (York Rd.), Timonium, 410-667-9200
In a traditional setting, this young Timonium enterprise offers a "varied Japanese menu" along with its signature raw fish and sticky rice; diners can mix and match – a piece or two of sushi, followed by an entree like teriyaki, tempura, dumpling and noodle dishes or hearty casseroles.

Elkridge Furnace Inn [S] 22 | 25 | 22 | $29
5745 Furnace Ave. (Levering Ave. & Washington Blvd.), Elkridge, 410-379-9336
■ This "beautiful old mansion", in a "charming" setting on "pretty" grounds near the Patapsco River, is a "special place for holidays and birthdays" and often booked for events; inside, there's a "working fireplace" and "good" Continental cooking, and while it's a bit "expensive, the desserts lessen the blow."

Ellicott Mills Brewing Co. ◐ [S] 17 | 19 | 17 | $20
8308 Main St. (bet. Ellicott Mills Dr. & Old Columbia Pike), Ellicott City, 410-313-8141
◪ A "welcome addition to Ellicott City", this "great"-looking microbrewery (converted from a turn-of-the-century warehouse) is hailed for its quaffing "atmosphere" and "interesting" bar food and for providing local yuppies with a "destination at night"; despite reports of "inconsistent" chow and service, it's got "potential."

ESPN Zone [S] — | — | — | M
Power Plant, 601 E. Pratt St. (Gay St.), 410-685-3776
They've turned the power on at this recent Disney production in Inner Harbor – a spectacular cave-like space lit-up by sports videos and wired for live cable sports network interviewing, where the 'boy food' (burgers and ribs) is definitely not relegated to the backfield; armchair recliners offer additional jock sightings and video viewing possibilities.

Ethel & Ramone's Cafe [S] ▽ 16 | 14 | 16 | $15
1615 Sulgrave Ave. (Kelly Ave.), 410-664-2971
■ With its "front porch", "funky" parlor setting and "quirky" ways, this Mt. Washington cafe is "nice for a tête à tête" over "homemade" soups, breads and treats; a rotating roster of young chefs turns out "New Age" Cal–Italian fare, but many go "for coffee and cake" rather than "actual food food."

Faidley's 22 | 9 | 14 | $13
Lexington Mkt., 400 W. Lexington St. (Paca St.), 410-727-4898
■ "Baltimore's finest crab cakes", "great crab soup", "the best shuckers in the business", and a glimpse of "real Bawlmer" make a "stand-up lunch" at this "classic" city market raw bar "worth the risk" of a visit to this neglected part of town; besides, it's one of the most "interesting places" left standing.

Baltimore   F | D | S | C

Fazzini's Italian Kitchen S   ▽ 22 | 9 | 17 | $13
Cranbrook Shopping Ctr., 578 Cranbrook Rd. (York Rd.), Cockeysville, 410-667-6104
■ "Pound for pound, dollar for dollar", this "family-run" Cockeysville strip mall joint turns out some of the "best Italian food" around; but "timing is important" if you're in a home meal replacement mode, as its "humongous portions and delicious selections" result in "long lines."

Fisherman's Wharf S   18 | 16 | 18 | $24
826 Dulaney Valley Rd. (Fairmount Ave.), Towson, 410-337-2909
■ Head for this "straightforward" Towson seafooder for "huge" "slabs" of "very fresh" fish, "good crab soup" and some "unbeatable" light fare bargains at the bar; its "great selection" comes with little in the way of decor and "sometimes spotty service", but it's the "only game in town for a fish dinner."

Fishery, The S   ▽ 17 | 14 | 15 | $29
1717 Eastern Ave. (Broadway), 410-327-9340
◪ In Fells Point, defenders of this Iberian hybrid enthuse over the "superb Spanish selections" and "good" Maryland-style seafood, while adversaries find it to be "touristy" and "not attentive" to its clientele; however, the "potent sangria" has made no enemies thus far.

Friendly Farms S   20 | 12 | 20 | $18
17434 Foreston Rd. (Mt. Carmel Rd.), Upperco, 410-239-7400
■ It's a "nice ride in the country" to Upperco, where traditional American "home cooking" ("great crab cakes and fried chicken") is dished out by little "old ladies" in a pass-the-bowls, "family-style" setting complete with a duck pond; a bit "limited", maybe, but it's an inexpensive opportunity to feed the kids something other than "chain restaurant food"; P.S. "no booze."

Gabler's S   ▽ 24 | 18 | 21 | $23
2200 Perryman Rd. (Old Philadelphia Rd.), Aberdeen, 410-272-0626
■ Nothing ever seems to change at this "fantastic" 60-year-old crab house near Aberdeen, where enthusiasts enjoy the "great view" of the Bush River, along with steamed "crabs à la Maryland" washed down with cold, long-neck beers; it's a seasonal-only "experience", a "stepping back" into the past, not just a seafood feast; N.B. reservations essential.

G & M Restaurant S   – | – | – | M
804 N. Hammonds Ferry Rd., Linthicum, 410-636-1777
Mavens swear by the "biggest, meatiest, backfin lump crab cakes for the money" "anywhere" – the "size of grapefruits", they've put this otherwise nondescript exurban spot on the area's gastronomic map; insiders ignore the long menu and order beer, crab and "nothing else."

Baltimore

F | D | S | C

Garry's Grill S
▽ | 19 | 14 | 18 | $15

553A Baltimore-Annapolis Blvd. (McKinsey Rd.), Severna Park, 410-544-0499
See review in Annapolis and Eastern Shore Directory.

Germano's Trattoria S
21 | 18 | 20 | $34

300 S. High St. (Fawn St.), 410-752-4515

▧ Locals consider this individualistic, "Tuscan-style" Little Italy bistro a "cut above" the "tourist traps" in the neighborhood; it's a "cheerful" corner townhouse with oversize posters enlivening the walls, "attentive" service and "many interesting dishes" to offer; some mutter about a "hit-or-miss" kitchen, but most just say "mmmm."

Gibby's S
19 | 14 | 16 | $23

22 W. Padonia Rd. (bet. I-83 & York Rd.), Timonium, 410-560-0703

■ Since it's no secret that this Timonium fish house offers "excellent" crabs and "plain seafood" with "good quality and portions for the price", it's not surprising that there are "long waits", an "incredible" decibel level and crowds that strain the capacity of its "no-decor" dining room; while hard-core fans say it's "fun with friends on Crab Night" ($1/crab Tuesday and Wednesday after 9 PM), the more demure declare takeout is the "deal."

Glasz Cafe S
– | – | – | I

6080 Falls Rd. (Lake Ave.), 410-377-9060

A tony crowd treats this "tiny" Falls Road shop as a community living room, dropping by for coffee, specialty sandwiches, salads and what disciples tout as the area's "best vegetarian" dishes; outsiders who go strictly for the fare may find it a bit pricey.

Globe Brewing Co. S
13 | 10 | 12 | $15

1321 Key Hwy. (Webster St.), 410-347-7964

■ With its "airplane hangar atmosphere", "uncomfortable" perches and a menu of bar snacks and seafood that still needs work, this Inner Harbor meet-and-mingle brewpub is little more than a "fun place to play pool" and have a drink – a "noisy cavern as a dining room is not my idea of a good time"; in sum, the "beer is good, that's it."

Golden Gate Noodle House S
– | – | – | I

6-8 Allegheny Ave. (York Rd.), Towson, 410-337-2557

The English-language menu at this no-nonsense Towson Chinese is a compendium of Hong Kong–style noodle soups, multiregional preparations of seafood and meats, and healthful choices; even more intriguing are the dishes that the Asian-American customers are eating – if the servers aren't too busy, get their advice.

Baltimore | F | D | S | C |

Golden West Cafe | - | - | - | I |
842 W. 36th St. (Elm St.), 410-889-8891
As soon as the sun rises on Hampden's main thoroughfare, arty locals start dropping by this "very pleasant" bean bar/cafe for "authentic New Mexico breakfasts", coffee breaks and light, veggie-friendly fare for lunch and dinner; be sure to check out the inviting mini-lounge cleverly carved out of the back room.

Grand Palace S | ▽ 24 | 13 | 21 | $17 |
5721 Ritchie Hwy. (Church St.), Glen Burnie, 410-636-8333
■ "Dim sum heaven" resides in a Brooklyn strip mall – this Cantonese's daily dim sum lunches are "so festive and delicious", patrons hardly notice that the dining room is like a "windowless cave"; it's also the "only place" in the area with a menu of "true Hong Kong cuisine."

Gringada S | ▽ 12 | 12 | 15 | $15 |
Harpers Choice Village Ctr., 54-85 Harpers Farm Rd. (Cedar Ln.), Columbia, 410-730-5780
◪ Columbia has seen some skirmishes over this "always crowded" Mexican, just about the "cheapest place with plates" in the area; its amigos admire the live entertainment and "authentic" dishes; opponents fire back that it's a "dreary" facsimile of Mexican cuisine.

Gunning's Crab House S | 19 | 11 | 16 | $21 |
3901 S. Hanover St. (Jeffrey St.), 410-354-0085
◪ The Gunning family has moved on, but this picturesque South Baltimore seafooder has retained its summertime patio and blue-collar, "wear your jeans" feel; its still a "solid" steamed crab emporium and its signature sugar-dusted, "battered pepper rings" and giant eclairs are also on hand; still, a picky few jeer that it's "over the hill."

Gunning's Seafood S | ▽ 18 | 11 | 16 | $19 |
7304 Parkway Dr. (Dorsey Rd./Rte. 176), Hanover, 410-712-9404
■ Local color may have been left behind in the move to this strip mall near BWI, but not the "Old Baltimore" family recipes, "big-haired waitresses" or steady supplies of "great", sweet, meaty crabs and other fresh seafood; perhaps there's nothing "gourmet" about steaming shellfish, but the Gunnings (who steam 'em the old-time way, in beer) do it better than most.

HAMILTON'S S | 25 | 23 | 22 | $38 |
Admiral Fell Inn, 888 S. Broadway (Thames St.), 410-522-2195
■ Supporters toast a "strong start for the former Milton Inn crew" and the "elegant, comfortable feeling" they've brought to this historic locale; it's already producing Contemporary American cuisine "excellent" enough for a "business dinner" or a "fine evening" out; most find it "enjoyable" but rough spots and a post-*Survey* manager change add variables to the equation.

HAMPTON'S [S] 27 | 28 | 27 | $54
Harbor Court Hotel, 550 Light St. (bet. Conway & Lee Sts.), 410-347-9744
■Voted No. 1 for decor and service in Baltimore, "first-class" formal dining "doesn't get any better" than at this premiere "event restaurant"; the breathtaking harbor views and "top-quality" New American menu leave patrons feeling "pampered"; P.S. "a drink in the Explorer's Lounge" starts the evening off in style.

Hampton's of Towson [S] ▽ 20 | 19 | 20 | $25
Hampton House, 204 E. Joppa Rd. (Fairmount Ave.), Towson, 410-821-8888
■This "comfortable" residential dining room is "popular" with Towson seniors who "go to dance" and enjoy "fine old-style dining" on "great prime rib, seafood" and other Americana; many take advantage of the $11.95 "early-bird special" (4–5:30 PM) for a "decent" meal and a "great", green view; Dad will love it.

Hampton Tea Room 🚭 ▽ 14 | 21 | 19 | $13
Hampton Mansion, 535 Hampton Ln. (Dulaney Valley Rd.), Towson, 410-583-7401
■It's "nice to take out-of-towners" to lunch or tea at this "charming" "Towson landmark" for a glimpse of Baltimore's genteel past; diners encounter traditional American dishes they haven't had "since childhood", served in an "old-fashioned" setting – the food isn't "great", but the place is.

Hard Rock Cafe 🌙 **[S]** 14 | 20 | 15 | $18
Power Plant, 601 E. Pratt St. (Market Pl.), 410-347-7625
See review in Washington, DC Directory.

Harryman House [S] 20 | 20 | 20 | $28
340 Main St. (1¼ mi. north of Franklin Blvd.), Reisterstown, 410-833-8850
■Cobbled from a historic dwelling ("ask for the 'cabin room'"), this "odd mix of bar food and upscale" New American dining is well-calibrated to Reisterstown's varied needs; in its "noisy bar" and "rustic" dining rooms, it plays "host" to "romantic" meetings, parents with kids and beery get-togethers with friends; overall it's a bit "hit-or-miss", but "relaxed."

Harvey's [S] 18 | 17 | 17 | $23
Greenspring Station, 2360 W. Joppa Rd. (Falls Rd.), Brooklandville, 410-296-9526
◪ "Where everybody knows your name" – or soon will, since seating at this sprawling suburban social center is "so close you could eat off the next table"; critics claim its wide-ranging California and spa menus translate into "too many cooks, uneven food."

Baltimore F | D | S | C

HAUSSNER'S   19 | 24 | 22 | $25
3242 Eastern Ave. (Clinton St.), 410-327-8365
◪ This vast Highlandtown "institution" is "a must-see", as much for the "people-watching" as the fabled "artwork" on the walls; the German–Old Maryland menu is less "exciting" and the place is "crowded" and "noisy"; however, the white-haired waitresses, like "kitsch central" itself, are "one of a kind"; P.S. don't miss the "'nudey' bar."

Helen's Garden S   23 | 21 | 22 | $16
2908 O'Donnell St. (Linwood Ave.), 410-276-2233
■ "Delightful owners" and "very original cooking" make this coffee bar and second-story American "an oasis of civility" in Canton; a "lovely spot for lunch or brunch" ("take your mother-in-law" or your squeeze), it looks "modern yet quaint", serves "healthy", "imaginative" food and delivers real bang for the buck.

HELMAND, THE S   25 | 21 | 23 | $22
806 N. Charles St. (bet. Madison & Read Sts.), 410-752-0311
■ "Highly recommended" for serving some of Baltimore's "best ethnic food" (the "things they can do with pumpkin") at "fantastic prices", this Mt. Vernon Afghan is also esteemed for its "intimate atmosphere" and "quick service"; out-of-towners even plan excursions "for its rack of lamb – the best anywhere."

Henninger's Tavern   22 | 21 | 20 | $24
1812 Bank St. (bet. Ann & Wolfe Sts.), 410-342-2172
■ Offering "rowhouse dining at its best", this Fells Point "low-key joint delivers knockout" Contemporary American cooking, although "simple and straightforward is the key" to getting the most from its menu; the atmosphere is "cool enough" for twenty to thirtysomethings and "normal enough to please" their parents, but "get there early" as there's no reserving and the 10 tables fill up fast.

Hoang's Seafood Grill & Sushi Bar S   21 | 15 | 18 | $23
1619 Sulgrave Ave. (Kelly Ave.), 410-466-1000
■ Sushi fanciers can "belly up to the bar" at this Mt. Washington Pan-Asian seafood specialist; others go for "anything on the grill" or the "appetizers, especially the spare ribs"; all are served in "generous portions" that nearly overwhelm this "very tiny place."

Holy Frijoles S   21 | 15 | 17 | $12
908 W. 36th St. (bet. Elm & Roland Aves.), 410-235-2326
■ Hampden's "funkiest" is one of Baltimore's "best cheap eats", feeding the young and hungry "tremendous portions" of "good", "fresh Tex-Mex" in a "hole-in-the-wall" BYO that is chronically "cramped" but "really fun"; the hip servers ("tattoos and nostril rings" are de rigueur) are "kid-friendly", but the little ones may get a "little testy" about the waits.

Baltimore F | D | S | C

Hull Street Blues Cafe S   22 | 18 | 22 | $19
1222 Hull St. (bet. Cuba St. & Fort Ave.), Locust Point, 410-727-7476

■ A neighborhood "treasure", this "everyone's welcome" tavern near Fort McHenry has a white tablecloth American dining room, a "large working fireplace" and one of Charm City's "best brunch" deals that's a self-serve "glutton fest"; the bar food plus works "for a quick lunch", but the real "surprise" is the grandmotherly dessert selection.

Hunan Manor S   24 | 19 | 21 | $18
7091 Deepage Dr. (Carved Stone Rd. & Snowden River Pkwy.), Columbia, 410-381-1134

■ In Columbia, "pleasant" dining rooms with a "solicitous" staff are scarce, so this "consistent" operation would be welcome even if it didn't produce some of the "very best Chinese food" in the vicinity (including "great vegetarian dishes"); capable of dealing with "large" business groups and hungry kids, it's "always busy" and may seem a bit "frayed"; P.S. there's an "excellent" Asian market next door.

Hunter's Lodge S   – | – | – | M
9445 Baltimore National Pike/Rte. 40 (1 mi. west of Rte. 29), Ellicott City, 410-461-4990

"Newcomer" in an opulently refurbished historic "log cabin" that's "incongruous" amid the nearby Route 40 strip malls, but noted for its "wonderful fresh fish" and "creative" Contemporary American–Mediterranean fare; with candlelit tables and interesting fabrics, it's a "needed alternative" to the area's dress-down venues.

Ikaros S   20 | 14 | 20 | $21
4805 Eastern Ave. (bet. Oldham & Ponca Sts.), 410-633-3750

■ Patrons don't leave Highlandtown's "Greek Sabatino's" hungry ("the doggy bag alone makes three more meals") or poor ("out-of-towners on a budget are always impressed" by the "bargain" tab); also a surprise are the "welcoming" waiters who let customers "try different" dishes; this old-timer is "supported by the Greek community", which may give it an edge over equally worthy challengers.

JEANNIER'S   24 | 19 | 22 | $31
Broadview Apts., 105 W. 39th St. (University Pkwy.), 410-889-3303

◢ The top in-town French refuses to be dismissed with quips about "maiden aunt heaven" and "olde-time elegance" – the eating's too good; its "quiet, dignified" dining room is well suited to "classics" like the "great crab omelet", as well as affordable "light fare with French flair"; those in a "peppier" mood can adjourn to the romantic bar.

Baltimore | F | D | S | C |

Jennings Cafe ☻ | ▽ 18 | 12 | 18 | $13 |
808 Frederick Rd. (Ingleside Ave.), Catonsville, 410-744-3824
■ "If you like red, you'll love" this "homey" Catonsville's decor – crimson counter, bar lights, seats and so on; those who appreciate "great, fat burgers", cheap "old-fashioned" American food (fried oysters) and bar smoke will enjoy it all the more; P.S. ask for "Peggy, Baltimore's best waitress."

Jerry D's Saloon ☻S | ▽ 17 | 12 | 18 | $14 |
7808 Harford Rd. (Taylor Ave.), 410-665-0525
◪ This loosened-tie Parkville "watering hole" encourages belt relaxation as well, to make "room for its great steak", "huge and delicious pork chop", Wednesday's "$9.95 lobster dinner" and Thursday night prime rib specials; the "guy"-type bar also offers "solid" fare, but as fans joke, its recent "expansion makes more room for smoke."

Jilly's S | 14 | 10 | 14 | $15 |
Enchanted Forest Shopping Ctr., 10030 Baltimore Nat'l Pike (Bethany Ln.), Ellicott City, 410-461-3093
1012 Reisterstown Rd. (Waldron Ave.), Pikesville, 410-653-0610
■ Although most have "very little good to say" about this Pikesville "sports bar wanna-be" (or its Ellicott City clone) – "too noisy", "smoky", "run down" – it's packed anyway; apparently its denizens are "more interested in the bar" action than the ribs, burgers and "casual" food, which is just as well, since there isn't much service.

Jimmy's S | 17 | 13 | 19 | $12 |
801 S. Broadway (Lancaster St.), 410-327-3273
■ "Stars of *Homicide*", "pols", hospital docs ("relaxing after a busy night") and other "interesting characters" hit this Fells Point diner for Charm City's "best grease" and draft beer; despite the hype, it remains "satisfying and homey", a "really blue-collar, one bread kind of place" for a "home-cooked, hearty feed at a reasonable price."

J. Leonard's Waterside S | ▽ 21 | 22 | 21 | $31 |
Harborview Marina, 500 Harborview Dr. (Key Hwy.), 410-752-6896
◪ "Excellent" harbor views and a pleasant postprandial "walk in good weather" are this marina location's perennial attractions, yet eateries come and go on the site; while this "elegant everything" seafooder offers "good food and competent service", and has fans praising it as the "best so far", they worry that "even the early bird is expensive."

Johansson's S | ▽ 20 | 20 | 18 | $20 |
4 W. Main St. (Rte. 27), Westminster, 410-876-0101
■ Ornate British pub, with the requisite "great beers on tap" and "ceiling fan in the bar", that boasts "surprisingly good" fare – "delicious" crab cakes and "great seafood" highlight an American menu; downstairs, the Down Under Club is a "very different" local scene.

Baltimore   F | D | S | C

John Steven, Ltd. S   20 | 18 | 16 | $19
1800 Thames St. (Ann St.), 410-327-5561
■ No Fells Point "pub crawl" skips this "traditional sailor's bar", with its "slightly scuzzy" barroom and "tourist"-pleasing patio; go for "succulent steamed shrimp", "funky", Americanized sushi and beer in the bar, or the "imaginative" "Cajun-seafood mix" in the "back room"; service is "relaxed but prompt" and prices are agreeable.

Josef's Country Inn S   23 | 20 | 21 | $29
2410 Pleasantville Rd. (Rte. 152), Fallston, 410-877-7800
✏ Restaurant "pro" Josef Gohring's (Peerce's Plantation) "attractive country location" in Harford County, where costumed waitresses serve rich German-Continental and "wild game dishes" in kitschy, somewhat "cramped", surroundings; most say it's "uneven", but a "good choice" for anyone who's in the area or in need of an excuse to take a "nice drive."

JOY AMERICA CAFE S   24 | 24 | 22 | $39
American Visionary Art Museum, 800 Key Hwy. (Covington St.), 410-244-6500
✏ "Let's hear it for vertical food" exult devotees of this "cutting edge" Contemporary American in the Inner Harbor's folk art museum, where the "complex towers" rising from the plates are "unique" and "definitely non-Baltimore" – ditto the minimalist decor; that said, some wallet-watchers whine that it's "worth one visit just to see, but the portions are small and pricey"; N.B. the post-*Survey* departure of its founding chef puts the above food rating in question.

J. Patrick's ●S⊉   ▽ 15 | 13 | 16 | $19
1371 Andre St. (Fort Ave.), 410-244-8613
■ "All the Irish relatives feel at home" at this "bit of the old sod" in Locust Point, a "dark, smoky" pub where the "spirit of fun" and "great" Gaelic music are infectious; the Irish-American food, however, "is not the reason for a visit" – it can be "good", but as one thoughtful regular puts it "it's got its off-and-on days, mainly off."

J. Paul's S   18 | 18 | 18 | $22
Harborplace, 301 Light St. Pavilion (Pratt St.), 410-659-1889
See review in Washington, DC Directory.

Jumbo Seafood S   22 | 16 | 19 | $18
48 E. Sudbrook Sq. (Old Court Rd.), Pikesville, 410-602-1441
■ Some of Baltimore's best Chinese is "best delivered" – otherwise, you may find yourself "sitting in your neighbor's lap" at this "busy, well-run" but "small" Pikesville spot; when crowded "it gets a little crazy", though the kitchen remains "dependable" and woks out "fantastic" dishes "for the whole family."

Baltimore   F | D | S | C

Kawasaki   21 | 18 | 20 | $25
413 N. Charles St. (bet. Franklin & Mulberry Sts.), 410-659-7600

■ "Top-rate sushi" in a "relaxed, comfortable atmosphere" is the draw at this Charles Street Japanese; supplementing the cold selections are cooked seafood, "good tempura", teriyaki and noodle dishes; loyalists praise the "great seating options" (sushi bar, tables or floor mats) and "solid", "friendly" service.

Kelly's ●S   ▽ 20 | 10 | 21 | $15
2108 Eastern Ave. (bet. Chester & Duncan Sts.), 410-327-2312

■ "Nobody is a stranger" at "fun"-loving Kelly and Mary Sheridan's East Baltimore pub, but you "never know what you are walking into" – everything from "Elvis impersonations" to karaoke; regulars laud some of "Baltimore's best crabs and cream of crab soup" at "low prices"; it's got "a lot of heart", not a lot of "upscale" trappings.

Kelsey's S   ▽ 18 | 15 | 17 | $19
Normandy Shopping Ctr., 8480 Baltimore Nat'l Pike (Center Ave.), Ellicott City, 410-418-9076

☑ A "very cozy" storefront, this Ellicott City Irish saloon resembles "a million others" – but few of them are to be found in these environs; the "great atmosphere", "reliable" American grub and "try-hard" demeanor keep it popular with merrymakers (and "too loud" and "crowded" for others); those in search of meal deals may find it "too expensive for a shopping center" spot.

King's Contrivance S   22 | 23 | 21 | $35
10150 Shaker Dr. (bet. Rtes. 29 & 32), Columbia, 410-995-0500

☑ Columbia's "special occasion restaurant", a "great old mansion" serving Continental fare, is a "very impressive" venue that attracts locals with a $19.95 pre-theater "bargain"; praise for its "elegant, fine dining" is not quite universal, however, with critics calling it "reliable but fusty", like a "medieval chamber", and "expensive"; still, it's "convenient" and heavily trafficked.

La Scala S   ▽ 22 | 18 | 24 | $25
411 S. High St. (Eastern Ave.), 410-783-9209

■ It's something of a sleeper, yet those who have discovered this "upscale", family-owned, "comfortable Italian eatery" proclaim it "the restaurant for me in Little Italy"; "good food", "nice Italian wines" and "attentive service" are only part of the story – the finish is the "world's best cannoli."

Baltimore

F | D | S | C

La Tavola S
21 | 16 | 18 | $29
248 Albemarle St. (Fawn St.), 410-685-1859
■ This young Italian's decorator could use a "color check" – its "purple and yellow" tones are a bit much even for "conventioneers"; but its grilled fish and "incredibly rich pastas" are "so good you could overlook the decor", so most do, crowning it "Little Italy's best new entry."

La Tesso Tana S
20 | 19 | 19 | $30
58 W. Biddle St. (Cathedral St.), 410-837-3630
■ "A must on symphony night", when this "intimate", step-down "gem" "convenient to the 'Music Halls'" hums with "interesting people" eating "innovative" Italian fare; to experience its quieter side, go "for an excellent lunch."

Legal Sea Food
19 | 17 | 18 | $30
100 E. Pratt St. (Calvert St.), 410-332-7360
See review in Washington, DC Directory.

LENNY'S CHOP HOUSE S
26 | 27 | 23 | $46
Harbor Inn Pier 5, 711 Eastern Ave. (President St.), 410-843-5555
■ When consummate restaurateur Lenny Kaplan (of Polo Grill and Classic Catering repute) inaugurated this "sleek", "classy" Inner Harbor steak and seafood house – acclaimed as the "most handsome room" in town, with the "best steak" – folks were primed for it to become a "place to see, be seen and feel important"; the above ratings bear this out, but the debut of nearby McCormick & Schmick's may bust a few of Lenny's chops.

Liberatore's Bistro S
21 | 21 | 20 | $27
Freedom Village Shopping Ctr., 6300 Georgetown Blvd. (Liberty Rd.), Eldersburg, 410-781-4114
New Town Village Ctr., 9712 Groffs Mills Dr. (Lakeside Blvd.), Owings Mills, 410-356-3100
Timonium Corporate Ctr., 9515 Deereco Rd. (Padonia Rd.), Timonium, 410-561-3300
■ Patrons get the "full Italian treatment" at these "flamboyant", suburban outposts, what with "cheerful" cherubs on the walls, "always entertaining" servers and "good standard Italian" cuisine; although most are happy to have such "attractive and pleasant" spots within briefcase-toting distance, a few carp about "hefty dinner prices."

LINWOOD'S S
27 | 26 | 25 | $41
McDonough Crossroads, 25 Crossroads Dr. (McDonough & Reisterstown Rds.), Owings Mills, 410-356-3030
■ A "class act", this "elegant" bistro ("no need to board the QE2") has fans dubbing it "amazingly consistent" for an "imaginative" California-style menu; this is where Owings Mills goes "for a celebration" overseen by a "well-trained staff", or to "watch all the action" from the bar; there's never "too much table-hopping" for its steady customers, who go to "eat well, see and be seen."

Baltimore

| | F | D | S | C |

Liquid Earth S
(fka Sacred Grounds) ▽ | 20 | 23 | 19 | $13 |
1626 Aliceanna St. (Broadway), 410-276-6606
■ Fells Point coffeehouse with a "unique offering of sin and health food": "homemade pies" vs. "lots of juices", "organic ingredients" and vegan bites; this "intimate", "ecologically-conscious" bean bar gives "trendy" twentysomethings a place to "cuddle up with a magazine."

Lista's S | 16 | 19 | 15 | $20 |
Brown's Wharf, 1637 Thames St. (Broadway), 410-327-0040
■ "Take a water taxi" to this "ordinary Mexican in an extraordinary setting" on the Fells Point waterfront where the "pretty" surroundings are the "major plus"; though a few go for "good food" and "fun", most find the "cookie-cutter" fare "so-so" and the "atmosphere too cluttered" and "too touristy", adding that the "service is not always good, but the view is."

Little Havana ● S | 15 | 16 | 15 | $20 |
1325 Key Hwy. (Webster St.), 410-837-9903
■ A "hot spot for 20 year olds" occupying an Inner Harbor commercial space grunged up to look "like a set from *Miami Vice*", this newcomer's Cuban theme is reflected in its cigar-friendliness and a few Caribbean dishes on its mainly bar food menu; admirers go for the "great decor and spicing", but others are puzzled: "why treat a good warehouse this way?"

Loco Hombre S | 19 | 15 | 16 | $18 |
413 W. Coldspring Ln. (Keswick Rd.), 410-889-2233
1777 Reisterstown Rd. (I-695), 410-486-4800
■ This wildly popular Roland Park Tex-Mex is annexing Alonso's operation next door, which just might relieve the chronic "waits", "noise" and crowding – but there's no guarantee; while LH seems to have hit on the proper mix of "good frozen margaritas" and "consistently tasty food" that satisfies all but aficionados ("ok if you don't know the real stuff"), the service suits far fewer; N.B. the Reisterstown branch is new and unrated.

Louie's Bookstore Cafe ● S | 17 | 19 | 13 | $16 |
518 N. Charles St. (bet. Centre & Franklin Sts.), 410-962-1224
■ With local "artistry on the walls", "classy music" performed nightly by Peabody Conservatory students and "all walks of life" wandering through the door, this "real bookstore" and cafe "adds a slight bohemian touch to Downtown Baltimore"; it's a "favorite for eating and meeting" that features "killer desserts", "healthy" American meals and Sunday brunch; service is "not their forte but definitely part of their charm."

Baltimore | F | D | S | C |

Luigi Petti ◧ | 18 | 16 | 17 | $23 |
1002 Eastern Ave. (Exeter St.), 410-685-0055
◪ "Nice patio dining", which is rarely found in Little Italy, would be enough to recommend this "pasta joint", even if it weren't reported that "Grandma makes the ravioli", the "people are friendly" and it serves a "good business meal"; some say the outdoor "environment beats" the Southern Italian menu, and views diverge enough to indicate the kitchen is "not consistent."

Maggie's ◧ | 19 | 17 | 18 | $21 |
310 E. Green St. (Washington Rd.), Westminster, 410-876-6868
◪ "Lunch amidst the greenery" at this old wooden bungalow in an offbeat Westminster location can be a "delight"; its "antique-looking" bar/dining room is filled with knickknacks (and, a few add, "uncomfortable chairs"), and "wonderful crab cakes" and salads add appeal.

Main Street Blues ◧ | – | – | – | M |
8089 Main St. (Tiber Alley), Ellicott City, 410-203-2830
This "brand new" New Orleans–inspired dining and live music venue sits "right on Main Street in Ellicott City", a picturesque thoroughfare lined with antique shops, watering holes and eateries; here, the focus is on barroom fun and Big Easy blues, fueled by bar bites, Creole-Cajun vittles and rich desserts; "looks like a winner."

Mama Lucia ◧ | 18 | 11 | 16 | $15 |
Valley Ctr., 9616 Reisterstown Rd. (Greenspring Valley Rd.), Owings Mills, 410-363-0496
■ Known for its "good shopping center pizza" and "pasta lunch specials", this scrubbed, cafeteria-style Italian also works for everyday "family dining", since "standard Little Italy" – style staples are "served in heaps", and the "price is right"; if you want "atmosphere", though, carry out.

Mamie's ◧ | ▽ 17 | 15 | 21 | $12 |
911 W. 36th St. (Roland Ave.), Hampden, 410-366-2996
■ "Fun, funky", "fast, filling" and "cheap", a meal in this kitschy "old movie theater basement" is akin to "eating in a '30s kitchen, but with room"; like nearby Cafe Hon (some of whose "servers and customers moved here"), its "eclectic" menu revisits old Baltimore classics and Mom's cooking ("broccoli was gray"), and its staff "tries hard to charm."

Mangia Mangia ◧ | – | – | – | I |
834 S. Luzerne Ave. (Hudson St.), 410-534-8999
With a giant pasta bowl painted on its outside wall and a menu that lets customers mix-and-match starches and sauces or design their own brick-oven pizzas, this young Canton spaghetti house energizes the genre; late hours and easygoing ways are likely to appeal to young strivers at the massive new American Can Co. shopping/office/entertainment complex across the way.

Baltimore   F | D | S | C

Mango Grove 🚬   ▽ 19 | 15 | 21 | $13
Dobbin Ctr., 6365B Dobbin Rd. (Rte. 175), Columbia, 410-884-3426
◪ Some surveyors say this Columbia outpost is a "good local place" to explore Southern India's pungent "vegetarian" cuisine in a no-frills atmosphere; but those who don't groove on this Grove gripe the food is "just ok."

Manor Tavern 🚬   19 | 19 | 18 | $28
15819 Old York Rd. (Manor Rd.), Monkton, 410-771-8155
■ A drink at the bar at this historic Hunt Country location is a "blue bloods and horses" affair; the "formal side", with "proper attire" a must, offers candlelit American-Continental cooking, while a "casual side", with a "charming" fireplace, features "reasonable, light fare"; it's "very popular", but "no bargain when it misses."

Marconi's   23 | 18 | 24 | $30
106 W. Saratoga St. (bet. Cathedral St. & Park Ave.), 410-727-9522
■ "Like Gibraltar, a sturdy Baltimore tradition" – this American's "delicious signature dishes" ("great lobster cardinale" and hot fudge sundaes) are still a "draw"; also compelling is the "old Baltimore atmosphere", which harks back to "H. L. Mencken's time", not to mention the servers ("average age only 65"); but, yes, there are a couple of curmudgeons who "never did like grainy chocolate sauce."

Margaret's Cafe 🚬   23 | 20 | 22 | $14
909 Fell St. (bet. Thames & Wolfe Sts.), 410-276-5605
■ Possibly Baltimore's "best venue for vegetarian cuisine", it's also the unofficial headquarters for the Fells Point Creative Alliance (don't miss their "terrific gallery upstairs"), which supplies this "laid-back" cafe with its "quirky and artsy" cast; a "personal touch", evident in the "creative, delicious" "home-cooked" meals, also makes it a "pleasant place to pass the time with tea and newspapers."

Martick's   21 | 18 | 17 | $25
214 W. Mulberry St. (Park Ave.), 410-752-5155
◪ "Bizarre", "but fun" – this West Baltimore institution "has to be experienced", but only if "you know the password" (it's a former speakeasy – ring the buzzer above the door) and are "in the mood for cobwebs" and a scary locale; its ringmaster, Morris Martick, "is a full-blown character", and his sorta French "menu is limited to the chef's whim", sometimes producing "great food" and sometimes not.

MATSURI   25 | 15 | 19 | $22
1105 S. Charles St. (Cross St.), 410-752-8561
■ "Wonderful sushi and sashimi", "good grilled items" and the "best box lunch in town" earn this "young, unstuffy" Cross Street spot Baltimore's top Japanese food rating; however, the "bargain" sushi has a price – surveyors report it's "crowded, small and very rushed."

189

Baltimore   F | D | S | C

Matthew's Pizza   – | – | – | I
3131 Eastern Ave. (East St.), 410-276-8755
The thick, bread-like crusts and wholesome toppings on this engaging, family-run storefront's pies evoke 'going-out-for-pizza' in the '60s memories; likewise, its retro prices – a pie with everything on it goes for $8.95, while the 'original' is still under $5.

McCabe's S   18 | 13 | 19 | $19
3845 Falls Rd. (38th St.), Hampden, 410-467-1000
■ When you can boast "Baltimore's best burger and bartender" and "great homemade desserts" in a "cozy pub" setting in Hampden, don't be surprised if there's "always a crowd"; it's the neighborhood's designated "great place to go" and insiders advise "eating at the bar" is the best bet.

McCafferty's S   21 | 21 | 20 | $32
1501 Sulgrave Ave. (Newbury St.), 410-664-2200
◪ "Beef meets Baltimore in an unchilly Mt. Washington setting", with a "clubby" bar for "out with the guys" boozing and "space between the tables" for "client" schmoozing; despite scattered gripes that this chop house is "sort of pricey", its "macho" meat eaters shrug: "thick steaks, strong drinks, comfy chairs – what more could a caveman want?"

McCormick & Schmick's S   – | – | – | M
Harbor Inn Pier 5, 711 Eastern Ave. (President St.), 410-234-1300
Floor-to-ceiling windows, sweeping waterfront views and a dockside outdoor cafe distinguish Baltimore's link in this high-end, Edwardian-feeling West Coast seafood chain; virtually a clubroom for Downtown since day one, its open, yet workman-like, manners are reflected in the clientele's loosened ties and rolled-up sleeves, but tourists tout it too.

M. GETTIER'S ORCHARD INN S   23 | 19 | 20 | $37
1528 E. Joppa Rd. (½ mi. west of Loch Raven Blvd.), Baynesville, 410-823-0384
◪ "Michael Gettier is an artist wherever he is located" say boosters of the star chef's latest effort; the goal is the "best of both worlds", a combination of his intimate "French touch" with the Orchard Inn's suburban location and moneyed clientele; however, the result draws a varied response, with pros praising the "exciting food" and others bemoaning "all Orchard Inn, not nearly enough Gettier"; "more professional" service needed say some.

Michael's Cafe ●S   18 | 16 | 17 | $23
2119 York Rd. (Timonium Rd.), Timonium, 410-252-2022
■ "Major hangout" seriously understates this "ever-expanding" Timonium "retreat's" ability to generate "fire hazard crowds" of "cigar nuts", "business" lunchers, "over 30" singles and "married couples on a date", all in a "friendly", "sports bar-ish" setting; foodwise, most go for the burgers, advising "don't get too fancy, they won't."

Baltimore

F	D	S	C

Milltowne Tavern S — | — | — | M
3733 Old Columbia Pike (Main St.), Ellicott City, 410-480-0894
On Ellicott City's historic Taylor's Row, this handsome, civilized young American grill caters to a "great variety" of appetites and pocketbooks ("from reasonable to expensive"), with "large portions" and "quality all the way around"; it establishes a "great atmosphere" with "wing chairs" in the bar and a stone-walled dining room, and seems to keep most visitors happy.

MILTON INN S 26 | 26 | 25 | $48
14833 York Rd. (2½ mi. north of Shawan Rd.), Sparks, 410-771-4366
■ New owners (Brass Elephant, King's Contrivance) have brightened this 18th-century destination without disturbing its "country atmosphere" or its tradition of "excellent" Maryland regional food and service; as "rustic and romantic" as ever, it's a premier special occasion place – the lovely "walk to the door", the smell of woodsmoke from the hearth room and the glow of candlelight are "only a hint of the wonderful things to come."

Minato S ▽ 22 | 17 | 19 | $24
800 N. Charles St. (Madison St.), 410-332-0332
■ A "great pre-theater place", this "dark, quiet", slightly "worn" Mt. Vernon subterranean is "eager to please" with a "nice selection" of all things Japanese and Vietnamese; the "food is inconsistent but usually good", especially the "great sushi and noodle dishes" and "super" spring rolls, which leads some to "order from both menus."

Morgan Millard S 18 | 18 | 18 | $23
4800 Roland Ave. (Upland Rd.), 410-889-0030
☒ Booths at this "very Roland Park" eatery "have to be reserved weeks in advance for Saturday night" – and don't even think about going "on Mother's Day"; while cynics sneer that the "floor is cracking", the service is "snippety" and the fare is "strictly white bread" American, the "blue-haired" ladies and "working lunch" yuppies who are regulars here call it "comforting", sometimes "charming" and "right out of an Anne Tyler" novel.

Morning Edition Cafe S 23 | 20 | 15 | $16
153 N. Patterson Park Ave. (Fayette St.), 410-732-5133
☒ "Take two newspapers" to fortify yourself against the "long lines" and "waiting room crunch" at this countrified Highlandtowner's "legendary" brunch; some question whether the "wait is justified", to which the "amazing food, fruity pancakes" and some of the "best omelet combos around" provide the strongest response; N.B. open Friday–Sunday only.

Baltimore

| | F | D | S | C |

MORTON'S OF CHICAGO ◐ 🅂   26 | 22 | 23 | $49
Sheraton Inner Harbor Hotel, 300 S. Charles St. (Conway St.), 410-547-8255
See review in Washington, DC Directory.

Mo's Crab & Pasta Factory ◐ 🅂   17 | 14 | 15 | $24
502 Albemarle St. (Eastern Ave.), 410-837-1600
Mo's Fisherman's Exchange 🅂
2025 E. Joppa Rd. (Satyr Hill Rd.), Parkville, 410-665-8800
**Mo's Fisherman's
Wharf Inner Harbor** ◐ 🅂
219 President St. (Stiles St.), 410-837-8600
Mo's Seafood Factory 🅂
2403 Belair Rd. (Mountain Rd.), Fallston, 410-893-6666
7146 Ritchie Hwy. (Furnace Branch Rd.), Glen Burnie, 410-768-1000 ◐
◪ Featuring "huge servings" of the "freshest seafood" "steamed, fried, broiled" or cooked in a variety of rich and garlicky ways, these fish factories don't offer much in the way of finesse, decor ("stuck in the '50s") or service, and they strike some as "too loud and commercial"; but if you like to "eat a lot of fish", they're a "good" catch.

Mr. Chan's 🅂   19 | 14 | 20 | $16
1010 Reisterstown Rd. (Sherwood Rd.), Pikesville, 410-484-1100
■ It's no secret that Pikesville's "steady" local Chinese offers "excellent" food, "efficient service" and "great lunch values" at the Sino-sushi buffet in its "serviceable" dining room; the lesser-known specialty is a "vegetarian menu" prepared with "very fresh veggies", which delights health fooders taking a break from meatless Sin Carne a few doors down.

Mt. Washington Tavern 🅂   – | – | – | I
5700 Newbury St. (Sulgrave Ave.), 410-367-6903
Mt. Washington watering hole and twentysomething stronghold in a "quaint, picturesque area of Baltimore"; pubby to the max, its "garden room provides instant charm" for beer, "lite fare" and fellowship.

Mughal Garden 🅂   22 | 17 | 21 | $21
920 N. Charles St. (bet. Eager & Read Sts.), 410-547-0001
■ Surveyors can't decide whether this Mt. Vernon Indian offers the best deal at its "lunch buffet heaven", where you can eat your way through a "great variety" of "wonderful", "tasty" dishes for a "very reasonable" price, or if it's "even better for dinner", when you can relax and let the waiters "make you feel like a queen"; P.S. the room is "nice", the neighborhood is not.

Baltimore   F | D | S | C

Nacho Mama's ☾ S   20 | 19 | 18 | $16
2907 O'Donnell St. (Linwood Ave.), 410-675-0898

■ With its zany "Elvis lives in Mexico" backdrop and a "nice", "inexpensive" "mix of Mexican and yuppie food" (crab quesadillas, jerk chicken), this Canton watering hole "doesn't try too hard", which is why it's such "rocking" fun; but regulars, who want the "cramped" place to themselves, warn "don't go when it's busy, which is all the time."

Nam Kang ☾ S   ▽ 21 | 11 | 17 | $17
2126 Maryland Ave. (21st St.), 410-685-6237

■ "You never know what will appear" on the table at this basement with "no decor" in Little Korea; while communication can be a challenge, whatever you choose (try a hot pot or Korean BBQ) is likely to be "spicy hot", "very fresh" and "very good"; in addition, the "best sushi for stuffing yourself" enhances the "very good value."

New No Da Ji S   19 | 12 | 18 | $17
2501 N. Charles St. (25th St.), 410-235-4846

☒ "Surprisingly good Korean food despite the all-you-can-eat atmosphere" draws a "big college crowd" to this dimly lit but "welcoming" North Charles Street Asian, where the "cheap, filling sushi" and "great buffet" lunch epitomize budget dining; however, its "'70s" interior and "bad location" are offsetting considerations.

New Towne Diner ☾ S   16 | 15 | 17 | $13
11316 Reisterstown Rd. (High Falcon Rd.), Owings Mills, 410-654-0066

☒ The "right food in the right location" explains this "bustling" Owings Mills diner's "fantastic growth" spurt; neighborhood "kids love the all-day breakfast", while their parents find it's an "easy night out", thanks to the "huge selection" of "good basic diner food", plus Italian and fish entrees and "reasonable prices"; however, critics counter that "service is uneven" and the food "so-so."

Nichiban   – | – | – | M
1035-37 S. Charles St. (Laight St.), 410-837-0818

"Great sushi" and "great atmosphere" – what more could you want from a Japanese? – well, in addition to lots of "fresh seafood and generous portions", this SoBo Nipponese has a full menu of noodles, chicken and beef, all served up in a charming, bento box–sized space.

Nichi Bei Kai [S] | 21 | 17 | 20 | $25 |
Columbia Mktpl., 9400 Snowden River Pkwy. (Oakland Mills Rd.), Columbia, 410-381-5800
1524 York Rd. (Seminary Ave.), Lutherville, 410-321-7090
◪ Some feel the "cook-at-the-table" show at these "noisy" suburban Japanese steakhouses is strictly for tourists and kids, and that the "lunch bargains" at the "great sushi bars" are more up to adult speed; still, if the knife-wielding chef's not "bland" that night, a communal steak-and-seafood meal can be "interactive" and even yield "good food."

Nick's Inner Harbor Seafood [S]≠ | 22 | 14 | 17 | $14 |
Cross St. Mkt., 1065 S. Charles St. (Cross St.), 410-685-2020
◪ "It's your basic blue-collar sushi bar in a blue-collar town", but only "before five", when "the gentrifiers" swarm into this Cross Street Market stall for happy hour, "fantastic", "cheap" sushi and "wonderful seafood"; many swear the "Federal Hill cultural mix is as much fun as the food is good", but others counter that it's basically "a smelly fish market."

North Star Tavern [S] | – | – | – | M |
808 Westminster Pike (½ mi. west of I-795), Reisterstown, 410-833-3994
This Reisterstown "country dining" location has transformed itself "one too many times" for some people to keep up with the changes; in its latest incarnation, it's acquired a "trendy, yuppie bar attitude" and an Old Maryland–style surf-and-turf menu; but, all in all, it's a "good pub after the game."

No Way Jose [S] | 17 | 15 | 16 | $16 |
1041 Marshall St. (Cross St.), 410-752-2837
◪ "Darn good 'ritas" and "cheap" Mexican eats keep this "crazy" Federal Hill cantina "always crowded" with the young and hungry; honchos go for the "A+ BBQ sauce, chips and salsa" and "tasty", "spicy" staples; however, a few grumps grumble "no way to serve food, you mean."

Obrycki's [S] | 21 | 15 | 17 | $28 |
1727 E. Pratt St. (bet. Ann St. & Broadway), 410-732-6399
◪ Though some locals claim it's "still the best", tourists are more likely to rate "Baltimore's most famous crab house" – a "landmark for steamed crab" – higher than natives; maybe that's because it puts "black pepper on crabs" instead of the more traditional seasonings, or because it's "getting too famous to maintain crabby standards" and too "expense account"–oriented for this "frowzy" block.

Ocean Pride [S] | 17 | 11 | 16 | $20 |
1534 York Rd. (Seminary Ave.), Lutherville, 410-321-7744
◪ Enthusiasts go for "great crabs year-round, good soups", "fried seafood by the bucket" and beer at this Lutherville "neighborhood joint", which boasts a "'70s" "ocean resort" atmosphere; it's said that "even the shrimp like it here", but a stubborn few still "don't get the attraction."

Olive Grove [S] ▽ 20 | 14 | 20 | $18

705 N. Hammonds Ferry Rd. (Nursery Rd.), Linthicum, 410-636-1385

■ Zealots drive 'round the Beltway for "fantastic crab cakes" and a "good" house salad at this Linthicum roadhouse, one of those "very homey" spots serving "quality food at very reasonable prices"; worker bees from nearby industrial parks refuel with the "excellent soup and salad lunch special."

One World Cafe [S] 19 | 20 | 17 | $11

904 S. Charles St. (Henrietta St.), 410-234-0235

■ It's in Federal Hill, but it "could be a coffeehouse in Seattle"; here as there, "Gen X relaxes" over an "exotic cuppa joe" or stokes up on "good vegetarian fare" like the "powerhouse tofu and hummus platter"; with its "interesting clientele" and "unhurried", "disinterested staff", it's *the* "cool, low-maintenance spot to meet a friend."

OPA! ◐ [S] 22 | 17 | 19 | $23

1911 Aliceanna St. (Wolfe St.), 410-522-4466

■ "*Opa* means olé in Greek", and that's how admirers salute this "fresh, modern" East Baltimore Hellene; the "outstanding whole grilled fish" illustrates why its simplicity, coupled with "feel like part of their family" hospitality, is hailed as a "delightful change from typical Greek restaurants" and a "good value if you wait long enough to be served."

Orchard Market & Cafe [S] 24 | 19 | 22 | $22

8815 Orchard Tree Ln. (Joppa Rd.), E. Towson, 410-339-7700

■ At an "intriguing" Persian market/cafe hidden "in a banal suburban" office park, the cuisine is a "feast for the mouth and eyes", as "fragrant as it is tasty" (think "duck with pomegranate and walnut sauce"); patrons "purr" about "a delightful experience", service with "panache" and a BYO policy that "certainly reduces cost."

OREGON GRILLE [S] 24 | 27 | 22 | $47

1201 Shawan Rd. (Beaver Dam Rd.), Hunt Valley, 410-771-0505

◪ This "classy, clubby" Hunt Country "high roller" showcasing chef Mark Henry's "genius" with Regional American cuisine is "fast becoming one of the best formal restaurants" in the area; though a minority feels it "still needs work", "when it's good, it's great"; the help may be "a bit young", but rest assured the "expensive" wines are not.

Orient [S] 20 | 13 | 18 | $17

319 York Rd. (Chesapeake Ave.), Towson, 410-296-9000

■ If you "work in Towson" or live nearby, you need no introduction to this "quick, convenient" answer to the "night no one wants to cook"; while its traditional Chinese dishes are "very good", the sleeper here is the "always fresh", "moderately priced sushi" that's served in "large portions."

Baltimore

| | F | D | S | C |

OUTBACK STEAKHOUSE S   19 | 15 | 18 | $22
Perry Hall Sq., 4215 Ebenezer Rd. (Belair Rd.), 410-529-7200
Tollgate Plaza, 615 Belair Rd. (Rte. 24), Bel Air, 410-893-0110
Target Shopping Ctr., 4420 Long Gate Pkwy. (St. John's Ln.), Ellicott City, 410-480-0472
134 Shawan Rd. (McCormick Rd.), Hunt Valley, 410-527-1540
See review in Washington, DC Directory.

Owl Bar ØS   17 | 22 | 17 | $22
The Belvedere, 1 E. Chase St. (N. Charles St.), 410-347-0888
■ "Beautiful, classic barroom" in the "old Belvedere" hotel with a "high ceiling", patterned brick walls and "unique atmosphere" that offers "nostalgia plus interesting light fare" (brick-oven pizza, burgers, raw bar) and some regional American entrees; complaints about "frat party" noise levels and "slow" service notwithstanding, revelers go for the legendary "yard of beer" or "just to keep it alive"; P.S. take advantage of on-site parking.

Panda S   – | – | – | M
6080 Falls Rd. (Lake Ave.), 410-377-4228
Worker bees buzzing along the Falls Road corridor alerted us to this honey of a place – a "good, reasonable Chinese" opposite Lake Roland; the civilized dining room offers a relaxing respite after a tough day, while the wide-ranging menu satisfies veggie-types as well as carnivores.

Paolo's S   20 | 19 | 18 | $25
Harborplace, 301 Light St. Pavilion (Pratt St.), 410-539-7060
Towson Commons, 1 W. Pennsylvania Ave. (York Rd.), Towson, 410-321-7000
See review in Washington, DC Directory.

PaperMoon Diner ØS   16 | 20 | 14 | $13
227 W. 29th St. (Remington Ave.), 410-889-4444
☒ "The novelty has worn off" this "freaky" Remington "playhouse" – patrons report it "can be very good, but quality fluctuates" and the "slacker" servers seem to be "lost in the '70s", albeit "with nose-rings"; nevertheless, steady traffic and an uptick in ratings testify to the 24-hour appeal of its "interesting diner/health food mix", not to mention the "weird" icons on the wall.

Peerce's Plantation S   22 | 22 | 22 | $36
12460 Dulaney Valley Rd. (Loch Raven Dr.), Phoenix, 410-252-3100
☒ A "picturesque" "country setting" and patio overlooking Loch Raven Reservoir are a "lovely" backdrop for a "dress-up meal" at this "special occasion" spot for the Continental "fine dining" vary (from "great to passable"), and while most feel "nicely taken care of", a few foes leave "unimpressed."

Peppermill [S] 18 15 19 $23

Heaver Plaza, 1301 York Rd. (Greenridge Rd.), Lutherville, 410-583-1107

■ Seniors and others who are mature enough to prize "good value" pack this "nothing fancy" Lutherville standby for "basic seafood", "local Maryland dishes" and "heart-healthy entrees"; a business lunch crowd is also on hand ("love their booths"), attracted by the "predictable" quality and "reasonable prices."

Perring Place [S] 20 14 20 $19

Perring Pkwy. & McLean Blvd., 410-661-0630

■ Serving "family-oriented" "comfort food" and "top-quality seafood" "in the Baltimore tradition" ("plenty for the price"), this is possibly the "best strip mall eatery in North Baltimore"; since it also offers "old-time" appeal, it "seems that a lot of 'we old codgers' enjoy" the place.

Peter's Inn ⊄ 24 17 21 $17

504 S. Ann St. (Eastern Ave.), 410-675-7313

■ This "divey", "tiny, good, cheap, hole-in-the-wall kinda place" in Fells Point overloads its "hip" customers' plates with "good, home-cooked", kinda Italian-Eclectic food of the "lots of garlic" variety; a former "biker bar" gone "artistic", it has lots of "character", but "no 'no smoking' section."

Phillips [S] 15 15 14 $24

Harborplace, 301 Light St. Pavilion (Pratt St.), 410-685-6600
White Marsh Mall, 822 Perry Hall Blvd. (Honeygo Blvd.), 410-931-0077

See review in Washington, DC Directory.

Piccolo's [S] 18 20 18 $25

Brown's Wharf, 1629 Thames St. (Broadway, on Pier), 410-522-6600

◪ "A fine view of tugboats with acceptable pasta" is the gist of the story on this "touristy" Fells Point "Continental-Italian" with a "great on-the-water" location and a "cruise ship dining room"; the majority reports the food is "lackluster", leading one local to lament that it's "a magical space that's never been used right."

PIERPOINT [S] 25 17 21 $35

1822 Aliceanna St. (bet. Ann & Wolfe Sts.), 410-675-2080

■ "Sophisticated and intimate" Fells Point boîte that showcases chef-owner Nancy Longo's "innovative Maryland cuisine"; her fans "love its smallness", which permits her to produce "tremendous food without the prices and atmosphere of a high-class restaurant"; while some respondents regret the "tight quarters", virtually all agree that "when it's good, it's very, very good", especially at brunch.

Baltimore | F | D | S | C |

Pisces S | – | – | – | E |
Hyatt Regency, 300 Light St. (bet. Conway & Pratt Sts.), 410-605-2835
This Inner Harbor hotel restaurant (formerly Berry & Elliot's), overlooking the city and harbor, has been energized with a "creative" seafood menu and spiffy decor that some say bring it closer to being "just what Baltimore needs – a great seafood restaurant with a view"; its brand of ambiance is also "good for drinks" or "when you don't want the night to end."

Planet Hollywood ◐ S | 11 | 20 | 13 | $20 |
Harborplace, 201 E. Pratt St. (Light St.), 410-685-7827
See review in Washington, DC Directory.

POLO GRILL S | 26 | 25 | 24 | $42 |
Inn at the Colonnade, 4 W. University Pkwy. (bet. Canterbury & Charles Sts.), 410-235-8200
■ A "really classy", "clubby", "truly professional operation" in a Homewood location, where Charm City's "big dogs" and "power players" come to nod and "be seen" (not heard – it's "too noisy"); the atmosphere is a bit "stuffy", but the "kitchen turns out well-done innovations on classic Continentals" that earn raves.

PRIME RIB S | 28 | 25 | 25 | $46 |
Horizon House, 1101 N. Calvert St. (Chase St.), 410-539-1804
■ The town "never tires" of this "swank", "old-fashioned supper club" (our version of the "Stork Club"), with its "sexy bar", glass-topped baby grand and "retro-chic decor"; "butter-soft steak" and the "best crab imperial around" win it top ratings for food (it's No. 2 for popularity) in this year's *Baltimore Survey*, devotees say it "blows away the chains" by making each diner "feel special."

Puffins/Sin Carne S | 20 | 16 | 18 | $23 |
1000 Reisterstown Rd. (Sherwood Ave.), Pikesville, 410-486-8811
☑ Sitting side by side in Pikesville, these "busy" Californian and Mexican sibs offer "different" takes on "healthy can be delicious" cooking; their "meatless but not flavorless" menus focus on vegetables and fish, "great breads" and desserts; a dip in ratings reflects complaints about a recent decline in "quality", but that doesn't seem to have slowed traffic – "all the girls lunch here."

Purim Oak S | ▽ 21 | 13 | 18 | $20 |
321 York Rd. (Chesapeake Ave.), Towson, 410-583-7770
■ "Stark, stark, stark" and "dark" – appearances don't matter to Towson bargain hunters cruising this Korean's all-you-can-eat buffet; it also boasts a "too large" (for novices) menu of "very authentic" food, plus some of the "best" sushi around.

Purple Orchid [S] 23 | 19 | 22 | $30
419 N. Charles St. (Franklin St.), 410-837-0080
■ On Charles Street's "Restaurant Row", this "quiet, upper-echelon" row house offers a "nice mix of French and Asian" fare, including "perfectly cooked, perfectly fresh fish" and "great presentations" of seasonal game; it's recommended for lunch with colleagues, a "first date" or whenever there's "someone you want to impress."

Rallo's [S] 16 | 14 | 18 | $11
838 E. Fort Ave. (Lawrence St.), 410-727-7067
■ A "typical", well-scrubbed, "white bread" sandwich shop in Locust Point "where they still call you 'hon'" and dish up a "great, cheap breakfast" and "basic home cooking" at lunch and dinner; for gastronomic time travel to its German past, join the "neighborhood" and savvy foodies for sour beef and dumplings on Thursday night.

Ralphie's Diner [S] 15 | 17 | 17 | $18
9690 Deereco Rd. (Padonia Rd.), Timonium, 410-252-3990
◪ "Imitation '50s decor", "iceberg lettuce", "lippy" service and a meat loaf and mashed potato menu propel this '90s "diner wanna-be in search of nostalgia" in a Timonium industrial park; but while its "great milk shakes" and "cute" for kids atmosphere are "good enough" for many, others advise "go to a real diner."

Ransome's Harbor Hill Cafe [S] 20 | 15 | 19 | $20
1032 Riverside Ave. (Cross St.), 410-576-9720
■ Although you can't go wrong with some of Baltimore's "best bar food" at this "great neighborhood" saloon near Federal Hill, there are "some surprises on the wine list and [American-Mediterranean] menu" that earn it city-wide regard; yet, "fresh-baked bread", "good food" and drink are only part of the "draw" – it has the kind of "local feel" that makes you "want to move there."

Red Brick Station ◐[S] - | - | - | I
8149 Honeygo Blvd. (Perry Hall Blvd.), White Marsh, 410-931-7827
In a trend-setting, small-town concept mall, this glass-fronted brewpub fills a dining and destination vacuum with hearty eats – burgers, steaks and such – that suit the suds and the revelers that pack the place.

Red Star [S] 16 | 14 | 15 | $19
906 S. Wolfe St. (Thames St.), 410-327-2212
◪ At night when it's "loud", "crowded" and "hard to get in the door", this Fells Point tavern evokes some of the raucous atmosphere of its original red-light district days; while some say its "interesting sandwiches" and American plates make it "good for lunch" when you can soak up its "engaging" vibes, a couple of "slippage" reports make others wonder if it's "comeback" time.

Baltimore   F | D | S | C

Regi's S   17 | 18 | 17 | $19
1002 Light St. (Hamburg St.), 410-539-7344
☒ Its "walk to Camden Yards" convenience, along with "remodeling" and "some great new American dishes", turned a Federal Hill "local bar" into a "trendy pub-type place"; although it "tastes good and feels good" to its yupscale clientele, some old-timers lament "oh, for the good old days" — now there's "no soul in the place or the food."

Ricciuti's S   ▽ 21 | 15 | 20 | $15
Hickory Ridge Village Ctr., 6420 Freetown Rd., Columbia, 410-531-0250
See review in Washington, DC Directory.

River Watch S   19 | 20 | 20 | $22
207 Nanticoke Rd. (Middleborough Rd.), Essex, 410-687-1422
■ "There's a good time to be had" eating steamed crabs or "awesome" crab cakes and "watching the boats" at the "Venice of Essex"; the crowds "love the summer parties outside", with "great dancing, live sounds", "good views" and the year-round bar scene.

Romano's Macaroni Grill S   19 | 19 | 19 | $19
6181 Columbia Crossing Circle (Dobbin Rd.), Columbia, 410-872-0626
9701 Beaver Dam Rd. (Padonia Rd.), Timonium, 410-628-7112
☒ "Keep the beeper on", there's a "long wait" for a table at this "noisy pasta hall" where a "jug of wine" on the table, a "nice, diverse menu" and "special attention" to kids spell "family" fun Italian-style in Timonium; but spoilsports sniff that while it may have a "facade of style", it's "not so cheap" for something with a "charmless chain feel"; N.B. the Columbia branch is new and unrated.

Rose's Cafe S   – | – | – | I
Meadow Mill, 3600 Clipper Mill Rd. (Union Ave.), 410-662-9513
The smell of baking cookies in Hampden's exciting Meadow Mill arts complex entices visitors into this casual comfort station for seasonal light fare and homey treats; here, Rose Lansing's (ex Cafe Hon) much-loved goodies are available during gallery hours and possibly even later.

Rothwell's S   22 | 16 | 20 | $26
106 W. Padonia Rd. (York Rd.), Timonium, 410-252-0600
☒ It's in a "strip mall", "looks a bit like a chain" and the "preppies" in the "loud bar" are playing the "singles" game; still, most maintain this Timonium watering hole serves some "surprisingly good" American food — "great innovative specials", pastas and grills — at "modest" prices.

Baltimore | F | D | S | C |

Rotisseria 🆂 ✍︎   ▽ | 25 | 7 | 18 | $9 |
219 S. Broadway (bet. Gough & Pratt Sts.), 410-563-3172
■ Since the "king of rotisserie chicken" reigns over a tiny Upper Fells Point "hole-in-the-wall", carryout is the caveat – "don't sit, don't talk, just get it"; this Peruvian's "excellent" charcoal-grilled birds come with generous sides of plaintains and beans and are cheaper than your own cooking; should you opt to eat in, the "fantastic chicken pita sandwich helps you forget the setting."

Ruby Lounge | – | – | – | M |
Park Plaza Bldg., 802 N. Charles St. (Madison St.), 410-539-8051
Outwardly little has changed at this "dark", "chic" Mt. Vernon supper club, despite several post-*Survey* shifts in ownership; but that's not surprising since its "groovy atmosphere" and Eclectic food are in sync with its trendy, martini-loving loyalists.

RUDYS' 2900 🆂 | 26 | 22 | 24 | $39 |
2900 Baltimore Blvd. (Rte. 91), Finksburg, 410-833-5777
■ At their "marvelous" Continental-American "classic" in Finksburg, the "two Rudys are always on their toes": Rudy Speckamp, a "champion" chef, keeps his "consistently fine food" fresh with regional and "Austrian innovations", while Rudy Paul and his "very knowledgeable staff" orchestrate a "special dining experience" for each table; though a few shrug "too far from town", most maintain it's "worth the trip."

Rusty Scupper 🆂 | 15 | 20 | 16 | $25 |
402 Key Hwy. (Covington St.), 410-727-3678
☒ Baltimore's "best harbor views" make this a "beautiful waterfront location" for tourists, as well as a spot for a "great Sunday brunch" and "happy hour" madness; but whereas some are satisfied with the "average" seafood, the common refrain is "if you could just eat the view."

RUTH'S CHRIS STEAK HOUSE 🆂 | 24 | 22 | 23 | $44 |
600 Water St. (bet. Gay St. & Market Pl.), 410-783-0033
See review in Washington, DC Directory.

Sabatino's ☾🆂 | 18 | 15 | 19 | $25 |
901 Fawn St. (S. High St.), 410-727-9414
☒ The "Bookmaker salad is a must" at this "longtime favorite in Little Italy" with a "huge menu" of "old-fashioned" Italian-American dishes; but, while some say "after that specialty", it's "pedestrian" and "past its prime", local pols and other "favored regulars" disagree, calling it "always good" and recommending that you also try it "for people-watching after the bars close."

201

Saigon [S] ▽ 22 | 8 | 19 | $16
3345 Belair Rd. (Erdman Ave.), 410-276-0055
◩ This "peasant" Vietnamese in "working man's Baltimore" is a "family-run restaurant and it shows in the careful preparation" of its "authentic" food and "attentive, if slightly inept, service"; for Indochine aficionados this "unlikely spot" is "the place to go for *pho*", those meal-sized soups that define "cheap" eats.

Samos 🚫 ▽ 25 | 9 | 20 | $11
600 S. Oldham St. (Fleet St.), 410-675-5292
■ A corner hangout where "waitresses, cops, bus drivers, and serious eaters" go for "superb", "cheap", homestyle Greek cooking; engaging owner Nick Georgales "wants only to be loved for his food", so everyone's betting that he can handle his post-*Survey* expansion; it's BYO so "take your own beer and one for Nick too."

Sanders' Corner [S] 15 | 18 | 18 | $15
2260 Cromwell Bridge Rd. (Loch Raven Dr.), Glen Arm, 410-825-5187
◩ Its outdoor deck, with a "phenomenal view" of Loch Raven woods, is an "escape" and a place to "meet for breakfast and lunch" (the interior is less inviting); although you "can't beat the prices or location", most feel that the American "food could improve", likewise the "spotty service."

San Sushi [S] ▽ 23 | 12 | 18 | $23
9832 York Rd. (Padonia Rd.), Timonium, 410-453-0140
San Sushi Too [S]
10 W. Pennsylvania Ave. (York Rd.), Towson, 410-825-0907
◩ Some of "Baltimore's best sushi" draws a knowledgeable contingent to Timonium's tiny, "aim-to-please" Japanese where they "ask Sam [Sesum] for an off-menu special" featuring the catch of the day or his brother Bruce, the top sushi chef, for custom-made creations; the Towson location is related, but some say it's more "hit and miss."

Schultz's Crab House [S] ▽ 23 | 12 | 19 | $20
1732 Old Eastern Ave. (Walkern Rd.), Essex, 410-687-1020
■ "You can't eat it all", but when it comes to freshly steamed, "good" quality crabs and traditional "cream of crab soup" at this Essex seafooder, customers give it their all; it's not surprising that this "knotty pine and linoleum joint" with "reasonable prices" and old-line help has been enjoying "neighborhood support" for years – it's the "real thing."

Scotto's [S] – | – | – | M
5 Bel Air S. Pkwy. (Rte. 24), Bel Air, 410-515-2233
Write-ins could hardly contain their excitement at finding this "sophisticated Italian between the Bel Air strip malls", where "incredible crab-stuffed ravioli" and other imaginative pastas and "great value" lunches can be consumed in pleasant cafe surroundings or taken home.

Baltimore   F D S C

Shanghai Lil's S — — — M
2933 O'Donnell St. (S. Potomac St.), 410-327-1300
Visual reminders of World War II are an arcane backdrop for this youthful Canton bar with a second-floor sushi scene; the Chinese menu reads like Sunday night in the 'burbs, but the trendy ambiance and inventive fusion specials are city slick.

Shogun S   ▽ 22 17 20 $22
(fka Jpn.)
316 N. Charles St. (Saratoga St.), 410-962-1130
■ Despite the "uninspiring" atmosphere, fans have no quarrel with the "good sushi" and "best deal" lunchbox specials that distinguish this Downtown entry; for Japanese raw or cooked, they say it's "the place to go", regardless of recurring management shuffles.

Shula's Steak House S   — — — M
Omni Inner Harbor Hotel, 101 W. Fayette St. (bet. Charles & Liberty Sts.), 410-385-6601
Although there's TV sports viewing and gridiron memorabilia aplenty at former Colt (and Dolphin) coach Don Shula's Downtown steakhouse, you'll also find suave surroundings and happy diners enjoying the beef and seafood fare; go casual in the less expensive sports bar, or join dressed-up theatergoers in the comfortable dining room.

Silk Road   ▽ 17 15 18 $19
336 N. Charles St. (bet. Mulberry & Saratoga Sts.), 410-385-9013
◪ "No one does vegetables like this" exult admirers of this young Charles Street Afghan that uses familiar ingredients in flavorful soups, pilafs and kebabs; yet, while most visitors appreciate its "great value" and much of the food, the feeling is that it's "not up" to its nearby compatriot "Helmand's level, but is still quite good."

Silk Road Cafe S   ▽ 17 8 15 $10
3215 N. Charles St. (33rd St.), 410-889-1319
■ A "Sunday night student bite" stop in an apartment complex near Johns Hopkins U; "kind people" provide cheap sustenance – "good" Asian noodles, warming soups and sandwiches – that's "perfect for a meal on-the-run."

Silver Diner ⊘S   14 15 16 $14
Towsontowne Ctr., 825 Dulaney Valley Rd. (Fairmount Ave.), Towson, 410-823-5566
See review in Washington, DC Directory.

Silver Spring Mining Co. S   ▽ 16 16 17 $18
705 Belair Rd. (Tollgate Rd.), Bel Air, 410-803-1040
8634 Belair Rd. (Link Ave.), Perry Hall, 410-256-6809
◪ When folks living near these stretches of Belair Road want a "night out with the kids" or a place to "hang out with friends", they "herd" together at these "brown food group roadhouses", largely because they're there; "typical burger and beer joints", they're "not bad for everyday" eats.

203

Baltimore   F | D | S | C

Sisson's S   19 | 18 | 18 | $21
36 E. Cross St. (bet. Charles & Light Sts.), 410-539-2093
■ Maryland's "first microbrewery" matches "great beer with fun Cajun-Creole fare" in a "noisy", "crowded" Cross Street pub where 'le bon temps rouler' Baltimore-style; however, if "spicing it up" is not your thing, there are "good ribs" and notable BBQ, plus a post-*Survey* chef change promises veggies, salads and some milder dishes.

SoBo Cafe S   - | - | - | I
6 W. Cross St. (S. Charles St.), 410-752-1518
Bold art and a bright, airy atmosphere make this young venture a place where interesting "locals hang out" in South Baltimore (SoBo); its daily-changing chalkboard menu of updated American comfort classics (mostly $10 or under) is so appealing, it's hard to save room for the temptingly displayed desserts.

Sotto Sopra S   22 | 24 | 20 | $35
405 N. Charles St. (Mulberry St.), 410-625-0534
■ The "gorgeous, stylish interior" is made even more so by the bevy of "beautiful people" who line this Charles Street gilded age dining room – its "fabulous" dark lighting makes it *the* "place to see and be seen"; the "sophisticated" owners combine "inventive" food with a "big city atmosphere" to create an "Italian with an attitude, but it works" fine.

Speakeasy S   18 | 19 | 19 | $22
2840 O'Donnell St. (Linwood Ave.), 410-276-2977
☑ When "Canton is the place to go", pros praise this "pretty", two-tier Mediterranean with an Edwardian air as an "upscale" option; however, foes feel a bit uneasy about the Speakeasy, saying the food has "lost its edge" and is "nothing special anymore."

Spike & Charlie's S   23 | 20 | 20 | $33
1225 Cathedral St. (Preston St.), 410-752-8144
■ "Near the theaters, but not so dressy you can't wear jeans", this New American "gets full marks for imagination" when it comes to "original" seasonal cuisine and a wine bar with "outstanding" bottles; while critics carp that "service is not its strong point", and others don't respond to its "less-is-more approach" to decor, for most it's an "after a show must"; P.S. "save room for homemade ice cream."

Steak and Ale S   16 | 15 | 17 | $22
60 W. Timonium Rd. (Deereco Rd.), Timonium, 410-252-6800
☑ "Reliable red meat and seafood", a "great salad bar" and a "bargain" early-bird menu ($7.49 – $10.99) keep this Timonium staple's "musty" mock-Tudor dining rooms full; factor in the "cozy", "private" space and "family-oriented" service to understand why "if you're hungry and in the area, you could do worse."

Stone Mill Bakery [S]⊅ 22 | 14 | 18 | $28
5127 Roland Ave. (Deepdene Rd.), 410-532-8669
Stone Mill Bakery & Ecole/Appetite
Greenspring Station, 10751 Falls Rd. (Greenspring Valley), Brooklandville, 410-821-1358
◪ Some surveyors say Billy Himmelrich's "excellent" artisanal breads, while still Baltimore's "best", aren't "as novel" these days, nor are his bakery/cafes "as charming", although their "wonderful veggie soup, good sandwiches" and pastries are popular for lunch; the French-inspired Tuesday–Saturday night BYO dinners in Ecole's "spare" space also evoke mixed feelings, with some calling the experience "tense", but others leaving "totally satisfied and stuffed."

Sunset ◐[S] ▽ 21 | 19 | 20 | $24
625 Greenway Ave. (Aquahart Rd.), Glen Burnie, 410-768-1417
■ "Good, old-fashioned dining" on seafood, red meat, "cream of crab soup and strawberry shortcake" has not been entirely eclipsed by suburban chains, as proven by this Glen Burnie American-Continental "standby"; "unbelievable amounts" of these "honest", "old-time" dishes are served by a "courteous staff" to longtime customers, whose major concern is about "prices going up."

Surfin' Bull [S] ▽ 23 | 15 | 25 | $23
2821 O'Donnell St. (Streeper St.), 410-675-9155
■ "Hidden" above a Canton bar, this Latino offers a "unique" "eating experience", with "wonderful" seafood, steak, "great specials" and homemade sangria; it's a "warm, friendly" "family affair" – with members "cooking, serving and cleaning up", "even the kids help" – and in "between courses, a waiter plays the guitar."

Sushi Café [S] ▽ 19 | 13 | 17 | $17
1120 S. Hollins St. (bet. Baltimore & Lombard), 410-837-2345
■ Little more than slot-sized, this Hollins Market counter slices some of the "most affordable and unusual sushi in town"; fans "go for the rolls" ("nobody does it better"), the "sushi boat deal" or for "late-night takeout"; one devotee even declares "I practically live in this place."

Sushi-Ya [S] 20 | 14 | 21 | $19
Valley Ctr., 9616 Reisterstown Rd. (Greenspring Valley Rd.), Owings Mills, 410-356-9996
■ The "owner always makes you feel so welcome" at this "small" but "pleasant" Owings Mills Japanese that customers feel like they've made a friend; his food is very user-friendly too – "everything is fresh and good", with "very solid sushi" and "great wasabi dumplings", plus it's a wallet-friendly BYO.

Baltimore   F | D | S | C

Suzie's Soba S   – | – | – | I
1009 W. 36th St. (Roland Ave.), 410-243-0051
This with-it Japanese set in spiffy new Hampden digs (Cafe Hon's original location) proves that ramen doesn't have to equal reconstituted noodles in cardboard cups; its fresh noodles, turning up in toppings and in soups, add an appealing Asian accent to the medley of fresh flavors bursting out along this street.

Swallow at the Hollow S   ▽ 14 | 11 | 17 | $14
5921 York Rd. (Northern Pkwy.), 410-532-7542
☒ "It's Tuesday and there's nothing in the fridge", and this "cheap, smoky", cave-like watering hole near the Senator movie theater is rocking; critics quip that as the "neighborhood has declined, so has the food", but the hefty burgers, bar bites (and even a "fabulous French onion soup") are basically ballast for the beer.

Szechuan   ▽ 22 | 14 | 21 | $17
1125 S. Charles St. (Cross St.), 410-752-8409
■ For more years than anyone cares to remember, this "hardworking" South Baltimore Chinese has been "calmly" wokking out "spicy", "clever" cooking on the "cheap"; the place is plain, but you're there "strictly for the food" anyway.

Szechuan Best S   22 | 14 | 19 | $16
8625 Liberty Rd. (Old Court Rd.), Randallstown, 410-521-0020
■ 'Cantonese Best' more accurately describes the "delicious", "authentic" food and "great weekend dim sum" at this Randallstown Chinese that's bigger on "bargain" dining than decor ("where orange fringe lamps go to die"); it's best to go with "Taiwanese friends" or ask about the "Chinese menu that [the staff] will translate gladly."

Szechuan House S   ▽ 23 | 14 | 24 | $16
Galleria Towers, 1427 York Rd. (Seminary Ave.), Lutherville, 410-825-8181
■ Sure, it's in a pedestrian shopping mall, but everything else – "great service, good food", "bargain" prices – about this Lutherville "American-style" Chinese is "excellent for a neighborhood place with easy parking"; P.S. act like a regular and "ask for stuff not on the menu."

Tapestry S   ▽ 17 | 14 | 15 | $24
1705 Aliceanna St. (Broadway), 410-327-7037
☒ A change in chefs and management at this "funky" Fells Point Contemporary American is leaving surveyors at loose ends: enthusiasts insist there's "still great food and wine" and add "check out the courtyard and the bar", but critics counter "something's missing" and also cite "disappointing service for the cost" of the meal.

Baltimore | F | D | S | C |

Tenosix S | 20 | 17 | 21 | $20 |
1006 Light St. (Hamburg St.), 410-528-2146
■ It's "great fun to watch the chefs from the bar" of this "relaxing" Federal Hill Eclectic with "oodles of noodles" to "satisfy many food moods"; in sum, a "pasta lover's dream" set in a "dinner party" atmosphere.

TERSIGUEL'S S | 25 | 23 | 24 | $40 |
8293 Main St. (Old Columbia Pike), Ellicott City, 410-465-4004
■ At their "charming", lace-curtained 1890 townhouse in Ellicott City, the Tersiguel family, who "has and meets high standards", "makes dining out a special warm occasion" that captures the spirit of the French countryside; their "wonderful cooking" is served in a "take-your-time atmosphere" that lets diners savor the meal and "excellent" wines; if it seems a bit "stuffy" at first, it soon "thaws."

Thai S | 24 | 15 | 21 | $18 |
3316-18 Greenmount Ave. (33rd St.), 410-889-7303
■ Baltimore's "best Thai" is an "extremely reliable", "reasonably priced" place with a "broad selection" of dishes and "friendly service"; carved screens and silk paintings brighten this "old" storefront that's in a "pretty rough" Waverly neighborhood; P.S. there's a "parking lot in back", and you can "enter the backdoor."

Thai Landing | 23 | 16 | 21 | $20 |
1207 N. Charles St. (bet. Biddle & Preston Sts.), 410-727-1234
■ While known for its "hot, hot, hot" Thai food (but "you can get it mild") and its "priceless" waiter, Charlie, this in-town Siamese is also touted for its "excellent value."

Thai Orient S | 21 | 20 | 20 | $18 |
Valley Ctr., 9616-I Reisterstown Rd. (Greenspring Valley Rd.), Owings Mills, 410-363-3488
◪ Elaborate "murals", crystal "chandeliers" and a "wide selection of Thai and Chinese" dishes make for "great neighborhood dining" Owing Mills–style; located in a shopping center known as the 'Pink Mall', if it were "more authentic and less suburban", it mightn't be such a hit.

That's Amore | 17 | 16 | 18 | $23 |
720 Kenilworth Dr. (Bosley Ave.), Towson, 410-825-5255
See review in Washington, DC Directory.

TIO PEPE S | 25 | 22 | 22 | $38 |
10 E. Franklin St. (bet. Charles & St. Paul Sts.), 410-539-4675
◪ An "institution" and the *Baltimore Survey*'s favorite restaurant, this Downtown Spanish-Continental is one of those places people love to hate – they complain about being "treated like cattle" and made to "wait with reservations" in a "whitewashed dungeon"; however, loyalists like the "great garlic shrimp", roast pig and "excellent" sangria served in "cozy nooks" that are synonymous with "classy" "celebrations" and "fun."

Tomato Palace [S] | 19 | 17 | 18 | $17
10221 Wincopin Circle (Rte. 175), Columbia, 410-715-0211
■ "Overlooking lovely Columbia Lake", this "lively", "family-friendly" pasta-and-pizza place has many virtues – "fresh", "tasty", "homemade" Italian fare, "great atmosphere" and a "reasonable price"; despite a few faults (it "can get crowded" and "noisy"), it's "a perfect meeting place" and "as good as a suburban restaurant gets."

Tony Cheng's Szechuan [S] | 21 | 20 | 20 | $24
801 N. Charles St. (Madison St.), 410-539-6666
■ This "lovely old Mt. Vernon townhouse", with "front windows on the passing scene on Charles Street", serves as an "elegant setting" for "really good" Chinese food; a few complaints about "no parking" may explain why some prefer it "for takeout tonight."

Trattoria Alberto ▽ 24 | 19 | 21 | $41
1660 Crain Hwy. (Underpass Rte. 100), Glen Burnie, 410-761-0922
■ Some of the area's "best" and most "expensive" Northern Italian pasta and veal are found in this "airy, appealing" dining room that's set in a "most unlikely", gussied-up Glen Burnie "strip center"; while the staff here will "remember your name", it may forget to tell you the "price of specials."

Troia the Bistro at the Walters [S] (CLOSED) | 19 | 22 | 18 | $26
600 N. Charles St. (Mt. Vernon Pl.), 410-752-2887
◪ With a skylit atrium, soothing fountain and the Walters Art Gallery as a "sophisticated" backdrop, this Italian is the quintessential "girls-do-lunch place"; while some aesthetes assert the room is "chilly and too spare" and the food "isn't as good" as its popular Towson counterpart, Cafe Troia, perhaps that will change now that chef-proprietor Gino Troia is focusing his attention here.

Turf Inn ◐[S] (CLOSED) | 16 | 15 | 16 | $23
2306 York Rd. (bet. Padonia & Timonium Rds.), 410-252-2911
◪ "Old standby" in Timonium for the kind of "reasonably priced" but "ordinary" Maryland and Italian cuisine that's getting hard to find; while the very pink decor "needs renovation", it's "nice to sit outside" on the patio.

Tuscany Grill [S] | – | – | – | M
2047 York Rd. (Timonium Rd.), Timonium, 410-252-3353
An attractive Mediterranean villa with a big bar and a menu of Tuscan-inspired pastas, pizza and antipasti; despite start-up problems with noise levels, service and a fledgling kitchen, give them credit for providing an alternative to mass-market Italian-American clones; N.B. it's no longer affiliated with the Downtown hotspot, Sotto Sopra.

Baltimore   F | D | S | C

Velleggia's S   19 | 17 | 18 | $23
829 E. Pratt St. (Albemarle St.), 410-685-2620
◪ Pros make the pilgrimage to this "Naples in Baltimore" "at least once each year" for "old standby favorites that are done well here", like lasagna and "sausage with green peppers"; however, critics counter that it offers a "generic taste of Little Italy" in a "noisy", "commercial" environment.

Vera's Bakery S   – | – | – | M
548 Baltimore-Annapolis Blvd. (McKinsey Rd.), Severna Park, 410-647-3337
"Amusing" ex-diplomats let the world come to their "tiny" bakery/cafe "hidden" in Severna Park, where fresh flowers and antique accents augur some of the area's "best", but least expensive, Brazilian and internationally inspired fare, wonderful breads and beautifully decorated special-occasion cakes; you can stuff yourself at their brunch buffet (under $10) or go for a romantic BYO dinner.

Viccino Bistro S   22 | 17 | 19 | $31
1317 N. Charles St. (Mt. Royal Ave.), 410-347-0349
■ "Before the symphony", this "attractive", "up-and-coming" North Charles Street Italian-American buzzes with admirers of the chef's "excellent" "ideas"; but a few feel the "difficult location" and bistro look "belie the cuisine."

Vito's Cafe S   18 | 15 | 18 | $20
Scott's Corner Shopping Ctr., 10249 York Rd. (Warren Rd.), Cockeysville, 410-666-3100
◪ Just "BYO", this bright, chipper Cockeysville strip mall Italian does the rest, with "big portions", "good pizza", "fast spaghetti" and "no surprises"; but wallet-watchers warn "it's a little pricey" for a place with "no ambiance."

Weber's on Boston S   – | – | – | M
845 S. Montford Ave. (Boston St.), 410-276-0800
It's "called Weber's again" and everyone's happy that this handsome American bistro in Canton, the "best any-night place by far", no longer has a Frenchified name "customers couldn't pronounce"; it's "always delivered on the basics" (a "good martini" and grills), along with a "variety of specials"; cassoulet, coq au vin and the "best onion soup" remain on the menu, and it would never tamper with the "great" Southern Sunday brunch.

Wild Mushroom   21 | 19 | 19 | $23
641 S. Montford Ave. (Foster Ave.), 410-675-4225
◪ "'Shrooms", "spores", "fungi" – the "mushroom rules" at this "quirky" Canton restoration featuring "innovative", veggie-oriented takes on New American cooking paired with Belgian beer; however, for some the "food doesn't taste as good as it first did [though it's] still very good", and they add that for a "funky" experience, the "bill can mount up."

Windows [S] 20 | 23 | 20 | $30

Renaissance Harborplace Hotel, 202 E. Pratt St. (bet. Calvert & South Sts.), 410-685-8439

■ "Some people are surprised" by the "club atmosphere" emanating from atop this Downtown hotel, where a "beautiful" harbor view, an "interesting" American menu and "great attention to detail" make it a "power center Monday–Friday"; P.S. it's also "lovely" for weekend brunch.

Windows on the Bay [S] ▽ 21 | 23 | 22 | $21

White Rock Marina, 1402 Colony Rd. (Ft. Smallwood Rd.), Pasadena, 410-255-1413

■ This "beautiful setting by the water" in Pasadena has a "straightforward way with seafood", "good drinks" and a "relaxing" ambiance; it's "best at sunset" on the screened-in patio or for one of the area's best New American brunches.

Wolford's Bakery & Cafe [S] ⊘ ▽ 20 | 12 | 17 | $11

31 W. Chesapeake Ave. (bet. Washington Ave. & York Rd.), Towson, 410-828-4760

■ Praised for providing "fresh soup and salad lunches", plus "yummy" sandwiches and pastries in "an area that needs" such options, this "family-owned" Towson storefront bakery is especially "pleasant" when sitting "outside" in nice weather; inside, there's a baked goods counter and a few tables and chairs.

Woman's Industrial Exchange 20 | 17 | 21 | $12

333 N. Charles St. (Pleasant St.), 410-685-4388

■ One goes to this "Old Baltimore" Downtown "landmark" as much for a "genteel", "one-of-a-kind" experience as for the "wonderful, old-fashioned" breakfasts and lunches; "little old ladies" serve Americana made "the way it should be" (chicken salad sandwiches with "aspic and homemade mayo") in a "character-laden" environment; P.S. few can resist buying "cakes and cupcakes on the way out."

Ze Mean Bean Café [S] 21 | 21 | 19 | $15

1739 Fleet St. (bet. Broadway & S. Ann St.), 410-675-5999

■ Fells Point coffeehouse and casual eatery offering coffee, chai and "excellent Eastern European chow" like pierogi and "wonderful salmon cakes; "comfy" surroundings reminiscent of "your grandmother's parlor" make it a "great place" to cozy-up with a good book or go for ze jazz brunch.

Zorba's Bar & Grill [S] 20 | 13 | 19 | $18

4710 Eastern Ave. (Oldham St.), 410-276-4484

■ "Suburban Greeks come back to the old neighborhood" in East Baltimore for "great" fish and lamb cooked over a "wood-burning grill" at this Hellenic social club; but there's "not a lot of seating" and "no ambiance", unless you count "Greek sports on TV."

Annapolis and the Eastern Shore

	F	D	S	C

Adam's Ribs S | 19 | 11 | 18 | $21
Eastport Shopping Ctr., 321-C Chesapeake Ave. (Bay Ridge Ave.), 410-267-0064
169 Mayo Rd. (Old Solomon Rd.), Edgewater, 410-956-2995
2200 Solomon's Island Rd. (Rte. 4), Prince Frederick, 410-586-0001
219 N. Fruitland Blvd. (Rte. 13), Salisbury, 410-749-6961
■ "Really good" ribs – "fall-off-the-bone tender and lean" specimens – taste best in a "no-frills", get-messy setting, as exemplified by these "family-dining" rib pits; here, "grab and go" eaters fill up on "basic BBQ", chicken and sides.

Angler S | ▽ 20 | 16 | 18 | $20
3015 Kent Narrows Way S. (Rte. 50, exit 42), Grasonville, 410-827-6717
■ At the "best down 'n' dirty stop on the way to the beach", a "local's bar and dining place", patrons have discovered "cheap, dependable fresh seafood" prepared "with authentic Eastern Shore simplicity"; "servers are very nice", plus there's plenty of "old waterman's" ambiance.

Bistro St. Michaels S | ▽ 26 | 22 | 25 | $33
403 S. Talbot St. (Mulberry St.), St. Michaels, 410-745-9111
☑ One of several "wonderful restaurants" that are putting St. Michaels on Maryland's gastronomic circuit, this atmospheric French has become something of a "neighborhood hangout"; lunch casually on a "phenomenal" fried oyster or soft-shell crab sandwich, or make it a "special place to dine" on contemporary Continental fare.

Buddy's Crabs & Ribs S | 17 | 15 | 17 | $17
100 Main St. (Market Space), 410-269-1800
☑ "Beer, crabs" and ribs require little in the way of elaborate atmosphere, but are enhanced by a "nice" nautical view, which explains the "busy feel" of this Annapolis "cafeteria-style", "on the dock" crab house, especially during its "generous" buffet brunch; beware, however, that it "grabs the tourist" trade, along with "too many teenagers at night."

Cafe Normandie S | 20 | 18 | 18 | $28
185 Main St. (Church Circle), 410-263-3382
☑ "Homestyle French without hauteur" at this "endearing" Annapolis bistro translates as a "cozy", lace-curtained setting with a fireplace and a Franglais menu that encompasses "great crêpes" and soft-shell crab; but, as a slip in *Survey* ratings suggests, it "has its ups and downs."

Annapolis and the Eastern Shore F | D | S | C

California Pizza Kitchen S   17 | 13 | 16 | $16
Annapolis Mall, Rte. 178 & Bestgate Rd., 410-573-2060
See review in Washington, DC Directory.

Calvert House S   ▽ 21 | 16 | 20 | $26
401 Solomons Island Rd. (Forest Dr.), Parole, 410-266-9210
■ Serving American "traditional fare in a pleasant atmosphere with good service" doesn't earn this Parole standby any headlines, but it's "nice" to know about; supporters say the seafood is some of the "best" around, singling out the crab cakes as the most "spectacular" dish.

Cantler's Riverside Inn S   22 | 15 | 18 | $20
458 Forest Beach Rd. (Brown's Wood Rd.), 410-757-1311
■ "It's worth getting lost to find" this "wonderful, on the river" site near Annapolis for "elbow-to-elbow crab picking"; the seafood arrives daily, and diners can enjoy a "great" open-air deck overlooking a wooded creek; maybe it's "not perfect" ("needs better parking"), but it's one of the "most relaxed crab places" in the vicinity; N.B. call for directions.

Carrol's Creek Cafe S   21 | 22 | 20 | $28
410 Severn Ave. (4th St.), 410-263-8102
◪ While this Contemporary American's cuisine is "quite good", for many "the gorgeous view of Annapolis and sailboats" from the window tables and deck is the "main reason for going"; a bit "more refined" and "creative" than most harbor venues, its "unbelievable brunch spread" might distract you from eyeing the "water and yachts."

Chart House S   19 | 21 | 19 | $30
300 Second St. (Severn Ave.), 410-268-7166
See review in Washington, DC Directory.

Chick & Ruth's Delly ●S⊟   17 | 14 | 17 | $12
165 Main St. (Conduit St.), 410-269-6737
■ "Campy" doesn't begin to describe this "middies and milk shakes", 24-hour Annapolis diner/deli "landmark" – the "only place to jaw a Reuben" while "meeting and greeting politicians", or to recite the *"Pledge of Allegiance"* over a breakfast infused with "nostalgia"; with its "old-fashioned" service and "local color" galore, it's like nowhere else, and that's not counting the owner's magic tricks.

Ciao S   - | - | - | M
51 West St. (Cathedral St.), 410-267-7912
This airy, "charming" Annapolis bistro offers an informal bar-buffet or carry-out lunch that makes for an intriguing introduction to the dishes on its full-service dinner menu; the kitchen borrows ideas from the Mediterranean for its pastas, paella, Greek chicken, salads, seafood and Moroccan tagines; P.S. the "great wine list" is a welcome feature.

Annapolis and the Eastern Shore | F | D | S | C |

Corinthian S | 23 | 23 | 23 | $33 |
Loews Annapolis Hotel, 126 West St. (Lafayette Ave.), 410-263-1299

■ Exemplifying Annapolis "hotel dining at its best", this Contemporary American offers "excellent steaks" and other "creative and well-prepared" selections in "romantic", softly lit surroundings; though some find its "tony" service and "hotel-ish" appointments a bit "soulless", "you can actually have a conversation" here.

Crab Claw S | 21 | 18 | 17 | $24 |
156 Mill St. (Talbot St.), St. Michaels, 410-745-2900

■ St. Michaels seafooder where watching the "best view" of river traffic "on the Chesapeake Bay" and eating "dependably fresh", spicy crabs can be "heaven in a casual way"; still, a few critics complain it's "cold there in winter" and "overrun by tourists" on summer weekends.

Fergie's S | ▽ 17 | 18 | 20 | $24 |
Oak Grove Marina, 2840 Solomons Island Rd./Rte. 2 (South River Rd.), Edgewater, 410-573-1371

■ "Sunsets across the South River" combined with "good early-bird prices" are the deal at this American stalwart; a "big hall" of a place, it's "convenient for large parties" (the local food and wine society meets here) and for business meals, when a "nice space" between tables and a "lovely view" matter as much as the "decent to very good" menu.

Garry's Grill S | ▽ 19 | 14 | 18 | $15 |
914 Bay Ridge Rd. (Georgetown Rd.), 410-626-0388

■ Known for "terrific breakfasts", fish and chips and tempting desserts, this American features "large portions served by a friendly staff", but surveyors split on whether the fare's "always wonderful" or "sounds better than it is"; remodeling has added a "much needed cozy touch."

Giolitti Deli S | ▽ 23 | 11 | 17 | $13 |
2068 Somerville Rd. (Solomons Island Rd.), 410-266-8600

■ This Italian deli's "stone-oven bakery" breads, "great sandwiches" and knowledgeable (if "disorganized") staff bring customers as "close to Italy as one will get in Annapolis" (not counting La Piccola Roma, its in-town relative); take home one of the "terrific sauces" from the market section – your pasta will thank you.

Griffin's at City Dock S | 17 | 19 | 19 | $20 |
22 Market Space (Main St.), 410-268-2576
Griffin's West St. Grill S
2049 West St. (Solomons Island Rd.), 410-266-7662

■ "Great-looking" spots to "drink beer" in good-looking "local" company, these polished pubs offer "outstanding" microbrews for washing down their "quick bite" American eats; a sit-down dinner may feel "like dining in a drum" if the place gets "loud", so consider the Sunday brunch.

Harris Crab House [S] 19 | 16 | 18 | $23

433 Kent Narrows Way N. (Rte. 50, exit 42), Grasonville, 410-827-9500

◪ "Sit on the top deck and watch the boats go by" while eating steamed "crabs the old way, with lots of beer" on the side, or "super combo specials of lobster and seafood" at this "traditional Maryland crab house" on Kent Narrows; built on the site of an old oyster plant, it offers an edible lesson in Chesapeake Bay history, yet some lament the loss of "personal touches" and the addition of "long waits."

Harrison's [S] 19 | 17 | 18 | $24

21551 Chesapeake House Dr. (Rte. 33), Tilghman Island, 410-886-2121

■ "Eastern shore charm" is personified by this venerable Tilghman Island refuge for "fishermen and duck hunters", where the megacalorie predawn breakfast is designed to keep you going all day; even for nonsporting types, it's "well worth the drive" for the "homestyle" Chesapeake cooking (fried chicken, "stewed tomatoes and crab cakes") and a "view to die for"; diners are in experienced hands – the place has been run by the same "wonderful family" for nearly 100 years.

Harry Browne's [S] 23 | 21 | 23 | $32

66 State Circle (bet. East St. & Maryland Ave.), 410-269-5124

■ Near the State House, this "romantic" Continental is a "good place to see and be seen" and is a "legislators' hangout" for "all the right reasons" – i.e. "the food is terrific" and "you're treated like a king even if you don't valet park the Rolls"; "don't be in a hurry", though – the cuisine is "usually a creative surprise" and that takes time; P.S. options include "jazz upstairs" and a "lovely" patio.

Holly's [S] ▽ 16 | 11 | 17 | $15

108 Jackson Creek Rd. (Rte. 50), Grasonville, 410-827-8711

■ "Maryland's finest chicken salad" and some of the state's "best home-cooked food" await those who aren't fooled by this old-fashioned Route 50 motel diner's "very ordinary" appearance; inside, besides hokey decor ("don't miss the table of laminated '50s cowboy" trading cards), you'll find the "locals" – this "Eastern Shore mainstay" is where they eat.

Imperial Hotel [S] ▽ 26 | 23 | 23 | $41

Imperial Hotel, 208 High St. (Cross St.), Chestertown, 410-778-5000

■ A visit is "worth the trip to Chestertown", especially if you stroll the streets of that colonial-era Chesapeake port as an aperitif to a "lovely" Contemporary American meal at this "very sophisticated" Victorian period piece; the "creative menus" feature "top-quality" regional ingredients and are matched by the presentation and the "best wine ever."

Annapolis and the Eastern Shore F | D | S | C

INN AT PERRY CABIN S   27 | 28 | 26 | $54
Inn at Perry Cabin, 308 Watkins Ln. (Talbot St.), St. Michaels, 410-745-2200
■ Join luminaries looking for privacy at this "elegant" Eastern Shore getaway; though the "dinner 'production'" strikes some as "pretentious", the modern Continental food, "great wine list" and "professional" service "befit the lovely surroundings" and do justice to the spectacular water view from the lovely patio.

Joss Cafe & Sushi Bar S   ▽ 25 | 19 | 23 | $21
195 Main St. (Church Circle), 410-263-4688
■ Annapolis sushi lovers wish we'd "stop telling everyone" about this "very small", "very friendly" and very good Japanese, with its "fine sushi" and "fresh, reliable" alternatives – it's "always busy" and they have trouble getting in; still, because the place is so tiny, when it's "quiet" it's a "good place to go alone."

LA PICCOLA ROMA S   25 | 21 | 23 | $32
200 Main St. (Church Circle), 410-268-7898
■ In historic Annapolis, as "in Rome", "high-end Italian" dining should be both "romantic" and "robust", and that's the aim at this "very good little" trattoria with "attentive" service; patrons "hunker down over antipasto", followed by "creative" entrees and desserts, or "stick to pasta" for a "good value."

Latitude 38 S   - | - | - | M
26342 Oxford Rd. (Bonfield Ave.), Oxford, 410-226-5303
Fine dining has found its locus in Oxford with this charming Contemporary American that's "popular with deckhands" who have spent a long day on the water; hand-painted, boat-themed murals set the mood for creative seafood and steak preparations.

LEWNES' STEAKHOUSE S   26 | 19 | 21 | $48
401 Fourth St. (Severn Ave.), 410-263-1617
■ For "great steaks in a seafood town", Annapolis carnivores proudly point to this "classic", which boasts "humongous, bring your appetite" portions of "outstanding meat" and men's-clubby vibes; devotees swear it's every bit "as good as the Palm" and, some say, just as "expensive."

Le Zinc S   - | - | - | E
101 Mill St. (Tilghman St.), Oxford, 410-226-5776
Once you negotiate this attractive Oxford bistro's "odd hours" (5 PM–9 PM Tuesday–Saturday) and "quirky" ways, you're in for some "excellent" fare; its mainly French menu changes weekly, running from soft-shell crab and barbecue of lamb to Vietnamese spring rolls, and is matched with interesting, offbeat wines.

Maria's Italian Ristorante [S] 20 | 18 | 19 | $23
12 Market Space (Randall St.), 410-268-2112
◪ "Maria [Priola] is great" and so is her "Italian the way Mama made it" food; her trattoria brings "Baltimore's Little Italy" to touristy Annapolis, and it's "a madhouse if you eat in the bar" – the "quiet surroundings" are inside; those in the know say "take an Italian-speaking friend and have the best of meals."

McGarvey's ◐ [S] 18 | 19 | 17 | $21
8 Market Space (Pinkney St.), 410-263-5700
■ In a town that takes justifiable pride in its watering holes, this "good Irish pub" by the Annapolis city dock is a "bar lover's dream" – "loud (in a fun way)", with "great American saloon food" (burgers, black bean soup, steaks), a raw bar and "good people-watching at the outside tables"; be prepared to "stand in line for a brew on a hot day."

Michael Rork's Town Dock [S] 24 | 18 | 22 | $30
125 Mulberry St. (Talbot St.), St. Michaels, 410-745-5577
◪ Michael Rork's followers "drive miles to get to" his St. Michaels town mooring, a "great" indoor-outdoor entertainment mecca with harbor views, a "peppy bar" and decor that some say "needs freshening"; the Eastern Shore American classics and daily specials are some of the "best around."

Middleton Tavern ◐ [S] 18 | 21 | 18 | $24
2 Market Space (Randall St.), 410-263-3323
◪ Tourists and boaters "sit outside" this colonial-era American tavern to "people-watch" over oyster shooters, raw bar nibbles and "good seafood" plates, soaking up the "George Washington ate here" atmosphere; locals love it best on "a cold afternoon by the fire" or for "casual yet refined dining upstairs" near the bar.

Morsels [S] – | – | – | M
205 N. Talbot St. (Mill St.), St. Michaels, 410-745-2911
Across the street from tony 208 Talbot in St. Michaels, this eye-catcher takes a casual, eclectic approach to New American fare and serves it up in a "neat, clean, bright dining" room; it's also an area "favorite for Sunday brunch."

Narrows [S] 24 | 22 | 21 | $27
3023 Kent Narrows Way S. (Rte. 50, exit 41), Grasonville, 410-827-8113
■ Eastern Shore "seafood on the water" is just about "as good as it gets" when you're looking out at the "boats in the Narrows" from this screened-in promontory; the menu features crab "bisque beyond belief", some of Maryland's "best crab cakes" and traditional specials that "can compete with the best"; though there's less "fisherman's atmosphere" in the dining room, it's "pleasant" too.

Annapolis and the Eastern Shore   F | D | S | C

Northwoods S   25 | 22 | 23 | $40
609 Melvin Ave. (Ridgely Ave.), 410-268-2609

■ This "lovely home-like setting" has long been considered the best place in Annapolis to "celebrate anything", from the passage of a bill to the passing of years; its adherents praise the prix fixe Continental dinner deals for offering "unbelievable value" on "hearty portions" of "delicious" food; while the "table-to-table distance" is a "little tight", the staff is willing to "go all out for you."

O'Brien's ◐ S   16 | 17 | 16 | $23
113 Main St. (Green St.), 410-268-6288

◪ A well-known "joint" for politico-spotting over seafood or a salad, it's also known for late-night revels of the twentysomething kind; yet the American pub fare gets "lackluster" reviews, and locals contend that "too many tourists" have discovered the place.

OUTBACK STEAKHOUSE S   19 | 15 | 18 | $22
Hechinger Plaza, 2207 Forest Dr. (Riva Rd.), 410-266-7229
See review in Washington, DC Directory.

Ram's Head Tavern S   19 | 20 | 17 | $20
33 West St. (bet. Calvert St. & Church Circle), 410-268-4545

■ "The premiere place to do lunch among the legislative staff" is a handsome, "trendy brewpub" that covers all bets with a "first-rate selection" of over 200 beers (including several "home brews"), and a menu that runs from "tasty pub" fare to seafood and steak; P.S. there's "lovely outdoor dining", plus "new live entertainment."

Red Hot & Blue S   19 | 15 | 17 | $18
201 Revell Hwy. (Rte. 50 at Old Bottom Rd.), 410-626-7427
See review in Washington, DC Directory.

Restaurant Michelangelo S   ▽ 23 | 22 | 22 | $30
2552 Riva Rd. (Aris Allen Blvd.), 410-573-0970

◪ Replacing Scirocco in an Annapolis-area locale that's starved for dress-up and business dining venues, this ambitious Mediterranean has gone Spanish and is now serving tapas and paella; reactions to its "transition" vary, with some declaring it a "masterpiece in the making" and a smaller group of holdouts saying it still "needs work."

Riordan's ◐ S   18 | 17 | 16 | $20
26 Market Space (Main St.), 410-263-5449

◪ "Way too noisy" for anyone over 40, this "close to the docks" watering hole has just what its "beer-drinking crowd" wants – a "bar scene" fueled by an "incredibly good hot crab dip" and "classic pub grub", as well as the "best prime rib" around for those who insist on a full meal; service is "casual" at best.

Annapolis and the Eastern Shore F | D | S | C

Robert Morris Inn S   21 | 23 | 21 | $34
314 N. Morris St. (Tredavon Rd.), Oxford, 410-226-5111
■ This "beautiful historic inn" at the "foot of the famous Oxford/Bellevue ferry", with its "burning fires and country food", remains a "must" for Oxford visitors; in its charmingly "down-at-the-heels" dining rooms, one finds "outstanding" examples of Eastern Shore American cuisine – the "crab cakes live up to their reputation", as does the genteel service.

RUTH'S CHRIS STEAK HOUSE S   24 | 22 | 23 | $44
301 Severn Ave. (3rd St.), 410-990-0033
See review in Washington, DC Directory.

Saigon Palace S   ▽ 21 | 16 | 18 | $21
W. Annapolis Shopping Ctr., 609-B Taylor Ave. (Rowe Blvd.), 410-268-4463
■ There is a scarcity of Asian restaurants in the Annapolis area, so this "delicious, creative" Vietnamese is especially prized; while the setting is a plain storefront, it offers "very good food for the price."

Tilghman Island Inn S   ▽ 22 | 22 | 22 | $29
21834 Coopertown Rd., Tilghman Island, 410-886-2141
■ Romantically "tucked away" at the tip of Tilghman Island, this Cape Cod–like inn takes advantage of the area's "great seafood" in its sophisticated Contemporary American cooking; eating a "lovely gourmet" meal by the fireplace or on the waterside deck epitomizes "relaxation"; there's also the fillip of a "great bar" and live music on weekends.

Treaty of Paris S   21 | 23 | 21 | $35
Maryland Inn, 16 Church Circle (Main St.), 410-216-6340
☑ Loyalists like this historic Annapolis inn for its "wonderful 18th-century atmosphere", "crab imperial, jazz" and "fab" Sunday brunch; like most treaties, however, it requires some compromise – the "cozy" setting leads to "intimate with strangers" seating, and a few feel its "tempting" "Maryland specialties" could be more "consistent."

208 TALBOT S   27 | 23 | 24 | $39
208 N. Talbot St. (bet. Dodson Ave. & North St.), St. Michaels, 410-745-3838
■ "Superb" is how surveyors summarize this St. Michaels New American whose "fine kitchen" exemplifies "culinary creativity at its best"; set in a "romantic" townhouse, diners feel like they're "eating in a private home", albeit one that's overseen by a "great" staff; overall, it's considered "the greatest treat", "très chic and worth every penny."

Vespucci S   – | – | – | E
87 Prince George St. (City Dock), 410-571-0100
Named after the 15th-century navigator, Amerigo Vespucci, an Italian spirit pervades the ornate dining rooms of this Annapolis maritime location; everything from valet parking to "quality ingredients" charts it as a fine destination.

Indexes to Baltimore Restaurants

Special Features and Appeals

TYPES OF CUISINE

Afghan
Helmand
Silk Road

American (New)
Antrim 1844
Baldwins Station
Bandaloops
Birds of a Feather
Brighton's
Carrol's Creek/A
Chameleon
Charleston
City Cafe
Corinthian/A
Corks
Donna's
Dooby's B&G
Hamilton's
Hampton's
Harryman House
Henninger's Tavern
Hunter's Lodge
Imperial Hotel/A
Inn at Perry Cabin/A
John Steven, Ltd.
Joy America
Latitude 38/A
Le Zinc/A
Linwood's
Louie's Bookstore
M. Gettier's Orchard
Michael Rork's/A
Morsels/A
Oregon Grill
Peter's Inn
Pierpoint
Polo Grill
Red Star
Regi's
Rudys' 2900
SoBo Cafe
Spike & Charlie's
Tapestry
Tilghman Island Inn/A
208 Talbot/A
Viccino Bistro
Weber's on Boston
Wild Mushroom
Windows
Windows on Bay

American (Regional)
Charleston
Fishery
Harrison's/A
Marconi's
Michael Rork's/A
Milton Inn
Oregon Grill
Peerce's Plantation
Pierpoint
Polo Grill
Robert Morris Inn/A
Sisson's

American (Traditional)
Alonso's
Angelina's
Ashley M's
Bare Bones
Baugher's
Bay Cafe
Bertha's
Bill Bateman's
Blue Moon Cafe
Boomerang Pub
Brighton's
Cafe Hon
Calvert House
Calvert House/A
Canopy
Capitol City Brewing
Chart House
Cheesecake Factory
Chick & Ruth's/A
Claddagh Pub
Clyde's
Corner Stable
Costas Inn
Crease
Dooby's B&G
DuClaw Brewing
Duda's Tavern
Ellicott Mills
ESPN Zone
Fergie's/A
Fisherman's Wharf
Friendly Farms
G & M Rest.
Garry's Grill
Globe Brewing Co.
Griffin's/A

Baltimore Indexes

Hampton's of Towson
Hampton Tea Room
Hard Rock Cafe
Harrison's/A
Harryman House
Harvey's
Helen's Garden
Holly's/A
Hull St. Blues
Hunter's Lodge
Jennings Cafe
Jerry D's Saloon
Jilly's
Jimmy's
Johansson's
John Steven, Ltd.
J. Patrick's
J. Paul's
Kelly's
Kelsey's
Lenny's Chop Hse.
Maggie's
Main St. Blues
Mamie's
Manor Tavern
Marconi's
McCabe's
McCafferty's
McCormick & Schmick's
McGarvey's/A
Michael's Cafe
Middleton Tavern/A
Milltowne Tavern
Morgan Millard
Morning Edition
Mt. Washington Tavern
Narrows/A
New Towne Diner
North Star Tavern
O'Brien's/A
Ocean Pride
Olive Grove
Oregon Grill
Owl Bar
PaperMoon Diner
Peerce's Plantation
Peppermill
Perring Place
Planet Hollywood
Prime Rib
Rallo's
Ralphie's Diner
Ram's Head Tavern/A
Ransome's
Red Brick Station
Regi's
Riordan's/A
Robert Morris Inn/A
Rose's Cafe
Rothwell's
Rusty Scupper
Sanders' Corner
Schultz's Crab Hse.
Shula's Steak Hse.
Silver Diner
Silver Spring Mining
SoBo Cafe
Stone Mill Bakery/Ecole
Sunset
Swallow at Hollow
Treaty of Paris/A
Vera's Bakery
Wolford's Bakery
Woman's Ind. Exch.
Ze Mean Bean

Asian
Cafe Zen
Hoang's
Nam Kang
Orient
Purim Oak
Purple Orchid
Shanghai Lil's
Suzie's Soba
Thai Orient

Bakeries
Baugher's
Della Notte
Garry's Grill
New Towne Diner
Rose's Cafe
Stone Mill Bakery/Ecole
Vera's Bakery
Wolford's Bakery

Bar-B-Q
Adam's Ribs
Bare Bones
Buddy's/A
Cafe Tattoo
Canopy
Corner Stable
Red Hot & Blue/A
Rotisseria

Brazilian
Vera's Bakery

221

Baltimore Indexes

Cajun/Creole
Main St. Blues
Sisson's

Californian
Bandaloops
California Pizza Kit.
Cheesecake Factory
Ethel & Ramone's
Harvey's
Linwood's
Paolo's
Puffins/Sin Carne

Caribbean
Braznell's

Chinese
Bamboo House
Cafe Zen
Golden Gate
Grand Palace
Hunan Manor
Jumbo Seafood
Mr. Chan's
Orient
Panda
Shanghai Lil's
Szechuan
Szechuan Best
Szechuan House
Thai Orient
Tony Cheng's

Coffeehouses
Adrian's
Café Pangea
City Cafe
Desert Cafe
Donna's
Ethel & Ramone's
Golden West
Helen's Garden
Liquid Earth
Louie's Bookstore
One World Cafe
ScBo Cafe
Ze Mean Bean

Coffee Shops/Diners
Blue Moon Cafe
Cafe Hon
Chick & Ruth's/A
Double T Diner
Holly's/A
Jimmy's
New Towne Diner
PaperMoon Diner
Rallo's
Ralphie's Diner
Silver Diner

Continental
Ashley M's
Bistro St. Michaels/A
Brass Elephant
Cacao Lane
Candle Light Inn
Elkridge Furnace
Harry Browne's/A
Inn at Perry Cabin/A
Josef's Country Inn
King's Contrivance
Manor Tavern
M. Gettier's Orchard
Northwoods/A
Peerce's Plantation
Rudys' 2900
Speakeasy
Sunset
Tio Pepe
Treaty of Paris/A

Crab Houses
A-1 Crab Haven
Bahama Mamas
Bo Brooks
Buddy's/A
Cantler's/A
Captain Harvey's
Costas Inn
Crab Claw/A
Gabler's
Gunning's Crab Hse.
Gunning's Seafood
Harris Crab House/A
Harrison's/A
Kelly's
Obrycki's
Ocean Pride
River Watch
Schultz's Crab Hse.

Cuban
Little Havana

Delis/Sandwich Shops
Attman's Deli
Chick & Ruth's/A
Garry's Grill
Giolitti Deli/A

Baltimore Indexes

Dim Sum
Grand Palace
Szechuan Best

Eastern European
Ze Mean Bean

Eclectic/International
Brewer's Art
Café Pangea
Dooby's B&G
Ethel & Ramone's
Glasz Cafe
Golden West
Henninger's Tavern
Joy America
Liquid Earth
Louie's Bookstore
Margaret's Cafe
Martick's
One World Cafe
Peter's Inn
Puffins/Sin Carne
Regi's
Ruby Lounge
Shanghai Lil's
SoBo Cafe
Speakeasy
Tapestry
Tenosix
Vera's Bakery

Ethiopian
Azeb's
Blue Nile

French
Bistro St. Michaels/A
Cafe Bretton
Cafe Normandie/A
Jeannier's
Le Zinc/A
Martick's
Purple Orchid
Tersiguel's

German
Haussner's
Josef's Country Inn

Greek
Acropolis
Black Olive
Ikaros

OPA!
Samos
Zorba's B&G

Hamburgers
(Best of many)
Alonso's
Claddagh Pub
Clyde's
Duda's Tavern
Jennings Cafe
John Steven, Ltd.
Kelsey's
McCabe's
Ram's Head Tavern/A
Samos
Weber's on Boston

Indian
Akbar
Ambassador Din. Rm.
Banjara
Bombay Grill
Cafe Bombay
Mango Grove
Mughal Garden

Irish
Claddagh Pub
J. Patrick's
Kelly's
Kelsey's

Italian
(N=Northern; S=Southern;
N&S=Includes both)
Amicci's (N&S)
Angelina's (N&S)
Ashley M's (N&S)
Bertucci's (N&S)
Boccaccio (N)
Brass Elephant (N)
Caesar's Den (N&S)
Cafe Troia (N&S)
Calvert House (N&S)
Casa Mia's (N&S)
Chiapparelli's (N&S)
Ciao Bella (N&S)
Dalesio's (N)
Da Mimmo (N&S)
Della Notte (N&S)
Due (N)
Fazzini's (N&S)
Germano's (N&S)
Giolitti Deli/A (N&S)

223

Baltimore Indexes

La Piccola Roma/A (N)
La Scala (N&S)
La Tavola (N&S)
La Tesso Tana (N&S)
Liberatore's (N&S)
Luigi Petti (S)
Mama Lucia (N&S)
Mangia Mangia (N&S)
Maria's/A (N&S)
Paolo's (N&S)
Piccolo's (N&S)
Ricciuti's (N&S)
Romano's (N&S)
Sabatino's (N&S)
Scotto's (N&S)
Sotto Sopra (N)
Tenosix (N&S)
That's Amore (N&S)
Tomato Palace (N&S)
Trattoria Alberto (N)
Troia/Walters (N&S)
Turf Inn (N&S)
Tuscany Grill (N&S)
Velleggia's (N&S)
Vespucci/A (N&S)
Viccino Bistro (N&S)
Vito's Cafe (N)

Japanese
Edo Sushi
Hoang's
Joss Cafe/A
Kawasaki
Matsuri
Minato
Nichiban
Nichi Bei Kai
Purim Oak
San Sushi
Shogun
Sushi Café
Sushi-Ya
Suzie's Soba

Korean
Nam Kang
New No Da Ji
Purim Oak

Latin American
Rotisseria
Vera's Bakery

Mediterranean
Al Pacino Cafe
Black Olive

Ciao/A
Desert Cafe
Hunter's Lodge
Rest. Michelangelo/A
Speakeasy

Mexican/Tex-Mex
Gringada
Holy Frijoles
Lista's
Loco Hombre
Nacho Mama's
No Way Jose
Puffins/Sin Carne

Middle Eastern
Al Pacino Cafe
Desert Cafe
Helmand
Orchard Market
Silk Road

Noodle Shops
Golden Gate
Hoang's
Silk Road Cafe
Suzie's Soba
Tenosix

Persian
Orchard Market

Pizza
Al Pacino Cafe
Bertucci's
California Pizza Kit.
Casa Mia's
Della Notte
Dooby's B&G
Due
Fazzini's
Mama Lucia
Mangia Mangia
Matthew's Pizza
O'Brien's/A
Owl Bar
Paolo's
Ruby Lounge
Tomato Palace
Tuscany Grill
Vito's Cafe

Seafood
(Best of many)
Angelina's
Angler/A
Anne Arundel Seafood

Baltimore Indexes

A-1 Crab Haven
Bahama Mamas
Bertha's
Black Olive
Bo Brooks
Calvert House
Candle Light Inn
Cantler's/A
Captain Harvey's
Carrol's Creek/A
Chart House
Corinthian/A
Costas Inn
Crab Claw/A
Faidley's
Fisherman's Wharf
Fishery
Gabler's
Gibby's
Gunning's Crab Hse.
Gunning's Seafood
Harris Crab House/A
Harrison's/A
Hoang's
Ikaros
J. Leonard's
John Steven, Ltd.
Josef's Country Inn
J. Paul's
Jumbo Seafood
Lenny's Chop Hse.
Marconi's
McCormick & Schmick's
Michael Rork's/A
Middleton Tavern/A
Mo's Fisherman's Exch.
Narrows/A
Nick's
O'Brien's/A
Ocean Pride
Perring Place
Pierpoint
Pisces
Polo Grill
Prime Rib
River Watch
Robert Morris Inn/A
Rusty Scupper
Schultz's Crab Hse.
Tilghman Island Inn/A
Windows on Bay

Southern/Soul
Charleston

Southwestern
Golden West
Joy America
No Way Jose

Spanish
Cafe Madrid
Fishery
Rest. Michelangelo/A
Surfin' Bull
Tio Pepe

Steakhouses
Claddagh Pub
Corinthian/A
Jerry D's Saloon
Lenny's Chop Hse.
Lewnes' Steakhse./A
McCabe's
McCafferty's
Morton's of Chicago
Nichi Bei Kai
Oregon Grill
Outback Steakhouse
Polo Grill
Prime Rib
Ruth's Chris
Shula's Steak Hse.
Steak & Ale
Surfin' Bull

Sushi
Bamboo House
Cafe Zen
Edo Sushi
Hoang's
John Steven, Ltd.
Joss Cafe/A
Kawasaki
Matsuri
Minato
Nam Kang
New No Da Ji
Nichiban
Nichi Bei Kai
Nick's
Orient
Purim Oak
San Sushi
Shanghai Lil's
Shogun
Sushi Café
Sushi-Ya
Szechuan Best

Baltimore Indexes

Thai
Bangkok Place
Ban Thai
San Sushi
Thai
Thai Landing
Thai Orient

Vegetarian
(Most Chinese, Indian and Thai restaurants)
Adrian's
Golden West

Helmand
Liquid Earth
Margaret's Cafe
One World Cafe
PaperMoon Diner
Puffins/Sin Carne
Wild Mushroom

Vietnamese
Hoang's
Saigon
Saigon Palace/A

Baltimore Indexes

NEIGHBORHOOD LOCATIONS

BALTIMORE

**Business District/
Downtown/
Convention Center/
Camden Yards/
Inner Harbor**
Brighton's
Cafe Bombay
California Pizza Kit.
Calvert House
Capitol City Brewing
Chart House
Cheesecake Factory
Donna's
ESPN Zone
Faidley's
Globe Brewing Co.
Hampton's
Hard Rock Cafe
J. Leonard's
Joy America
J. Paul's
Lenny's Chop Hse.
Little Havana
Marconi's
Martick's
McCormick & Schmick's
Morton's of Chicago
Mo's Fisherman's Wharf
Paolo's
Phillips
Pisces
Planet Hollywood
Rusty Scupper
Ruth's Chris
Shula's Steak Hse.
Tio Pepe
Windows

Canton
Bay Cafe
Claddagh Pub
Dooby's B&G
Helen's Garden
Kelly's
Mangia Mangia
Nacho Mama's
Shanghai Lil's
Speakeasy
Surfin' Bull
Weber's on Boston
Wild Mushroom

**Downtown/Charles St./
Mt. Vernon**
Akbar
Al Pacino/Cafe Isis
Ashley M's
Azeb's
Ban Thai
Bombay Grill
Brass Elephant
Brewer's Art
City Cafe
Donna's
Helmand
Kawasaki
La Tesso Tana
Louie's Bookstore
Minato
Mughal Garden
Nam Kang
New No Da Ji
Owl Bar
Prime Rib
Purple Orchid
Ruby Lounge
Shogun
Silk Road
Sotto Sopra
Spike & Charlie's
Thai Landing
Tony Cheng's
Troia/Walters
Viccino Bistro
Woman's Ind. Exch.

East Baltimore
Attman's Deli
Braznell's
Obrycki's
Rotisseria

**Federal Hill/
South Baltimore**
Bandaloops
Banjara
Boomerang Pub
Corks
Gunning's Crab Hse.
Hull St. Blues
J. Patrick's
Matsuri
Nichiban
Nick's
No Way Jose
One World Cafe

227

Baltimore Indexes

Rallo's
Ransome's
Regi's
Sisson's
SoBo Cafe
Sushi Café
Szechuan
Tenosix

Fells Point
Adrian's
Bertha's
Birds of a Feather
Black Olive
Blue Moon Cafe
Cafe Madrid
Duda's Tavern
Fishery
Hamilton's
Henninger's Tavern
Jimmy's
John Steven, Ltd.
Liquid Earth
Lista's
Margaret's Cafe
OPA!
Peter's Inn
Piccolo's
Pierpoint
Red Star
Tapestry
Ze Mean Bean

Hampden/Roland Park/ Homewood/ Charles Village
Alonso's
Ambassador Din. Rm.
Blue Nile
Cafe Hon
Café Pangea
Donna's
Golden West
Holy Frijoles
Jeannier's
Loco Hombre
Mamie's

McCabe's
Morgan Millard
PaperMoon Diner
Polo Grill
Rose's Cafe
Silk Road Cafe
Stone Mill Bakery
Suzie's Soba

Harbor East/Little Italy
Amicci's
Boccaccio
Caesar's Den
Charleston
Chiapparelli's
Ciao Bella
Dalesio's
Da Mimmo
Della Notte
Germano's
La Scala
La Tavola
Luigi Petti
Mo's Crab & Pasta
Sabatino's
Velleggia's

Highlandtown/Greektown
Acropolis
Haussner's
Ikaros
Matthew's Pizza
Morning Edition
Samos
Zorba's B&G

Mt. Washington/ Lake Roland
Al Pacino Cafe
Desert Cafe
Ethel & Ramone's
Glasz Cafe
Hoang's
McCafferty's
Mt. Washington Tavern
Panda

OUTER BALTIMORE

Brooklandville
Harvey's
Joey Chiu's
Stone Mill Bakery/Ecole

BWI/Linthicum/Elkridge
Elkridge Furnace
G & M Rest.

Gunning's Seafood
Olive Grove

Columbia
Akbar
Bertucci's
Bombay Peacock Grill
Clyde's

228

Baltimore Indexes

Gringada
Hunan Manor
King's Contrivance
Mango Grove
Nichi Bei Kai
Ricciuti's
Romano's
Tomato Palace

Ellicott City/Catonsville

Bare Bones
Cacao Lane
Candle Light Inn
Canopy
Double T Diner
Ellicott Mills
Hunter's Lodge
Jennings Cafe
Jilly's
Kelsey's
Main St. Blues
Milltowne Tavern
Outback Steakhouse
Tersiguel's

Essex/Dundalk

A-1 Crab Haven
Bahama Mamas
Costas Inn
River Watch
Schultz's Crab Hse.

Glen Burnie/Severna Park/Pasadena

Adam's Ribs
Anne Arundel Seafood
Cafe Bretton
Canopy
Double T Diner
Garry's Grill
Grand Palace
Mo's Seafood Factory
Sunset
Trattoria Alberto
Vera's Bakery
Windows on Bay

Hunt Valley/North Baltimore Co.

Friendly Farms
Manor Tavern
Milton Inn
Oregon Grill
Outback Steakhouse
Peerce's Plantation

Lutherville/Timonium/Cockeysville

Al Pacino/Cafe Isis
Bamboo House
Bertucci's
Corner Stable
Donna's
Edo Sushi
Fazzini's
Gibby's
Liberatore's
Michael's Cafe
Nichi Bei Kai
Ocean Pride
Peppermill
Ralphie's Diner
Romano's
Rothwell's
San Sushi
Steak & Ale
Szechuan House
Turf Inn
Tuscany Grill
Vito's Cafe

North Baltimore/York Road Corridor

Bangkok Place
Cafe Zen
Egyptian Pizza
Swallow at Hollow
Thai

Northeast Baltimore/Parkville/Perry Hall/Baynesville

Angelina's
Bo Brooks
Cafe Tattoo
Jerry D's Saloon
M. Gettier's Orchard
Mo's Fisherman's Exch.
Orchard Market
Outback Steakhouse
Perring Place
Saigon
Sanders' Corner
Silver Spring Mining

Owings Mills/Reisterstown

Bertucci's
Canopy
Captain Harvey's

229

Baltimore Indexes

Due
Harryman House
Liberatore's
Linwood's
Mama Lucia
New Towne Diner
North Star Tavern
Rudys' 2900
Sushi-Ya
Thai Orient

Pikesville
Al Pacino/Cafe Isis
Donna's
Jilly's
Jumbo Seafood
Loco Hombre
Mr. Chan's
Puffins/Sin Carne

Randallstown/ Eldersburg/ Sykesville
Akbar
Baldwins Station
Canopy
Liberatore's
Szechuan Best

Towson
Bill Bateman's
Cafe Troia
Casa Mia's
Crease
Fisherman's Wharf

Golden Gate
Hampton's of Towson
Hampton Tea Room
Orient
Paolo's
Purim Oak
San Sushi Too
Silver Diner
That's Amore
Wolford's Bakery

Westminster/ Taneytown
Antrim 1844
Baugher's
Canopy
Chameleon
Johansson's
Maggie's

White Marsh/Belair/ Harford County
Bertucci's
Double T Diner
DuClaw Brewing
Gabler's
Josef's Country Inn
Mo's Seafood Factory
Outback Steakhouse
Phillips
Red Brick Station
Scotto's
Silver Spring Mining

ANNAPOLIS/EASTERN SHORE

Annapolis
Adam's Ribs
Buddy's
Cafe Normandie
California Pizza Kit.
Calvert House
Cantler's
Carrol's Creek
Chart House
Chick & Ruth's
Ciao
Corinthian
Fergie's
Garry's Grill
Giolitti Deli
Griffin's

Harry Browne's
Joss Cafe
La Piccola Roma
Lewnes' Steakhse.
Maria's
McGarvey's
Middleton Tavern
Northwoods
O'Brien's
Outback Steakhouse
Ram's Head Tavern
Red Hot & Blue
Rest. Michelangelo
Riordan's
Ruth's Chris
Saigon Palace

Baltimore Indexes

Treaty of Paris
Vespucci

**Kent Narrows/
Near Eastern Shore/
St. Michaels/Chestertown**
Adam's Ribs
Angler
Bistro St. Michaels
Crab Claw
Harris Crab House
Harrison's

Holly's
Imperial Hotel
Inn at Perry Cabin
Latitude 38
Le Zinc
Michael Rork's
Morsels
Narrows
Robert Morris Inn
Tilghman Island Inn
208 Talbot

Baltimore Indexes

SPECIAL FEATURES AND APPEALS

Breakfast
(All hotels and the following standouts)
Baugher's
Blue Moon Cafe
Cafe Hon
Chick & Ruth's/A
Donna's
Double T Diner
Holly's/A
Jimmy's
Morning Edition
New Towne Diner
One World Cafe
Rallo's
Woman's Ind. Exch.

Brunch
(Best of many)
Cafe Hon
Carrol's Creek/A
Clyde's
Hampton's
Harryman House
Helen's Garden
Hull St. Blues
Joy America
Kelsey's
Louie's Bookstore
Margaret's Cafe
Morning Edition
Peerce's Plantation
Pierpoint
Pisces
Polo Grill
Ransome's
Treaty of Paris/A
Vera's Bakery
Weber's on Boston
Windows

Buffet Served
(Check prices, days and times)
Akbar
Ambassador Din. Rm.
Banjara
Boomerang Pub
Ciao/A
Della Notte
Mango Grove
Mughal Garden
New No Da Ji
Orchard Market
Phillips
Purim Oak
Saigon
Szechuan Best
Tuscany Grill
Windows

Business Dining
Bamboo House
Boccaccio
Bombay Grill
Brass Elephant
Brighton's
Cafe Bombay
Calvert House
Charleston
Corinthian/A
Hampton's
Helmand
Hunan Manor
King's Contrivance
La Piccola Roma/A
Lenny's Chop Hse.
Lewnes' Steakhse./A
Liberatore's
Linwood's
McCafferty's
Morton's of Chicago
Oregon Grill
Pierpoint
Polo Grill
Prime Rib
Rudys' 2900
Ruth's Chris
Sabatino's
Shula's Steak Hse.
Thai Landing
Viccino Bistro
Windows
Woman's Ind. Exch.

BYO
Adrian's
Al Pacino Cafe
Blue Moon Cafe
Blue Nile
Cafe Zen
Edo Sushi
Ethel & Ramone's

232

Baltimore Indexes

Fazzini's
Holy Frijoles
Mamie's
Orchard Market
Stone Mill Bakery/Ecole
Sushi-Ya
Vera's Bakery
Vito's Cafe
Ze Mean Bean

Caters
(Best of many)
Attman's Deli
Brass Elephant
Cafe Hon
Cafe Troia
Due
Elkridge Furnace
Giolitti Deli/A
Josef's Country Inn
Joy America
King's Contrivance
La Tesso Tana
Linwood's
Mama Lucia
Orchard Market
Peerce's Plantation
Pierpoint
Puffins/Sin Carne
Rudys' 2900
Samos
Spike & Charlie's
Vera's Bakery

Cigar Friendly
(Best of many)
Antrim 1844
Baldwins Station
Boomerang Pub
Brewer's Art
Cafe Tattoo
Charleston
Claddagh Pub
Corks
Ellicott Mills
Globe Brewing Co.
Hamilton's
Hampton's
Harryman House
Lenny's Chop Hse.
Lewnes' Steakhse./A
Oregon Grill
Owl Bar
Polo Grill

Prime Rib
Ruth's Chris
Shula's Steak Hse.

Dancing/Entertainment
(Check days, times and performers for entertainment; D=dancing; best of many)
Adrian's (varies)
Angelina's (guitar)
Antrim 1844 (piano)
A-1 Crab Haven (piano)
Baldwins Station (varies)
Bare Bones (bands)
Bay Cafe (varies)
Bertha's (jazz)
Bombay Grill (sitar)
Cacao Lane (varies)
Cafe Tattoo (bands)
Costas Inn (karaoke)
Fergie's/A (piano)
Gunning's Seafood (karaoke)
Hampton's (jazz/piano)
Hampton's of Towson (piano)
Harry Browne's/A (varies)
Harryman House (jazz)
Harvey's (varies)
Hunter's Lodge (varies)
Imperial Hotel/A (jazz)
Johansson's (bands)
J. Patrick's (varies)
Kelly's (karaoke)
Lenny's Chop Hse. (piano)
Louie's Bookstore (classical)
Luigi Petti (piano)
Main St. Blues (blues)
McCafferty's (piano)
M. Gettier's Orchard (piano)
Michael Rork's/A (D/varies)
Middleton Tavern/A (bands)
Morning Edition (varies)
O'Brien's/A (D/varies)
One World Cafe (folk/jazz)
Oregon Grill (piano)
Phillips (piano)
Piccolo's (bands)
Pisces (DJ)
Prime Rib (bass/piano)
Ram's Head Tavern/A (D/varies)
Red Brick Station (varies)
Red Star (DJ/tarot cards)
River Watch (bands)
Surfin' Bull (guitar)
Tilghman Island Inn/A (jazz)

233

Baltimore Indexes

Trattoria Alberto (classical)
Treaty of Paris/A (jazz)
Vespucci/A (D)
Weber's on Boston (guitar)
Windows (jazz)
Windows on Bay (bands)
Ze Mean Bean (varies)

Delivers*/Takeout
(Nearly all Asians, coffee shops, delis, diners and pasta/pizzerias deliver or do takeout; here are some interesting possibilities; D=delivery, T=takeout; *call to check range and charges, if any)

Adam's Ribs (T)
Al Pacino Cafe (D,T)
Anne Arundel Seafood (T)
Ashley M's (T)
Attman's Deli (D,T)
Bare Bones (T)
Baugher's (T)
Bill Bateman's (T)
Bo Brooks (T)
Canopy (T)
Chiapparelli's (T)
City Cafe (T)
Corner Stable (T)
Della Notte (T)
Due (T)
Faidley's (T)
Fazzini's (D,T)
Fisherman's Wharf (T)
Fishery (T)
Gibby's (T)
Giolitti Deli/A (T)
Gunning's Crab Hse. (T)
Gunning's Seafood (T)
Harris Crab House/A (T)
Haussner's (T)
Helen's Garden (T)
Holly's/A (T)
Linwood's (T)
Mama Lucia (T)
Mamie's (D,T)
Mo's Fisherman's Exch. (T)
Mr. Chan's (T)
Nick's (T)
Ocean Pride (T)
One World Cafe (T)
Orchard Market (T)
Orient (T)
Rotisseria (T)
Sabatino's (T)
Samos (D,T)
San Sushi (T)
Schultz's Crab Hse. (T)
Silk Road (T)
Silk Road Cafe (D,T)
Vera's Bakery (T)
Vito's Cafe (T)
Wild Mushroom (T)
Ze Mean Bean (T)

Dessert/Ice Cream
Adrian's
Baugher's
Blue Moon Cafe
Cafe Hon
Café Pangea
Charleston
Cheesecake Factory
City Cafe
Donna's
Haussner's
Henninger's Tavern
Holly's/A
Linwood's
Louie's Bookstore
New Towne Diner
One World Cafe
Pierpoint
Rose's Cafe
Sanders' Corner
Spike & Charlie's
Vera's Bakery
Wolford's Bakery
Woman's Ind. Exch.

Dining Alone
(Other than hotels, coffee shops, sushi bars and places with counter service)

Blue Moon Cafe
Cafe Hon
Café Pangea
City Cafe
Donna's
Faidley's
Joss Cafe/A
Louie's Bookstore
Nick's
One World Cafe
Tenosix
Woman's Ind. Exch.
Ze Mean Bean

Family Style
Friendly Farms
Harrison's/A

Baltimore Indexes

Fireplaces
Antrim 1844
Brewer's Art
Fishery
Hull St. Blues
Johansson's
John Steven, Ltd.
Manor Tavern
Milton Inn
North Star Tavern
Ocean Pride
Oregon Grill
Peerce's Plantation
Sanders' Corner
Steak & Ale
Tilghman Island Inn/A
Velleggia's
Ze Mean Bean

Game In Season
Birds of a Feather
Boccaccio
Boomerang Pub
Brass Elephant
Charleston
Corks
Ellicott Mills
Hamilton's
Hampton's
Harryman House
Joy America
McCabe's
M. Gettier's Orchard
Milton Inn
Oregon Grill
Pierpoint
Polo Grill
Purple Orchid
Sotto Sopra
Spike & Charlie's
Tersiguel's
Viccino Bistro

Health/Spa Menus
(Most places cook to order to meet any dietary request; call in advance to check; almost all Chinese, Indian and other ethnics have health-conscious meals, as do the following)
Kelly's
Liquid Earth
Margaret's Cafe
One World Cafe
Pierpoint
Puffins/Sin Carne
Wild Mushroom

Historic Interest
(Year opened; *building)
1722 North Star Tavern*
1740 Milton Inn*
1740 Ram's Head Tavern/A*
1744 Elkridge Furnace*
1750 Middleton Tavern/A*
1762 Hamilton's*
1772 Treaty of Paris/A*
1774 O'Brien's/A
1790 Black Olive*
1790 Harryman House*
1797 Hampton Tea Room*
1800 Candle Light Inn
1820 Bertha's*
1820 La Piccola Roma/A*
1844 Antrim 1844*
1849 Corks*
1850 Brass Elephant*
1850 Martick's*
1850 Wild Mushroom*
1851 Oregon Grill*
1860 Cacao Lane*
1860 Woman's Ind. Exch.*
1871 208 Talbot/A*
1880 Henninger's Tavern
1880 Manor Tavern*
1883 Baldwins Station
1886 Sanders' Corner*
1890 Tersiguel's*
1896 Morgan Millard*
1897 Brewer's Art*
1900 King's Contrivance*
1902 Imperial Hotel/A*
1903 Owl Bar*
1904 Ellicott Mills*
1904 Sotto Sopra*
1905 Hunter's Lodge
1913 Johansson's*
1920 Marconi's
1938 Gabler's*
1941 Peerce's Plantation

Hotel Dining
Admiral Fell Inn
   Hamilton's
Antrim 1844 Country Inn
   Antrim 1844

Baltimore Indexes

Belvedere
  Owl Bar
Harbor Court Hotel
  Brighton's
  Hampton's
Hyatt Regency
  Pisces
Imperial Hotel
  Imperial Hotel/A
Inn at Perry Cabin
  Inn at Perry Cabin/A
Inn at the Colonnade
  Polo Grill
Loews Annapolis
  Corinthian/A
Maryland Inn
  Treaty of Paris/A
Omni Inner Harbor
  Shula's Steak Hse.
Renaissance Harborplace
  Windows
Sheraton Inner Harbor
  Morton's of Chicago

"In" Places
Black Olive
Brewer's Art
Café Pangea
Harry Browne's/A
Linwood's
Manor Tavern
McCormick & Schmick's
Middleton Tavern/A
Milton Inn
Nacho Mama's
Polo Grill
SoBo Cafe
Sotto Sopra
Ze Mean Bean

Jacket Required
Hampton's
Marconi's
Prime Rib
Tio Pepe
Valley Inn

Late Late – After 12:30
(All hours are AM)
Bill Bateman's (1)
Chick & Ruth's/A (24 hrs.)
Costas Inn (1)
Dooby's B&G (1)
Double T Diner (24 hrs.)
Duda's Tavern (1)
Ellicott Mills (2)
Harryman House (2)
John Steven, Ltd. (1:30)
McGarvey's/A (1:30)
Nam Kang (4)
New Towne Diner (1)
PaperMoon Diner (24 hrs.)
Sabatino's (3)
Silver Diner (3)
Sunset (12:45)

Meet for a Drink
(Most top hotels and the following standouts)
Bay Cafe
Bertha's
Brewer's Art
Capitol City Brewing
Carrol's Creek/A
Chart House
John Steven, Ltd.
J. Paul's
Kelly's
Lewnes' Steakhse./A
Manor Tavern
McCormick & Schmick's
McGarvey's/A
Nick's
Owl Bar
Pisces
Ram's Head Tavern/A

Noteworthy Newcomers
Ashley M's
Black Olive
Cafe Madrid
Charleston
Ciao/A
Edo Sushi
ESPN Zone
Golden West
Hamilton's
Hard Rock Cafe
Hunter's Lodge
J. Paul's
Lenny's Chop Hse.
Main St. Blues
Mangia Mangia
McCormick & Schmick's
Milltowne Tavern
Morton's of Chicago
Oregon Grill

Baltimore Indexes

Pisces
Planet Hollywood
Red Brick Station
Rose's Cafe
Shanghai Lil's
Shula's Steak Hse.
SoBo Cafe
Suzie's Soba
Tapestry
Tuscany Grill

Offbeat

Bertha's
Cafe Tattoo
Haussner's
Holy Frijoles
Joy America
Kelly's
Liquid Earth
Marconi's
Margaret's Cafe
Martick's
One World Cafe
PaperMoon Diner
Peter's Inn
SoBo Cafe

Outdoor Dining

(G=garden; P=patio;
S=sidewalk; T=terrace;
W=waterside; best of many)
Ambassador Din. Rm. (P,S)
Angler/A (W)
Antrim 1844 (T)
Baldwins Station (W)
Bay Cafe (P,W)
Black Olive (G)
Cacao Lane (T)
Cafe Troia (S)
Candle Light Inn (P)
Cantler's/A (P,W)
Capitol City Brewing (P)
Carrol's Creek/A (P,W)
Chart House (P)
Cheesecake Factory (P)
Clyde's (P,W)
Crab Claw/A (P,W)
Elkridge Furnace (P)
Fergie's/A (W)
Gabler's (T,W)
Globe Brewing Co. (P,W)
Gunning's Crab Hse. (P)
Harris Crab House/A (P,W)
Harrison's/A (T,W)

Harry Browne's/A (P)
Harryman House (P)
Harvey's (P)
Imperial Hotel/A (G)
Inn at Perry Cabin/A (T,W)
J. Leonard's (W)
John Steven, Ltd. (P)
Josef's Country Inn (P)
Joy America (P)
J. Paul's (P)
La Piccola Roma/A (S)
Latitude 38/A (P)
Le Zinc/A (T)
Liberatore's (S)
Lista's (T,W)
Louie's Bookstore (S)
Luigi Petti (G)
Manor Tavern (T)
McGarvey's/A (S)
Michael Rork's/A (P,W)
Middleton Tavern/A (S)
Milton Inn (P)
Morsels/A (P)
Northwoods/A (T)
O'Brien's/A (S)
One World Cafe (P)
Orchard Market (S)
Oregon Grill (P)
Paolo's (T,W)
PaperMoon Diner (S)
Peerce's Plantation (P)
Phillips (T,W)
Piccolo's (P,W)
Ram's Head Tavern/A (P)
Regi's (S)
River Watch (P,W)
Robert Morris Inn/A (W)
Rusty Scupper (W)
Sanders' Corner (P)
Tapestry (P,S)
Tomato Palace (P,W)
Windows on Bay (W)

Outstanding Views

Baldwins Station
Bay Cafe
Cantler's/A
Carrol's Creek/A
Chart House/A
Cheesecake Factory
Crab Claw/A
Hampton's
Inn at Perry Cabin/A
J. Leonard's

237

Baltimore Indexes

Joy America
J. Paul's
McCormick & Schmick's
Michael Rork's/A
Narrows/A
Paolo's
Peerce's Plantation
Phillips
Piccolo's
Pisces
Rusty Scupper
Sanders' Corner
Tilghman Island Inn/A
Tomato Palace
Windows
Windows on Bay

Parking/Valet

(L=parking lot;
V=valet parking;
*=validated parking)

Acropolis (L)
Adam's Ribs (L)
Ambassador Din. Rm. (V)
Angler/A (L)
Anne Arundel Seafood (L)
Antrim 1844 (L)
Baldwins Station (L)
Bamboo House (L)
Bangkok Place (L)
Bare Bones (L)
Bo Brooks (L)
Boccaccio (L,V)
Brass Elephant (L)
Braznell's (L)
Caesar's Den (V)
Cafe Normandie/A*
California Pizza Kit. (L)
Calvert House/A (L)
Candle Light Inn (L)
Canopy (L)
Cantler's/A (L)
Capitol City Brewing (V)
Carrol's Creek/A (L)
Charleston (V)
Chart House/A (L)
Chiapparelli's (V)
Ciao Bella (V)
Clyde's (L)
Corinthian/A (L,V)
Corks (V)
Corner Stable (L)
Costas Inn (L)
Crab Claw/A (L)

Dalesio's (V)
Da Mimmo (V)
Della Notte (L)
Double T Diner (L)
DuClaw Brewing (L)
Due (L)
Faidley's (L)
Fazzini's (L)
Fergie's/A (V)
Fisherman's Wharf (L)
Fishery (L)
Friendly Farms (L)
Gabler's (L)
G & M Rest. (L)
Garry's Grill (L)
Germano's (V)
Gibby's (L)
Giolitti Deli/A (L)
Grand Palace (L)
Gringada (L)
Hamilton's (V)
Hampton's (V)
Hampton's of Towson (L)
Harris Crab House/A (L)
Harryman House (L)
Helmand (L)
Holly's/A (L)
Hunan Manor (L)
Imperial Hotel/A (L)
Jerry D's Saloon (L)
Jilly's (L)
J. Leonard's (L)
Johansson's (L)
Josef's Country Inn (L)
Kelsey's (L)
King's Contrivance (L)
La Scala (V)
Latitude 38/A (L)
Lenny's Chop Hse. (V)*
Liberatore's (L)
Linwood's (L)
Little Havana (L)
Louie's Bookstore (L)
Luigi Petti (V)
Maggie's (L)
Mama Lucia (L)
Mango Grove (L)
Manor Tavern (L)
Marconi's (V)
McCafferty's (L,V)
McCormick & Schmick's (L,V)
M. Gettier's Orchard (L)
Michael's Cafe (L,V)
Milton Inn (L)

Baltimore Indexes

Morgan Millard (L)
Mo's Fisherman's Exch. (L)*
Mt. Washington Tavern (L)
Mughal Garden*
New Towne Diner (L)
Nichi Bei Kai (L)
North Star Tavern (L)
Northwoods/A (L)
Obrycki's (L)*
Ocean Pride (L)
Olive Grove (L)
Orchard Market (L)
Oregon Grill (L)
Outback Steakhouse (L)
Owl Bar (L,V)
PaperMoon Diner (L)
Peerce's Plantation (L,V)
Peppermill (L)
Perring Place (L)
Pisces (V)
Polo Grill (L,V)
Prime Rib (L)*
Puffins/Sin Carne (L)
Purim Oak (L)
Purple Orchid*
Ralphie's Diner (L)
Red Brick Station (L)
Robert Morris Inn/A (L)
Romano's (L)
Rothwell's (L)
Ruth's Chris (V)
Sabatino's (V)
Saigon Palace/A (L)
Sanders' Corner (L)
San Sushi (L)
Scotto's (L)
Shogun (L)*
Shula's Steak Hse. (L,V)
Silver Spring Mining (L)
Sisson's (L,V)*
Sotto Sopra (V)
Steak & Ale (L)
Sushi-Ya (L)
Szechuan Best (L)
Szechuan House (L)
Thai Orient (L)
Treaty of Paris/A (V)
Turf Inn (L)
Tuscany Grill (L)
Viccino Bistro (V)
Vito's Cafe (L)
Windows (L)*
Windows on Bay (L)
Wolford's Bakery*

Parties & Private Rooms
(Any nightclub or restaurant charges less at off-times; * indicates private rooms available; best of many)

Antrim 1844*
Baldwins Station*
Baugher's*
Black Olive*
Boccaccio*
Brass Elephant*
Caesar's Den*
Candle Light Inn*
Carrol's Creek/A*
Charleston*
Chiapparelli's*
Clyde's*
Corks*
Friendly Farms*
Germano's*
Hamilton's*
Harry Browne's/A*
Harryman House*
Haussner's*
Jerry D's Saloon*
J. Leonard's*
Johansson's*
Josef's Country Inn*
King's Contrivance*
La Tavola*
La Tesso Tana*
Lenny's Chop Hse.*
Liberatore's*
Manor Tavern*
M. Gettier's Orchard*
Michael Rork's/A*
Milton Inn*
North Star Tavern*
Oregon Grill*
Peerce's Plantation*
Rudys' 2900*
Spike & Charlie's*
Tersiguel's*
Tio Pepe*
Wild Mushroom*

People-Watching
Brewer's Art
Café Pangea
Cafe Tattoo
Cheesecake Factory
City Cafe
Double T Diner
Holy Frijoles

239

Baltimore Indexes

John Steven, Ltd.
Linwood's
Louie's Bookstore
McGarvey's/A
Middleton Tavern/A
O'Brien's/A
Paolo's
Polo Grill
Sabatino's
Sotto Sopra

Power Scenes
Boccaccio
Charleston
Chick & Ruth's/A
Corinthian/A
Due
Harry Browne's/A
Holly's/A
Lenny's Chop Hse.
Lewnes' Steakhse./A
Linwood's
McCormick & Schmick's
Morton's of Chicago
Oregon Grill
Polo Grill
Ruth's Chris
Sabatino's
Windows

Pre-Theater Dining
(Call to check prices, days and times)
Brass Elephant
Brewer's Art
Candle Light Inn
La Tesso Tana
Sotto Sopra
Spike & Charlie's
Steak & Ale
Thai Landing
Turf Inn

Prix Fixe Menus
(Call to check prices, days and times)
Antrim 1844
Brass Elephant
Cafe Troia
Gunning's Seafood
Hampton's
J. Leonard's
Joy America
Steak & Ale

Stone Mill Bakery/Ecole
Tersiguel's
Treaty of Paris/A
208 Talbot/A

Pubs/Bars/Microbreweries
DuClaw Brewing
Duda's Tavern
Ellicott Mills
Hamilton's
Johansson's
John Steven, Ltd.
Kelly's
Ram's Head Tavern/A
Sisson's

Quiet Conversation
Adrian's
Calvert House
Calvert House/A
Corinthian/A
Desert Cafe
Hampton's
Hampton Tea Room
One World Cafe
Trattoria Alberto
Woman's Ind. Exch.
Ze Mean Bean

Raw Bars
Anne Arundel Seafood
Bertha's
Bill Bateman's
Chart House
Faidley's
Globe Brewing Co.
Griffin's/A
McGarvey's/A
Middleton Tavern/A
Mt. Washington Tavern
Nick's
O'Brien's/A
Ocean Pride
Owl Bar
Rusty Scupper
Schultz's Crab Hse.
Turf Inn
Windows

Reservations Essential
Antrim 1844
A-1 Crab Haven
Black Olive
Gabler's

240

Baltimore Indexes

Hampton's
Harryman House
Helmand
Inn at Perry Cabin/A
J. Leonard's
Kelly's (crab's)
Manor Tavern
Milton Inn
Stone Mill Bakery/Ecole
Tersiguel's
Tio Pepe

Romantic Spots
Antrim 1844
Desert Cafe
Harry Browne's/A
La Tesso Tana
Milton Inn
Prime Rib
Treaty of Paris/A

Saturday Lunch
Ambassador Din. Rm.
Amicci's
Angler/A
Anne Arundel Seafood
Baldwins Station
Banjara
Ban Thai
Baugher's
Bay Cafe
Bertha's
Bombay Grill
Brighton's
Cacao Lane
Caesar's Den
Cafe Hon
Cafe Normandie/A
Café Pangea
Cafe Zen
Candle Light Inn
Cantler's/A
Carrol's Creek/A
Chameleon
Cheesecake Factory
Chiapparelli's
City Cafe
Clyde's
Corner Stable
Crab Claw/A
Della Notte
Duda's Tavern
Ellicott Mills
Faidley's

Friendly Farms
Gabler's
Germano's
Grand Palace
Hampton Tea Room
Harris Crab House/A
Harry Browne's/A
Harryman House
Harvey's
Haussner's
Helen's Garden
Hoang's
Holly's/A
Holy Frijoles
Hull St. Blues
Hunan Manor
Imperial Hotel/A
Inn at Perry Cabin/A
Johansson's
John Steven, Ltd.
Josef's Country Inn
Joss Cafe/A
Joy America
J. Paul's
La Piccola Roma/A
La Tavola
Latitude 38/A
Liberatore's
Linwood's
Manor Tavern
Margaret's Cafe
Maria's/A
McCormick & Schmick's
M. Gettier's Orchard
Michael Rork's/A
Morning Edition
Narrows/A
Nick's
Orchard Market
Oregon Grill
Paolo's
Peerce's Plantation
Polo Grill
Sabatino's
San Sushi
Tersiguel's
Tilghman Island Inn/A
Tomato Palace
Treaty of Paris/A
Troia/Walters
Wild Mushroom
Windows
Ze Mean Bean

241

Baltimore Indexes

Sunday Dining – Best Bets
(B=brunch; L=lunch; D=dinner; plus all hotels and most Asians)
Akbar (L,D)
Ambassador Din. Rm. (L,D)
Baldwins Station (B,L,D)
Baugher's (L,D)
Cantler's/A (L,D)
Carrol's Creek/A (B,D)
Clyde's (B,L,D)
Corinthian/A (B,L,D)
Crab Claw/A (L,D)
Friendly Farms (L,D)
Gabler's (L,D)
Germano's (L,D)
Grand Palace (L,D)
Hampton's (B,D)
Harris Crab House/A (L,D)
Harrison's/A (L,D)
Harry Browne's/A (B,L,D)
Harryman House (B,D)
Harvey's (B,D)
Helen's Garden (L,D)
Hoang's (L,D)
Hunan Manor (L,D)
Imperial Hotel/A (B,L)
Inn at Perry Cabin/A (L,D)
Jerry D's Saloon (B,L,D)
John Steven, Ltd. (L,D)
Josef's Country Inn (B,D)
Joss Cafe/A (L,D)
Joy America (B)
Kelly's (D)
Kelsey's (B,L,D)
La Tavola (L,D)
Latitude 38/A (L,D)
Louie's Bookstore (B,L,D)
Manor Tavern (B,L,D)
Marconi's (B,D)
Margaret's Cafe (B,L,D)
McCabe's (L,D)
M. Gettier's Orchard (L,D)
Michael Rork's/A (B,L,D)
Morning Edition (B,L)
Narrows/A (B,L,D)
Obrycki's (L,D)
Oregon Grill (B,D)
Peerce's Plantation (B,D)
Pierpoint (B,D)
Polo Grill (B,L,D)
River Watch (L,D)
Tersiguel's (L,D)
Tilghman Island Inn/A (L,D)
Treaty of Paris/A (B,L,D)
Troia/Walters (B,L)
Weber's on Boston (B,L,D)
Windows (B,L,D)
Ze Mean Bean (B,L,D)

Senior Appeal
Baugher's
Calvert House/A
Chiapparelli's
Friendly Farms
Liberatore's
Northwoods/A
Peppermill
Perring Place
Steak & Ale
Turf Inn
Velleggia's

Singles Scenes
Bay Cafe
Brewer's Art
Capitol City Brewing
Crease
Donna's
Ellicott Mills
Globe Brewing Co.
Jilly's
Johansson's
John Steven, Ltd.
J. Paul's
McGarvey's/A
Michael's Cafe
Nacho Mama's
Nick's
O'Brien's/A
Ram's Head Tavern/A
Riordan's/A
River Watch
Shanghai Lil's
Weber's on Boston

Sleepers
(Good to excellent food, but little known)
Angler/A
Anne Arundel Seafood
Azeb's
Birds of a Feather
Calvert House/A
Chameleon
Corinthian/A
Dooby's B&G

Baltimore Indexes

Elkridge Furnace
Fazzini's
Gabler's
Giolitti Deli/A
Hampton's of Towson
Helen's Garden
Imperial Hotel/A
Joss Cafe/A
Kelly's
La Scala
Latitude 38/A
Minato
Nam Kang
Olive Grove
Perring Place
Purim Oak
Rotisseria
Saigon
Saigon Palace/A
Samos
San Sushi
Sunset
Surfin' Bull
Szechuan
Szechuan House
Tenosix
Thai Orient
Tilghman Island Inn/A
Wolford's Bakery
Zorba's B&G

Teflons
(Get lots of business, despite so-so food, i.e. they have other attractions that prevent criticism from sticking)
Bay Cafe
Capitol City Brewing
Cheesecake Factory
Hard Rock Cafe
Paolo's
Phillips
Planet Hollywood
Silver Diner
Velleggia's

Smoking Prohibited
(May be permissible at bar or outdoors)
Adrian's
Al Pacino Cafe
Ambassador Din. Rm.
Anne Arundel Seafood
Bangkok Place
Bistro St. Michaels/A
Black Olive
Blue Moon Cafe
Brighton's
Cafe Zen
Candle Light Inn
Cheesecake Factory
Donna's
Due
Edo Sushi
Elkridge Furnace
Ethel & Ramone's
Fazzini's
Friendly Farms
Gabler's
Garry's Grill
Glasz Cafe
Golden Gate
Golden West
Holy Frijoles
Joy America
King's Contrivance
La Piccola Roma/A
Liquid Earth
Loco Hombre
Mango Grove
Morgan Millard
Mughal Garden
New No Da Ji
New Towne Diner
Nichi Bei Kai
Northwoods/A
Orchard Market
Puffins/Sin Carne
Purple Orchid
Robert Morris Inn/A
Romano's
Rose's Cafe
Stone Mill Bakery/Ecole
Sushi-Ya
Szechuan Best
Szechuan House
Tersiguel's
Tomato Palace
Troia/Walters
Vera's Bakery
Viccino Bistro
Ze Mean Bean

Teas
Bertha's
Brighton's
Hampton Tea Room
Inn at Perry Cabin/A

Baltimore Indexes

Vera's Bakery
Ze Mean Bean

Teenagers & Other Youthful Spirits
Bill Bateman's
Buddy's/A
Cheesecake Factory
ESPN Zone
Hard Rock Cafe
Planet Hollywood

Visitors on Expense Accounts
Antrim 1844
Boccaccio
Brass Elephant
Charleston
Corinthian/A
Da Mimmo
Hamilton's
Hampton's
Inn at Perry Cabin/A
J. Leonard's
Joy America
King's Contrivance
Lewnes' Steakhse./A
Linwood's
M. Gettier's Orchard
Morton's of Chicago
Pierpoint
Polo Grill
Prime Rib
Rudys' 2900
Ruth's Chris
Tersiguel's
Tio Pepe
Wild Mushroom

Wheelchair Access
(Most places now have wheelchair access; call in advance to check)

Winning Wine Lists
Boccaccio
Caesar's Den
Cafe Madrid
Charleston
Corks
Hamilton's
Hampton's
Harry Browne's/A
Inn at Perry Cabin/A
M. Gettier's Orchard
Milton Inn
Oregon Grill
Polo Grill
Prime Rib
Rudys' 2900
Spike & Charlie's
Tersiguel's

Worth a Trip
Chestertown
  Imperial Hotel/A
St. Michaels
  Inn at Perry Cabin/A
  Michael Rork's/A
  208 Talbot/A
Sykesville
  Baldwins Station
Taneytown
  Antrim 1844
Westminster
  Baugher's
Tilghman Island
  Harrison's/A
  Tilghman Island Inn/A

Young Children
(Besides the normal fast-food places; * indicates children's menu available)
Baldwins Station*
Bare Bones*
Baugher's
Bertucci's
California Pizza Kit.
Canopy
Cheesecake Factory
Fazzini's*
Friendly Farms*
Hard Rock Cafe
Loco Hombre
Mama Lucia*
Outback Steakhouse*
Planet Hollywood
Silver Diner
Tomato Palace*

244

Rating Sheets

To aid in your participation in our next *Survey*

| F | D | S | C |

⌐⌐⌐⌐

Restaurant Name _____
Phone _____
Comments _____
_____
_____

⌐⌐⌐⌐

Restaurant Name _____
Phone _____
Comments _____
_____
_____

⌐⌐⌐⌐

Restaurant Name _____
Phone _____
Comments _____
_____
_____

⌐⌐⌐⌐

Restaurant Name _____
Phone _____
Comments _____
_____
_____

⌐⌐⌐⌐

Restaurant Name _____
Phone _____
Comments _____
_____
_____

⌐⌐⌐⌐

Restaurant Name _____
Phone _____
Comments _____
_____
_____

F | D | S | C

⌐⌐⌐⌐

Restaurant Name _____
Phone _____
Comments _____
_____
_____

⌐⌐⌐⌐

Restaurant Name _____
Phone _____
Comments _____
_____
_____

⌐⌐⌐⌐

Restaurant Name _____
Phone _____
Comments _____
_____
_____

⌐⌐⌐⌐

Restaurant Name _____
Phone _____
Comments _____
_____
_____

⌐⌐⌐⌐

Restaurant Name _____
Phone _____
Comments _____
_____
_____

⌐⌐⌐⌐

Restaurant Name _____
Phone _____
Comments _____
_____
_____

		F	D	S	C

⌐⌐⌐⌐

Restaurant Name _____
Phone _____
Comments _____
_____
_____

⌐⌐⌐⌐

Restaurant Name _____
Phone _____
Comments _____
_____
_____

⌐⌐⌐⌐

Restaurant Name _____
Phone _____
Comments _____
_____
_____

⌐⌐⌐⌐

Restaurant Name _____
Phone _____
Comments _____
_____
_____

⌐⌐⌐⌐

Restaurant Name _____
Phone _____
Comments _____
_____
_____

⌐⌐⌐⌐

Restaurant Name _____
Phone _____
Comments _____
_____
_____

	F	**D**	**S**	**C**

⌐⌐⌐⌐

Restaurant Name _____
Phone _____
Comments _____
_____
_____

⌐⌐⌐⌐

Restaurant Name _____
Phone _____
Comments _____
_____
_____

⌐⌐⌐⌐

Restaurant Name _____
Phone _____
Comments _____
_____
_____

⌐⌐⌐⌐

Restaurant Name _____
Phone _____
Comments _____
_____
_____

⌐⌐⌐⌐

Restaurant Name _____
Phone _____
Comments _____
_____
_____

⌐⌐⌐⌐

Restaurant Name _____
Phone _____
Comments _____
_____
_____

F | D | S | C

⌐⌐⌐⌐

Restaurant Name _____
Phone _____
Comments _____
_____
_____

⌐⌐⌐⌐

Restaurant Name _____
Phone _____
Comments _____
_____
_____

⌐⌐⌐⌐

Restaurant Name _____
Phone _____
Comments _____
_____
_____

⌐⌐⌐⌐

Restaurant Name _____
Phone _____
Comments _____
_____
_____

⌐⌐⌐⌐

Restaurant Name _____
Phone _____
Comments _____
_____
_____

⌐⌐⌐⌐

Restaurant Name _____
Phone _____
Comments _____
_____
_____

| F | D | S | C |

⌐⌐⌐⌐

Restaurant Name _____
Phone _____
Comments _____
_____
_____

⌐⌐⌐⌐

Restaurant Name _____
Phone _____
Comments _____
_____
_____

⌐⌐⌐⌐

Restaurant Name _____
Phone _____
Comments _____
_____
_____

⌐⌐⌐⌐

Restaurant Name _____
Phone _____
Comments _____
_____
_____

⌐⌐⌐⌐

Restaurant Name _____
Phone _____
Comments _____
_____
_____

⌐⌐⌐⌐

Restaurant Name _____
Phone _____
Comments _____
_____
_____

Wine Vintage Chart 1985-1996

This chart is designed to help you select wine to go with your meal. It is based on the same 0 to 30 scale used throughout this *Survey*. The ratings (prepared by our friend Howard Stravitz, a law professor at the University of South Carolina) reflect both the quality of the vintage and the wine's readiness for present consumption. Thus, if a wine is not fully mature or is over the hill, its rating has been reduced. We do not include 1987 because, with the exception of '87 cabernets, those vintages are not recommended.

	'85	'86	'88	'89	'90	'91	'92	'93	'94	'95	'96
WHITES											
French:											
Burgundy	27	28	20	29	24	18	26	19	25	25	26
Loire Valley	–	–	–	25	24	15	19	22	23	24	24
Champagne	28	25	24	26	28	–	–	24	–	25	26
Sauternes	22	28	29	25	26	–	–	–	18	22	24
California:											
Chardonnay	–	–	–	–	23	21	26	25	22	23	22
REDS											
French:											
Bordeaux	27	26	25	28	28	–	19	23	24	25	24
Burgundy	24	–	26	27	29	21	23	25	22	23	24
Rhône	26	20	26	28	27	26*	16	23*	23	24	22
Beaujolais	–	–	–	–	–	22	13	21	22	24	21
California:											
Cab./Merlot	27	26	16	22	28	26	25	24	24	23	22
Zinfandel	–	–	–	–	–	20	20	20	22	20	21
Italian:											
Tuscany	27	16	25	–	26	19	–	20	19	24	19
Piedmont	26	–	24	27	27	–	–	19	–	25	25

*Rating and recommendation is only for Northern Rhône wine in 1991 and Southern Rhône wine in 1993.

Bargain sippers take note: Some wines are reliable year in, year out, and are reasonably priced as well. These wines are best bought in the most recent vintages. They include: Alsatian Pinot Blancs, Côtes du Rhône, Muscadet, Bardolino, Valpolicella and inexpensive Spanish Rioja and California Zinfandel.